C000133746

A CHANGED MAN
& OTHER STORIES

THOMAS HARDY

A CHANGED MAN
& OTHER STORIES

ALAN SUTTON

First published 1913

First published in this edition in the United Kingdom in 1984 by
Alan Sutton Publishing Ltd · Phoenix Mill · Far Thrupp · Stroud
Gloucestershire

Reprinted 1987, 1993

Copyright © in this edition
Alan Sutton Publishing Limited, 1984

British Library Cataloguing in Publication Data

Hardy, Thomas, 1840–1928
   A changed man.—(Pocket classics)
   I. Title
   823′.8[F]   PR4740

   ISBN 0-86299-149-8

Cover picture: detail from Jealousy and Flirtation *by Haynes King. Victoria and
Albert Museum, London*

Typesetting and origination by
Alan Sutton Publishing Limited.
Photoset Bembo 9/10
Printed in Great Britain by
The Guernsey Press Company Limited,
Guernsey, Channel Islands.

CONTENTS

BIOGRAPHICAL NOTE

THOMAS HARDY (1840–1928) is the master of the English regional novel, describing in his 'Wessex' series of novels, against a background of strong local colour, the life and loves, 'the fret and fever', of rustic characters. An idealized and traditional Dorset countryside is the setting, at one level, of a gentle group of tales of 'singular charm' (Henry James), which are often deeply romantic and sentimentalized documents of social history illustrating Hardy as a keen observer of the manners, speech and rhythms of a rural England just beginning to be affected by the Industrial Revolution. Yet, at another level, these are novels of tragic ambition exploring with mature complexity the passions of their principal characters – victims of vanity, cowardice, derision and disaster – and their struggles against nature and community, flesh and spirit, 'struggles into love and struggles with love . . . novels about becoming complete' (D.H. Lawrence). He classified these novels into three groups:– Novels of Character and Environment, Romances and Fantasies, and Novels of Ingenuity – which well describe their principal methods and themes. Hardy himself regarded his verse as of more importance than his prose fiction, and his position as a formative influence on the development of the modern movement in poetry has been much rehabilitated in recent years.

He was born on June 2 1840 in a cottage at Upper Bockhampton, near Dorchester, the son and grandson of master stonemasons. He attended local schools at Dorchester and at the age of nine played the fiddle at weddings and dances. His early vocation was architecture, and he was articled (1856–61) to the Dorchester architect John Hicks. He continued to educate himself, studying Greek, Latin and theology in the early hours of the morning, and had begun writing poetry by his late 'teens. From 1862 to 1867 he worked in London for the architect Arthur Blomfield, reading widely, attending evening classes, and studying the paintings in the National Gallery.

In 1867 he returned to Dorset, having written his celebrated poem 'Neutral Tones' earlier that year. At his parents' house in Bockhampton he wrote his first novel, *The Poor Man and the Lady*, which he failed to publish, although it was admired. In 1869, now working in Weymouth, he began *Desperate Remedies*, to be published in 1871. In 1870 he was sent by the architect Crickmay to Cornwall, where he met Emma Lavinia Gifford, whom he was to marry in August 1874. His novels began to be successfully serialized after Leslie Stephen invited him to contribute his first popular success, *Far from the Madding Crowd*, anonymously to *The Cornhill Magazine* (1873/ 4). Finally he was able to abandon architectural practice and devote himself wholly to his writing, producing his greatest achievements as a novelist from 1878 to 1895, when he published his now famous works, such as *The Return of the Native* (1878), *The Mayor of Casterbridge* (1886), *The Woodlanders* (1887), *Tess of the d'Urbervilles* (1891), and *Jude the Obscure* (1895), in addition to the many short stories written mainly between 1888 and 1891.

In 1883 work was started on Max Gate, near Dorchester, the house where he was to remain, except for periodic visits to London and abroad, until his death. In 1893 he visited Dublin and met Florence Henniker, with whom he collaborated and developed an affectionate friendship. Estrangement from his wife was exacerbated by the publication of *Jude the Obscure*; its sympathetic treatment of the morality of adultery aroused the indignant censure of a scandalized Victorian public, which so disappointed Hardy as to compel him to return henceforth from his novel-writing to poetry.

In 1897 he began to prepare his first collection of verse, *Wessex Poems* (1898), which included poems both recent and dating back to the mid-1860s; this was followed by *Poems of the Past and the Present* (1901). Between 1903 and 1908 he published in three parts *The Dynasts,* an epic-drama of the Napoleonic Wars written in blank verse. This was highly acclaimed at the time and public recognition was given to him when he was awarded the Order of Merit in 1910. In 1912 he carried out one of the most thorough-going of his many revisions of the Wessex novels. His wife died in that year and her death was the occasion of an outpouring of poems written 'in expiation'. He was to marry Florence Dugdale in 1914 (under whose name Hardy's autobiography was published), and from then to the end of his life he reworked and composed material for the seven collections of verse which ended with the posthumous publication of *Winter Words* in 1928, the year of his death. He died on January 11 1928: his ashes were buried at Westminster Abbey and his heart in his first wife's grave in Stinsford churchyard.

NICHOLAS MANDER

A CHANGED MAN

I

The person who, next to the actors themselves, chanced to know most of their story, lived just below 'Top o' Town' (as the spot was called) in an old substantially-built house, distinguished among its neighbours by having an oriel window on the first floor, whence could be obtained a raking view of the High Street, west and east, the former including Laura's dwelling, the end of the Town Avenue hard by (in which were played the odd pranks hereafter to be mentioned), the Port-Bredy road rising westwards, and the turning that led to the cavalry barracks where the Captain was quartered. Looking eastward down the town from the same favoured gazebo, the long perspective of houses declined and dwindled till they merged in the highway across the moor. The white riband of road disappeared over Grey's Bridge a quarter of a mile off, to plunge into innumerable rustic windings, shy shades, and solitary undulations up hill and down dale for one hundred and twenty miles till it exhibited itself at Hyde Park Corner as a smooth bland surface in touch with a busy and fashionable world.

To the barracks aforesaid had recently arrived the —th Hussars, a regiment new to the locality. Almost before any acquaintance with its members had been made by the town-speople, a report spread that they were a 'crack' body of men, and had brought a splendid band. For some reason or other the town had not been used as the headquarters of cavalry for many years, the various troops stationed there having consisted of casual detachments only; so that it was with a sense of honour that everybody – even the small furniture-broker from whom the married troopers hired tables and chairs – received the news of their crack quality.

In those days the Hussar regiments still wore over the left

1

shoulder that attractive attachment, or frilled half-coat, hanging loosely behind like the wounded wing of a bird, which was called the pelisse, though it was known among the troopers themselves as a 'sling jacket.' It added amazingly to their picturesqueness in women's eyes, and, indeed, in the eyes of men also.

The burgher who lived in the house with the oriel window sat during a great many hours of the day in that projection, for he was an invalid, and time hung heavily on his hands unless he maintained a constant interest in proceedings without. Not more than a week after the arrival of the Hussars his ears were assailed by the shout of one schoolboy to another in the street below.

'Have 'ee heard this about the Hussars? They are haunted! Yes – a ghost troubles 'em; he has followed 'em about the world for years.'

A haunted regiment: that was a new idea for either invalid or stalwart. The listener in the oriel came to the conclusion that there were some lively characters amonge the —th Hussars.

He made Captain Maumbry's acquaintance in an informal manner at an afternoon tea to which he went in a wheeled chair – one of the very rare outings that the state of his health permitted. Maumbry showed himself to be a handsome man of twenty-eight or thirty, with an attractive hint of wickedness in his manner that was sure to make him adorable with good young women. The large dark eyes that lit his pale face expressed this wickedness strongly, though such was the adaptability of their rays that one could think they might have expressed sadness or seriousness just as readily, if he had had a mind for such.

An old and deaf lady who was present asked Captain Maumbry bluntly: 'What's this we hear about you? They say your regiment is haunted.'

The Captain's face assumed an aspect of grave, even sad, concern. 'Yes,' he replied, 'it is too true.'

Some younger ladies smiled till they saw how serious he looked, when they looked serious likewise.

'Really?' said the old lady.

'Yes. We naturally don't wish to say much about it.'

'No, no; of course not. But – how haunted?'

'Well: the – *thing*, as I'll call it, follows us. In country quarters or town, abroad or at home, it's just the same.'

'How do you account for it?'

'H'm.' Maumbry lowered his voice. 'Some crime committed by certain of our regiment in past years, we suppose.'

'Dear me. . . . How very horrid, and singular!'

'But, as I said, we don't speak of it much.'

'No . . . no.'

When the Hussar was gone, a young lady, disclosing a long-suppressed interest, asked if the ghost had been seen by any of the town.

The lawyer's son, who always had the latest borough news, said that, though it was seldom seen by any one but the Hussars themselves, more than one townsman and woman had already set eyes on it, to his or her terror. The phantom mostly appeared very late at night, under the dense trees of the town-avenue nearest the barracks. It was about ten feet high; its teeth chattered with a dry naked sound, as if they were those of a skeleton; and its hip-bones could be heard grating in their sockets.

During the darkest weeks of winter several timid persons were seriously frightened by the object answering to this cheerful description, and the police began to look into the matter. Whereupon the appearances grew less frequent, and some of the Boys of the regiment thankfully stated that they had not been so free from ghostly visitation for years as they had become since their arrival in Casterbridge.

This playing at ghosts was the most innocent of the amusements indulged in by the choice young spirits who inhabited the lichened, red-brick building at the top of the town bearing 'W.D.' and a broad arrow on its quoins. Far more serious escapades – levities relating to love, wine, cards, betting – were talked of, with no doubt more or less of exaggeration. That the Hussars, Captain Maumbry included, were the cause of bitter tears to several young women of the town and country is unquestionably true, despite the fact that the gaieties of the young men wore a more staring colour in this old-fashioned place than they would have done in a large and modern city.

II

Regularly once a week they rode out in marching order.

Returning up the town on one of these occasions, the romantic pelisse flapping behind each horseman's shoulder in the soft south-west wind, Captain Maumbry glanced up at the oriel. A mutual nod was exchanged between him and the person who sat there reading. The reader and a friend in the room with him followed the troop with their eyes all the way up the street, till, when the soldiers were oppostie the house in which Laura lived, that young lady became discernible in the balcony.

'They are engaged to be married, I hear,' said the friend.

'Who – Maumbry and Laura? Never – so soon?'

'Yes.'

'He'll never marry. Several girls have been mentioned in connection with his name. I am sorry for Laura.'

'Oh, but you needn't be. They are excellently matched.'

'She's only one more.'

'She's one more, and more still. She has regularly caught him. She is a born player of the game of hearts, and she knew how to beat him in his own practices. If there is one woman in the town who has any chance of holding her own and marrying him, she is that woman.'

This was true, as it turned out. By natural proclivity Laura had from the first entered heart and soul into military romance as exhibited in the plots and characters of those living exponents of it who came under her notice. From her earliest young womanhood civilians, however promising, had no chance of winning her interest if the meanest warrior were within the horizon. It may be that the position of her uncle's house (which was her home) at the corner of West Street nearest the barracks, the daily passing of the troops, the constant blowing of trumpet-calls a furlong from her windows, coupled with the fact that she knew nothing of the inner realities of military life, and hence idealized it, had also helped her mind's original bias for thinking men-at-arms the only ones worthy of a woman's heart.

Captain Maumbry was a typical prize; one whom all surrounding maidens had coveted, ached for, angled for, wept for, had by her judicious management become subdued to her purpose; and in addition to the pleasure of marrying the man she loved, Laura had the joy of feeling herself hated by the mothers of all the marriageable girls of the neighbourhood.

The man in the oriel went to the wedding; not as a guest, for at this time he was but slightly acquainted with the parties; but mainly because the church was close to his house; partly, too, for a reason which moved many others to be spectators of the ceremony; a subconsciousness that, though the couple might be happy in their experiences, there was sufficient possibility of their being otherwise to colour the musings of an onlooker with a pleasing pathos of conjecture. He could on occasion do a pretty stroke of rhyming in those days, and he beguiled the time of waiting by pencilling on a blank page of his prayer-book a few lines which, though kept private then, may be given here:–

AT A HASTY WEDDING

(*Triolet*)

If hours be years the twain are blest,
    For now they solace swift desire.
By lifelong ties that tether zest
If hours be years. The twain are blest
Do eastern suns slope never west.
    Nor pallid ashes follow fire.
If hours be years the twain are blest
    For now they solace swift desire.

As if, however, to falsify all prophecies, the couple seemed to find in marriage the secret of perpetuating the intoxication of a courtship which, on Maumbry's side at least, had opened without serious intent. During the winter following they were the most popular pair in and about Casterbridge – nay in South Wessex itself. No smart dinner in the country houses of the younger and gayer families within driving distance of the borough was complete without their lively presence; Mrs.

Maumbry was the blithest of the whirling figures at the
county ball; and when followed that inevitable incident of
garrison town life, an amateur dramatic entertainment, it was
just the same. The acting was for the benefit of such and such
an excellent charity – nobody cared what, provided the play
were played – and both Captain Maumbry and his wife were
in the piece, having been in fact, by mutual consent, the
originators of the performance. And so with laughter, and
thoughtlessness, and movement, all went merrily. There was
a little backwardness in the bill-paying of the couple; but in
justice to them it must be added that sooner or later all owings
were paid.

III

At the chapel-of-ease attended by the troops there arose above
the edge of the pulpit one Sunday an unknown face. This was
the face of a new curate. He placed upon the desk, not the
familiar sermon book, but merely a Bible. The person who
tells these things was not present at that service, but he soon
learnt that the young curate was nothing less than a great
surprise to his congregation; a mixed one always, for though
the Hussars occupied the body of the building, its nooks and
corners were crammed with civilians, whom, up to the
present, even the least uncharitable would have described as
being attracted thither less by the services than by the soldiery.

Now there arose a second reason for squeezing into an
already overcrowded church. The persuasive and gentle elo-
quence of Mr. Sainway operated like a charm upon those
accustomed only to the higher and dryer styles of preaching,
and for a time the other churches of the town were thinned of
their sitters.

At this point in the nineteenth century the sermon was the
sole reason for churchgoing amongst a vast body of religious
people. The liturgy was a formal preliminary, which, like the
Royal proclamation in a court of assize, had to be got through
before the real interest began; and on reaching home the
question was simply: Who preached, and how did he handle
his subject? Even had an archbishop officiated in the service

proper nobody would have cared much about what was said
or sung. People who had formerly attended in the morning
only began to go in the evening, and even to the special
addresses in the afternoon.

One day when Captain Maumbry entered his wife's drawing-room, filled with hired furniture, she thought he was
somebody else, for he had not come upstairs humming the
most catching air afloat in musical circles or in his usual
careless way.

'What's the matter, Jack?' she said without looking up from
a note she was writing.

'Well – not much, that I know.'

'O, but there is,' she murmured as she wrote.

'Why – this cursed new lath in a sheet – I mean the new
parson! He wants us to stop the band-playing on Sunday
afternoons.'

Laura looked up aghast.

'Why, it is the one thing that enables the few rational beings
hereabouts to keep alive from Saturday to Monday!'

'He says all the town flock to the music and don't come
to the service, and the pieces played are profane, or mun-
dane, or inane, or something – not what ought to be played
on Sunday. Of course 'tis Lautmann who settles those
things.'

Lautmann was the bandmaster.

The barrack-green on Sunday afternoons had, indeed,
become the promenade of a great many townspeople cheerfully inclined, many even of those who attended in the
morning at Mr. Sainway's service; and little boys who ought
to have been listening to the curate's afternoon lecture were
too often seen rolling upon the grass and making faces behind
the more dignified listeners.

Laura heard no more about the matter, however, for two or
three weeks, when suddenly remembering it she asked her
husband if any further objections had been raised.

'O – Mr. Sainway. I forgot to tell you. I've made his
acquaintance. He is not a bad sort of man.'

Laura asked if either Maumbry or some others of the
officers did not give the presumptuous curate a good setting
down for his interference.

'O well – we've forgotten that. He's a stunning preacher, they tell me.'

The acquaintance developed apparently, for the Captain said to her a little later on, 'There's a good deal in Sainway's argument about having no band on Sunday afternoons. After all, it is close to his church. But he doesn't press his objections unduly.'

'I am surprised to hear you defend him!'

'It was only a passing thought of mine. We naturally don't wish to offend the inhabitants of the town if they don't like it.'

'But they do.'

The invalid in the oriel never clearly gathered the details of progress in this conflict of lay and clerical opinion; but so it was that, to the disappointment of musicians, the grief of out-walking lovers, and the regret of the junior population of the town and country round, the band-playing on Sunday afternoons ceased in Casterbridge barrack-square.

By this time the Maumbrys had frequently listened to the preaching of the gentle if narrow-minded curate; for these light-natured, hit-or-miss, rackety people went to church like others for respectability's sake. None so orthodox as your unmitigated worldling. A more remarkable event was the sight to the man in the window of Captain Maumbry and Mr. Sainway walking down the High Street in earnest conversation. On his mentioning this fact to a caller he was assured that it was a matter of common talk that they were always together.

The observer would soon have learnt this with his own eyes if he had not been told. They began to pass together nearly every day. Hitherto Mrs. Maumbry, in fashionable walking clothes, had usually been her husband's companion; but this was less frequent now. The close and singular friendship between the two men went on for nearly a year, when Mr. Sainway was presented to a living in a densely-populated town in the midland counties. He bade the parishioners of his old place a reluctant farewell and departed, the touching sermon he preached on the occasion being published by the local printer. Everybody was sorry to lose him; and it was with genuine grief that his Casterbridge congregation learnt later on that soon after his induction to his benefice, during some bitter weather, he had fallen seriously ill of inflammation of the lungs, of which he eventually died.

We now get below the surface of things. Of all who had known the dead curate, none grieved for him like the man who on his first arrival had called him a 'lath in a sheet.' Mrs. Maumbry had never greatly sympathized with the impressive parson; indeed, she had been secretly glad that he had gone away to better himself. He had considerably diminished the pleasures of a woman by whom the joys of earth and good company had been appreciated to the full. Sorry for her husband in his loss of a friend who had been none of hers, she was quite unprepared for the sequel.

'There is something that I have wanted to tell you lately, dear,' he said one morning at breakfast with hesitation. 'Have you guessed what it is?'

She had guessed nothing.

'That I think of retiring from the army.'

'What!'

'I have thought more and more of Sainway since his death, and of what he used to say to me so earnestly. And I feel certain I shall be right in obeying a call within me to give up this fighting trade and enter the Church.

'What – be a parson?'

'Yes.'

'But what should *I* do?'

'Be a parson's wife.'

'Never!' she affirmed.

'But how can you help it?'

'I'll run away rather!' she said vehemently.

'No, you mustn't,' Maumbry replied, in the tone he used when his mind was made up. 'You'll get accustomed to the idea, for I am constrained to carry it out, though it is against my worldly interests. I am forced on by a Hand outside me to tread in the steps of Sainway.'

'Jack,' she asked, with calm pallor and round eyes; 'do you mean to say seriously that you are arranging to be a curate instead of a soldier?'

'I might say a curate *is* a soldier – of the church militant; but I don't want to offend you with doctrine. I distinctly say, yes.'

Late one evening, a little time onward, he caught her sitting by the dim firelight in her room. She did not know he had entered; and he found her weeping. 'What are you crying about, poor dearest?' he said.

She started. 'Because of what you have told me!'

The Captain grew very unhappy; but he was undeterred.

In due time the town learnt, to its intense surprise, that Captain Maumbry had retired from the —th Hussars and gone to Fountall Theological College to prepare for the ministry.

IV

'O, the pity of it! Such a dashing soldier – so popular – such an acquisition to the town, – the soul of social life here! And now! . . . One should not speak ill of the dead, but that dreadful Mr. Sainway – it was too cruel of him!'

This is a summary of what was said when Captain, now the Reverend, John Maumbry was enabled by circumstances to indulge his heart's desire of returning to the scene of his former exploits in the capacity of a minister of The Gospel. A low-lying district of the town, which at that date was crowded with improverished cottagers, was crying for a curate, and Mr. Maumbry generously offered himself as one willing to undertake labours that were certain to produce little result, and no thanks, credit, or emolument.

Let the truth be told about him as a clergyman; he proved to be anything but a brilliant success. Painstaking, single-minded, deeply in earnest as all could see, his delivery was laboured, his sermons were dull to listen to, and alas, too, too long. Even the dispassionate judges who sat by the hour in the bar-parlour of the White Hart – an inn standing at the dividing line between the poor quarter aforesaid and the fashionable quarter of Maumbry's former triumphs, and hence affording a position of strict impartiality – agreed in substance with the young ladies to the westward, though their views were somewhat more tersely expressed: 'Surely, God A'mighty spwiled a good sojer to make a bad pa'son when he shifted Cap'n Ma'mbry into a sarpless!'

The latter knew that such things were said, but he pursued his daily labours in and out of the hovels with serene unconcern.

It was about this time that the invalid in the oriel became more than a mere bowing acquaintance of Mrs. Maumbry's. She had returned to the town with her husband, and was living with him in a little house in the centre of his circle of ministration, when by some means she became one of the invalid's visitors. After a general conversation while sitting in his room with a friend of both, an incident led up to the matter that still rankled deeply in her soul. Her face was now paler and thinner than it had been; even more attractive, her disappointments having inscribed themselves as meek thoughtfulness on a look that was once a little frivolous. The two ladies had called to be allowed to use the window for observing the departure of the Hussars, who were leaving for barracks much nearer to London.

The troopers turned the corner of Barrack Road into the top of High Street, headed by their band playing 'The girl I left behind me' (which was formerly always the tune for such times, though it is now nearly disused). They came and passed the oriel, where an officer or two, looking up and discovering Mrs. Maumbry, saluted her, whose eyes filled with tears as the notes of the band waned away. Before the little group had recovered from that sense of the romantic which such spectacles impart, Mr. Maumbry came along the pavement. He probably had bidden his former brethren-in-arms a farewell at the top of the street, for he walked from that direction in his rather shabby clerical clothes, and with a basket on his arm which seemed to hold some purchases he had been making for his poorer parishioners. Unlike the soldiers he went along quite unconscious of his appearance or of the scene around.

The contrast was too much for Laura. With lips that now quivered, she asked the invalid what he thought of the change that had come to her.

It was difficult to answer, and with a wilfulness that was too strong in her she repeated the question.

'Do you think,' she added, 'that a woman's husband has a right to do such a thing, even if he does feel a certain call to it?'

Her listener sympathized too largely with both of them to be anything but unsatisfactory in his reply. Laura gazed longingly out of the window towards the thin dusty line of Hussars, now smalling towards the Mellstock Ridge. 'I,' she said, 'who should have been in their van on the way to London, am doomed to fester in a hole in Durnover Lane!'

Many events had passed and many rumours had been current concerning her before the invalid saw her again after her leave-taking that day.

V

Casterbridge had known many military and civil episodes; many happy times, and times less happy; and now came the time of her visitation. The scourge of cholera had been laid on the suffering country, and the low-lying purlieus of this ancient borough had more than their share of the infliction. Mixen Lane, in the Durnover quarter, and in Maumbry's parish, was where the blow fell most heavily. Yet there was a certain mercy in its choice of a date, for Maumbry was the man for such an hour.

The spread of the epidemic was so rapid that many left the town and took lodgings in the villages and farms. Mr. Maumbry's house was close to the most infected street, and he himself was occupied morn, noon, and night in endeavours to stamp out the plague and in alleviating the sufferings of the victims. So, as a matter of ordinary precaution, he decided to isolate his wife somewhere away from him for a while.

She suggested a village by the sea, near Budmouth Regis, and lodgings were obtained for her at Creston, a spot divided from the Casterbridge valley by a high ridge that gave it quite another atmosphere, though it lay no more than six miles off.

Thither she went. While she was rusticating in this place of safety, and her husband was slaving in the slums, she struck up an acquaintance with a lieutenant in the —st Foot, a Mr. Vannicock, who was stationed with his regiment at the Budmouth infantry barracks. As Laura frequently sat on the shelving beach, watching each thin wave slide up to her, and hearing, without heeding, its gnaw at the pebbles in its retreat, he often took a walk that way.

The acquaintance grew and ripened. Her situation, her history, her beauty, her age – a year or two above his own – all tended to make an impression on the young man's heart, and a reckless flirtation was soon in blithe progress upon that lonely shore.

It was said by her detractors afterwards that she had chosen her lodging to be near this gentleman, but there is reason to believe that she had never seen him till her arrival there. Just now Casterbridge was so deeply occupied with its own sad affairs – a daily burying of the dead and destruction of contaminated clothes and bedding – that it had little inclination to promulgate such gossip as may have reached its ears on the pair. Nobody long considered Laura in the tragic cloud which overhung all.

Meanwhile, on the Budmouth side of the hill the very mood of men was in contrast. The visitation there had been slight and much earlier, and normal occupations and pastimes had been resumed. Mr. Maumbry had arranged to see Laura twice a week in the open air, that she might run no risk from him; and, having heard nothing of the faint rumour, he met her as usual one dry and windy afternoon on the summit of the dividing hill, near where the high road from town to town crosses the old Ridge-way at right angles.

He waved his hand, and smiled as she approached, shouting to her: 'We will keep this wall between us, dear.' (Walls formed the field-fences here.) 'You mustn't be endangered. It won't be for long, with God's help!'

'I will do as you tell me, Jack. But you are running too much risk yourself, aren't you? I get little news of you; but I fancy you are.'

'Not more than others.'

Thus somewhat formally they talked, an insulating wind beating the wall between them like a mill-weir.

'But you wanted to ask me something?' he added.

'Yes. You know we are trying in Budmouth to raise some money for your sufferers; and the way we have thought of is by a dramatic performance. They want me to take a part.'

His face saddened. 'I have known so much of that sort of thing, and all that accompanies it! I wish you had thought of some other way.'

She said lightly that she was afraid it was all settled. 'You object to my taking a part, then? Of course –'

He told her that he did not like to say he positively objected. He wished they had chosen an oratorio, or lecture, or anything more in keeping with the necessity it was to relieve.

'But,' said she impatiently, 'people won't come to oratorios or lectures! They will crowd to comedies and farces.'

'Well, I cannot dictate to Budmouth how it shall earn the money it is going to give us. Who is getting up this performance?'

'The boys of the —st.'

'Ah, yes; our old game!' replied Mr. Maumbry. 'The grief of Casterbridge is the excuse for their fivolity. Candidly, dear Laura, I wish you wouldn't play in it. But I don't forbid you to. I leave the whole to your judgment.'

The interview ended, and they went their ways northward and southward. Time disclosed to all concerned that Mrs. Maumbry played in the comedy as the heroine, the lover's part being taken by Mr. Vannicock.

VI

Thus was helped on an event which the conduct of the mutually-attracted ones had been generating for some time.

It is unnecessary to give details. The —st Foot left for Bristol, and this precipitated their action. After a week of hesitation she agreed to leave her home at Creston and meet Vannicock on the ridge hard by, and to accompany him to Bath, where he had secured lodgings for her, so that she would be only about a dozen miles from his quarters.

Accordingly, on the evening chosen, she laid on her dressing-table a note for her husband, running thus:–

DEAR JACK – I am unable to endure this life any longer, and I have resolved to put an end to it. I told you I should run away if you persisted in being a clergyman, and now I am doing it. One cannot help one's nature. I have resolved to throw in my lot with Mr. Vannicock, and I hope rather than expect you will forgive me. – L.

Then with hardly a scrap of luggage, she went, ascending to the ridge in the dusk of early evening. Almost on the very spot where her husband had stood at their last tryst she beheld the outline of Vannicock, who had come all the way from Bristol to fetch her.

'I don't like meeting here – it is so unlucky!' she cried to him. 'For God's sake let us have a place of our own. Go back to the milestone, and I'll come on.'

He went back to the milestone that stands on the north slope of the ridge, where the old and new roads diverge, and she joined him there.

She was taciturn and sorrowful when he asked her why she would not meet him on the top. At last she inquired how they were going to travel.

He explained that he proposed to walk to Mellstock Hill, on the other side of Casterbridge, where a fly was waiting to take them by a cross-cut into the Ivell Road, and onward to that town. The Bristol railway was open to Ivell.

This plan they followed, and walked briskly through the dull gloom till they neared Casterbridge, which place they avoided by turning to the right at the Roman Amphitheatre and bearing round to Durnover Cross. Thence the way was solitary and open across the moor to the hill whereon the Ivell fly awaited them.

'I have noticed for some time,' she said, 'a lurid glare over the Durnover end of the town. It seems to come from somewhere about Mixen Lane.'

'The lamps,' he suggested.

'There's not a lamp as big as a rushlight in the whole lane. It is where the cholera is worst.'

By Standfast Corner, a little beyond the Cross, they suddenly obtained an end view of the lane. Large bonfires were burning in the middle of the way, with a view to purifying the air; and from the wretched tenements with which the lane was lined in those days persons were bringing out bedding and clothing. Some was thrown into the fires, the rest placed in wheelbarrows and wheeled into the moor directly in the track of the fugitives.

They followed on, and came up to where a vast copper was set in the open air. Here the linen was boiled and disinfected.

By the light of the lanterns Laura discovered that her husband was standing by the copper, and that it was he who unloaded the barrow and immersed its contents. The night was so calm and muggy that the conversation by the copper reached her ears.

'Are there many more loads tonight?'

'There's the clothes o' they that died this afternoon, sir. But that might bide till tomorrow, for you must be tired out.'

'We'll do it at once, for I can't ask anybody else to undertake it. Overturn that load on the grass and fetch the rest.

The man did so and went off with the barrow. Maumbry paused for a moment to wipe his face, and resumed his homely drudgery amid this squalid and reeking scene, pressing down and stirring the contents of the copper with what looked like an old rolling-pin. The steam therefrom laden with death, travelled in a low trail across the meadow.

Laura spoke suddenly: 'I won't go tonight after all. He is so tired, and I must help him. I didn't know things were so bad as this!'

Vannicock's arm dropped from her waist, where it had been resting as they walked. 'Will you leave?' she asked.

'I will if you say I must. But I'd rather help too.' There was no expostulation in his tone.

Laura had gone forward. 'Jack,' she said, 'I am come to help!'

The weary curate turned and held up the lantern. 'O – what, is it you, Laura?' he asked in surprise. 'Why did you come into this? You had better go back – the risk is great.'

'But I want to help you, Jack. Please let me help! I didn't come by myself – Mr. Vannicock kept me company. He will make himself useful too, if he's not gone on. Mr. Vannicock!'

The young lieutenant came forward reluctantly. Mr Maumbry spoke formally to him adding as he resumed his labour, 'I thought the —st Foot had gone to Bristol.'

'We have. But I have run down again for a few things.'

The two newcomers began to assist, Vannicock placing on the ground the small bag containing Laura's toilet articles that he had been carrying. The barrow-man soon returned with another load, and all continued work for nearly a half-hour, when a coachman came out from the shadows to the north.

'Beg pardon, sir,' he whispered to Vannicock, 'but I've waited so long on Mellstock hill that at last I drove down to the turnpike; and seeing the light here, I ran on to find out what had happened.'

Lieutenant Vannicock told him to wait a few minutes, and the last barrow-load was got through. Mr. Maumbry stretched himself and breathed heavily, saying, 'There; we can do no more.'

As if from the relaxation of effort he seemed to be seized with violent pain. He pressed his hands to his sides and bent forward.

'Ah! I think it has got hold of me at last,' he said with difficulty. 'I must try to get home. Let Mr. Vannicock take you back, Laura.'

He walked a few steps, they helping him, but was obliged to sink down on the grass.

'I am – afraid – you'll have to send for a hurdle, or shutter, or something,' he went on feebly, 'or try to get me into the barrow.'

But Vannicock had called to the driver of the fly, and they waited until it was brought on from the turnpike hard by. Mr. Maumbry was placed therein. Laura entered with him, and they drove to his humble residence near the Cross, where he was got upstairs.

Vannicock stood outside by the empty fly awhile but Laura did not reappear. He thereupon entered the fly and told the driver to take him back to Ivell.

VII

Mr. Maumbry had over-exerted himself in the relief of the suffering poor, and fell a victim – one of the last – to the pestilence which had carried off so many. Two days later he lay in his coffin.

Laura was in the room below. A servant brought in some

letters, and she glanced them over. One was the note from herself to Maumbry, informing him that she was unable to endure life with him any longer and was about to elope with Vannicock. Having read the letter she took it upstairs to where the dead man was, and slipped it into his coffin. The next day she buried him.

She was now free.

She shut up his house at Durnover Cross and returned to her lodgings at Creston. Soon she had a letter from Vanni-cock, and six weeks after her husband's death her lover came to see her.

'I forgot to give you back this – that night,' he said presently, handing her the little bag she had taken as her whole luggage when leaving.

Laura received it and absently shook it out. There fell upon the carpet her brush, comb, slippers, nightdress, and other simple necessaries for a journey. They had an intolerably ghastly look now, and she tried to cover them.

'I can now,' he said, 'ask you to belong to me legally – when a proper interval has gone – instead of as we meant.'

There was languor in his utterance, hinting at a possibil-ity that it was perfunctorily made. Laura picked up her articles, answering that he certainly could so ask her – she was free. Yet not her expression either could be called an ardent response. Then she blinked more and more quickly and put her handkerchief to her face. She was weeping violently.

He did not move or try to comfort her in any way. What had come between them? No living person. They had been lovers. There was now no material obstacle whatever to their union. But there was the insistent shadow of that unconscious one; the thin figure of him, moving to and fro in front of the ghastly furnace in the gloom of Durnover Moor.

Yet Vannicock called upon Laura when he was in the neighbourhood, which was not often; but in two years, as if on purpose to further the marriage which everybody was expecting, the —st Foot returned to Budmouth Regis.

Thereupon the two could not help encountering each other at times. But whether because the obstacle had been the source

of the love, or from a sense of error, and because Mrs.
Maumbry bore a less attractive look as a widow than before,
their feelings seemed to decline from their former incandesc-
ence to a mere tepid civility. What domestic issues supervened
in Vannicock's further story the man in the oriel never knew;
but Mrs. Maumbry lived and died a widow.

1900

THE WAITING SUPPER

I

Whoever had perceived the yeoman standing on Squire Everard's lawn in the dusk of that October evening fifty years ago, might have said at first sight that he was loitering there from idle curiosity. For a large five-light window of the manor-house in front of him was unshuttered and uncurtained, so that the illuminated room within could be scanned almost to its four corners. Obviously nobody was ever expected to be in this part of the grounds after nightfall.

The apartment thus swept by an eye from without was occupied by two persons; they were sitting over dessert, the tablecloth having been removed in the old-fashioned way. The fruits were local, consisting of apples, pears, nuts, and such other products of the summer as might be presumed to grow on the estate. There was strong ale and rum on the table, and but little wine. Moreover, the appointments of the dining-room were simple and homely even for the date, betokening a countrified household of the smaller gentry, without much wealth or ambition – formerly a numerous class, but now in great part ousted by the territorial landlords.

One of the two sitters was a young lady in white muslin, who listened somewhat impatiently to the remarks of her companion, an elderly, rubicund personage, whom the merest stranger could have pronounced to be her father. The watcher evinced no signs of moving, and it became evident that affairs were not so simple as they first had seemed. The tall farmer was in fact no accidental spectator, and he stood by premeditation close to the trunk of a tree, so that had any traveller passed along the road without the park gate, or even round the lawn to the door, that person would scarce have noticed the other, notwithstanding that the gate was quite near at hand, and the park little larger than a paddock. There

was still light enough in the western heaven to brighten
faintly one side of the man's face, and to show against the
trunk of the tree behind the admirable cut of his profile; also
to reveal that the front of the manor-house, small though it
seemed, was solidly built of stone in that never-to-be-surpas-
sed style for the English country residence – the mullioned
and transomed Elizabethan.

The lawn, although neglected, was still as level as a
bowling green – which indeed it might once have served for;
and the blades of grass before the window were raked by the
candle-shine, which stretched over them so far as to touch
the yeoman's face in front.

Within the dining-room there were also, with one of the
twain, the same signs of a hidden purpose that marked the
farmer. The young lady's mind was straying as clearly into
the shadows as that of the loiterer was fixed upon the room –
nay, it could be said that she was quite conscious of his
presence outside. Impatience caused her foot to beat silently
on the carpet, and she more than once rose to leave the table.
This proceeding was checked by her father, who would put
his hand upon her shoulder and unceremoniously press her
down into her chair, till he should have concluded his
observations. Her replies were brief enough, and there was
factitiousness in her smiles of assent to his views. A small iron
casement between two of the mullions was open, and some
occasional words of the dialogue were audible without.

'As for drains – how can I put in drains? The pipes don't
cost much, that's true; but the labour in sinking the trenches
is ruination. And then the gates – they should be hung to
stone posts, otherwise there's no keeping them up through
harvest.' The Squire's voice was strongly toned with the
local accent, so that he said 'draïns' and 'geäts' like the rustics
on his estate.

The landscape without grew darker, and the young man's
figure seemed to be absorbed into the trunk of the tree. The
small stars filled in between the larger, the nebulæ between
the small stars, the trees quite lost their voice; and if there
was still a sound, it was from the cascade of a stream which
stretched along under the trees that bounded the lawn on its
northern side.

At last the young girl did get to her feet and secure her retreat. 'I have something to do, papa,' she said. 'I shall not be in the drawing-room just yet.'

'Very well,' replied he. 'Then I won't hurry.' And closing the door behind her, he drew his decanters together and settled down in his chair.

Three minutes after that a woman's shape emerged from the drawing-room window, and passing through a wall-door to the entrance front, came across the grass. She kept well clear of the dining-room window, but enough of its light fell on her to show, escaping from the dark-hooded cloak that she wore, stray verges of the same light dress which had figured but recently at the dinner-table. The hood was contracted tight about her face with a drawing-string, making her countenance small and baby-like, and lovelier even than before.

Without hesitation she brushed across the grass to the tree under which the young man stood concealed. The moment she had reached him he enclosed her form with his arm. The meeting and embrace, though by no means formal, were yet not passionate; the whole proceeding was that of persons who had repeated the act so often as to be unconscious of its performance. She turned within his arm, and faced in the same direction with himself, which was towards the window; and thus they stood without speaking, the back of her head leaning against his shoulder. For a while each seemed to be thinking his and her diverse thoughts.

'You have kept me waiting a long time, dear Christine,' he said at last. 'I wanted to speak to you particularly, or I should not have stayed. How came you to be dining at this time o' night?'

'Father has been out all day, and dinner was put back till six. I know I have kept you; but Nicholas, how can I help it sometimes, if I am not to run any risk? My poor father insists upon my listening to all he has to say; since my brother left he has had nobody else to listen to him; and tonight he was particularly tedious on his usual topics – draining, and tenant-farmers, and the village people. I must take daddy to London; he gets so narrow always staying here.'

'And what did you say to it all?'

'Well, I took the part of the tenant-farmers, of course, as the beloved of one should in duty do.' There followed a little break or gasp, implying a strangled sigh.

'You are sorry you have encouraged that beloving one?'

'O no, Nicholas . . . What is it you want to see me for particularly?'

'I know you *are* sorry, as time goes on, and everything is at a dead-lock, with no prospect of change, and your rural swain loses his freshness! Only think, this secret understanding between us has lasted near three year, ever since you was a little over sixteen.'

'Yes, it has been a long time.'

'And I an untamed, uncultivated man, who has never seen London, and knows nothing about society at all.'

'Not uncultivated, dear Nicholas. Untravelled, socially unpractised, if you will,' she said, smiling. 'Well, I did sigh; but not because I regret being your promised one. What I do sometimes regret is that the scheme, which my meetings with you are but a part of, has not been carried out completely. You said, Nicholas, that if I consented to swear to keep faith with you, you would go away and travel, and see nations, and peoples, and cities, and take a professor with you, and study books and art, simultaneously with your study of men and manners; and then come back at the end of two years, when I should find that my father would by no means be indisposed to accept you as a son-in-law. You said your reason for wishing to get my promise before starting was that your mind would then be more at rest when you were far away, and so could give itself more completely to knowledge than if you went as my unaccepted lover only, fuming with anxiety as to how I should be when you came back. I saw how reasonable that was; and solemnly swore myself to you in consequence. But instead of going to see the world you stay on and on here to see me.'

'And you don't want me to see you?'

'Yes – no – it is not that. It is that I have latterly felt frightened at what I am doing when not in your actual presence. It seems so wicked not to tell my father that I have a lover close at hand, within touch and view of both of us; whereas if you were absent my conduct would not seem quite so treacherous. The realities would not stare at one so. You would be a pleasant dream to me, which I should be free to indulge in without reproach of my conscience; I should live in hopeful expectation of your returning fully qualified to boldy claim me of my father. There, I have been terribly frank, I know.'

He in his turn had lapsed into gloomy breathings now. 'I did plan it as you state,' he answered. 'I did mean to go away the moment I had your promise. But, dear Christine, I did not foresee two or three things. I did not know what a lot of pain it would cost to tear myself from you. And I did not know that my stingy uncle – heaven forgive me calling him so! – would so flatly refuse to advance me money for my purpose – the scheme of travelling with a first-rate tutor costing a formidable sum o' money. You have no idea what it would cost!'

'But I have said that I'll find the money.'

'Ah, there,' he returned, 'you have hit a sore place. To speak truly, dear, I would rather stay unpolished a hundred years than take your money.'

'But why? Men continually use the money of the women they marry.'

'Yes; but not till afterwards. No man would like to touch your money at present, and I should feel very mean, if I were to do so in present circumstances. That brings me to what I was going to propose. But no – upon the whole I will not propose it now.'

'Ah! I would guarantee expenses, and you won't let me! The money is my personal possession: it comes to me from my late grandfather, and not from my father at all.'

He laughed forcedly and pressed her hand. 'There are more reasons why I cannot tear myself away,' he added. 'What would become of my uncle's farming? Six hundred acres in this parish, and five hundred in the next – a constant traipsing from one farm to the other; he can't be in two places at once. Still, that might be got over if it were not for the other matters. Besides, dear, I still should be a little uneasy, even though I have your promise, lest somebody should snap you up away from me.'

'Ah, you should have thought of that before. Otherwise I have committed myself for nothing.'

'I should have thought of it,' he answered gravely. 'But I did not. There lies my fault, I admit it freely. Ah, if you would only commit yourself a little more, I might at least get over that difficulty! But I won't ask you. You have no idea how much you are to me still; you could not argue so coolly if you had. What property belongs to you I hate the very sound of; it is you I care for. I wish you hadn't a farthing in the world but what I could earn for you!'

'I don't altogether wish that,' she murmured.

'I wish it, because it would have made what I was going to propose much easier to do than it is now. Indeed I will not propose it, although I came on purpose, after what you have said in your frankness.'

'Nonsense, Nic. Come, tell me. How can you be so touchy?'

'Look at this then, Christine dear.' He drew from his breast-pocket a sheet of paper and unfolded it, when it was observable that a seal dangled from the bottom.

'What is it?' She held the paper sideways, so that what there was of window-light fell on its surface. 'I can only read the Old English letters – why – our names! Surely it is not a marriage-licence?'

'It is.'

She trembled. 'O Nic! how could you do this – and without telling me!'

'Why should I have thought I must tell you? You had not spoken "frankly" then as you have now. We have been all to each other more than these two years, and I thought I would propose that we marry privately, and that I then leave you on the instant. I would have taken my travelling-bag to church, and you would have gone home alone. I should not have started on my adventures in the brilliant manner of our original plan, but should have roughed it a little at first; my great gain would have been that the absolute possession of you would have enabled me to work with spirit and purpose, such as nothing else could do. But I dare not ask you now – so frank as you have been.'

She did not answer. The document he had produced gave such unexpected substantiality to the venture with which she had so long toyed as a vague dream merely, that she was, in truth, frightened a little. 'I – don't know about it!' she said.

'Perhaps not. Ah, my little lady, you are wearying of me!'

'No, Nic,' responded she, creeping closer. 'I am not. Upon my word, and truth, and honour, I am not, Nic.'

'A mere tiller of the soil, as I should be called,' he continued, without heeding her. 'And you – well, a daughter of one of the – I won't say oldest families, because that's absurd, all families are the same age – one of the longest chronicled families about here, whose name is actually the name of the place.'

'That's not much, I am sorry to say! My poor brother – but I won't speak of that. . . . Well,' she murmured mischievously, after a pause, 'you certainly would not need to be uneasy if I were to do this that you want me to do. You would have me safe enough in your trap then; I couldn't get away!'

'That's just it!' he said vehemently. 'It *is* a trap – you feel it so, and that though you wouldn't be able to get away from me you might particularly wish to! Ah, if I had asked you two years ago you would have agreed instantly. But I thought I was bound to wait for the proposal to come from you as the superior!'

'Now you are angry, and take seriously what I meant purely in fun. You don't know me even yet! To show you that you have not been mistaken in me, I *do* propose to carry out this licence. I'll marry you, dear Nicholas, tomorrow morning.'

'Ah, Christine! I am afraid I have stung you on to this, so that I cannot –'

'No, no, no!' she hastily rejoined; and there was something in her tone which suggested that she had been put upon her mettle and would not flinch. 'Take me whilst I am in the humour. What church is the licence for?'

'That I've not looked to see – why our parish church here, of course. Ah, then we cannot use it! We dare not be married here.'

'We do dare,' said she. 'And we will too, if you'll be there.'

'*If* I'll be there!'

They speedily came to an agreement that he should be in the church-porch at ten minutes to eight on the following morning, awaiting her; and that, immediately after the conclusion of the service which would make them one, Nicholas should set out on his long-deferred educational tour, towards the cost of which she was resolving to bring a substantial subscription with her to church. Then, slipping from him, she went indoors by the way she had come, and Nicholas bent his steps homewards.

II

Instead of leaving the spot by the gate, he flung himself over the fence, and pursued a direction towards the river under the trees. And it was now, in his lonely progress, that he showed for the first time outwardly that he was not altogether unworthy of her. He wore long waterboots reaching above his knees, and, instead of making a circuit to find a bridge by which he might cross the Froom – the river aforesaid – he made straight for the point whence proceeded the low roar that was at this hour the only evidence of the stream's existence. He speedily stood on the verge of the waterfall which caused the noise, and stepping into the water at the top of the fall, waded through with the sure tread of one who knew every inch of his footing, even though the canopy of trees rendered the darkness almost absolute, and a false step would have precipitated him into the pool beneath. Soon reaching the boundary of the grounds, he continued in the same direct line to traverse the alluvial valley, full of brooks and tributaries to the main stream – in former times quite impassable, and impassable in winter now. Sometimes he would cross a deep gully on a plank not wider than the hand; at another time he ploughed his way through beds of spear-grass where at a few feet to the right or left he might have been sucked down in a morass. At last he reached firm land on the other side of this watery tract, and came to his house on the rise behind – Elsenford – an ordinary farmstead, from the back of which rose indistinct breathings, belchings, and snortings, the rattle of halters, and other familiar features of an agriculturist's home.

While Nicholas Long was packing his bag in an upper room of this dwelling, Miss Christine Everard sat at a desk in her own chamber at Froom-Everard manor-house, looking with pale fixed countenance at the candles.

'I ought – I must now!' she whispered to herself. 'I should not have begun it if I had not meant to carry it through! It runs in the blood of us, I suppose.' She alluded to a fact unknown to her lover, the clandestine marriage of an aunt under circumstances somewhat similar to the present. In a few minutes she had penned the following note:–

October 13, 183–

DEAR MR. BEALAND – Can you make it convenient to yourself to meet me at the Church tomorrow at eight? I name the early hour because it would suit me better than later on in the day. You will find me in the chancel, if you can come. An answer yes or no by the bearer of this will be sufficient.

CHRISTINE EVERARD

She sent the note to the rector immediately, waiting at a small side-door of the house till she heard the servant's footsteps returning along the lane, when she went round and met him in the passage. The rector had taken the trouble to write a line, and answered that he would meet her with pleasure.

A dripping fog which ushered in the next morning was highly favourable to the scheme of the pair. At that time of the century Froom-Everard House had not been altered and enlarged; the public lane passed close under its walls; and there was a door opening directly from one of the old parlours – the south parlour, as it was called – into the lane which led to the village. Christine came out this way, and after following the lane for a short distance entered upon a path within a belt of plantation, by which the church could be reached privately. She even avoided the churchyard gate, walking along to a place where the turf without the low wall rose into a mound, enabling her to mount upon the coping and spring down inside. She crossed the wet graves, and so glided round to the door. He was there, with his bag in his hand. He kissed her with a sort of surprise, as if he had expected that at the last moment her heart would fail her.

Though it had not failed her, there was, nevertheless, no great ardour in Christine's bearing – merely the momentum of an antecedent impulse. They went up the aisle together, the bottle-green glass of the old lead quarries admitting but little light at that hour, and under such an atmosphere. They stood by the altar-rail in silence, Christine's skirt visibly quivering at each beat of her heart.

Presently a quick step ground upon the gravel, and Mr. Bealand came round by the front. He was a quiet bachelor, courteous towards Christine, and not at first recognizing in Nicholas a neighbouring yeoman (for he lived aloofly in the next parish), advanced to her without revealing any surprise at her unusual request. But in truth he was surprised, the keen interest taken by many country young women at the present day in church decoration and festivals being then unknown.

'Good morning,' he said; and repeated the same words to Nicholas more mechanically.

'Good morning,' she replied gravely. 'Mr Bealand, I have a serious reason for asking you to meet me – us, I may say. We wish you to marry us.'

The rector's gaze hardened to fixity, rather between than upon either of them, and he neither moved nor replied for some time.

'Ah!' he said at last.

'And we are quite ready.'

'I had no idea –'

'It has been kept rather private,' she said calmly.

'Where are your witnesses?'

'They are outside in the meadow sir. I can call them in a moment,' said Nicholas.

'Oh – I see it is – Mr. Nicholas Long,' said Mr. Bealand, and turning again to Christine, 'Does your father know of this?'

'Is it necessary that I should answer that question, Mr. Bealand?'

'I am afraid it is – highly necessary.'

Christine began to look concerned.

'Where is the licence?' the rector asked; 'since there have been no banns.'

Nicholas produced it, Mr. Bealand read it, an operation which occupied him several minutes – or at least he made it appear so; till Christine said impatiently, 'We are quite ready, Mr. Bealand. Will you proceed? Mr. Long has to take a journey of a great many miles today.'

'And you?'

'No. I remain.'

Mr. Bealand assumed firmness. 'There is something wrong in this,' he said. 'I cannot marry you without your father's presence.'

'But have you a right to refuse us?' interposed Nicholas. 'I believe we are in a position to demand your fulfilment of our request.'

'No, you are not! Is Miss Everard of age? I think not. I think she is months from being so. Eh, Miss Everard?'

'Am I bound to tell that?'

'Certainly. At any rate you are bound to write it. Meanwhile I refuse to solemnize the service. And let me entreat you two young people to do nothing so rash as this, even if by going to some strange church, you may do so without discovery. The tragedy of marriage –'

'Tragedy?'

'Certainly. It is full of crises and catastrophes, and ends with the death of one of the actors. The tragedy of marriage, as I was saying, is one I shall not be a party to your beginning with such light hearts, and I shall feel bound to put your father on his guard, Miss Everard. Think better of it, I entreat you! Remember the proverb, "Marry in haste and repent at leisure."'

Christine, spurred by opposition, almost stormed at him. Nicholas implored; but nothing would turn that obstinate rector. She sat down and reflected: By-and-by she confronted Mr. Bealand.

'Our marriage is not to be this morning, I see,' she said. 'Now grant me one favour, and in return I'll promise you to do nothing rashly. Do not tell my father a word of what has happened here.'

'I agree – if you undertake not to elope.'

She looked at Nicholas, and he looked at her. 'Do you wish to elope, Nic?' she asked.

'No,' he said.

So the compact was made, and they left the church singly, Nicholas remaining till the last, and closing the door. On his way home, carrying the well-packed bag which was just now to go no further, the two men who were mending water-carriers in the meadows approached the hedge, as if they had been on the alert all the time.

'You said you mid want us for zummat, sir?'

'All right – never mind,' he answered through the hedge. 'I did not require you after all.'

III

At a manor not far away there lived a queer and primitive couple who had lately been blessed with a son and heir. The christening took place during the week under notice, and this had been followed by a feast to the parishioners. Christine's father, one of the same generation and kind, had been asked to drive over and assist in the entertainment, and Christine, as a matter of course, accompanied him.

When they reached Athelhall, as the house was called, they found the usually quiet nook a lively spectacle. Tables had been spread in the apartment which lent its name to the whole building – the hall proper – covered with a fine open-timbered roof, whose braces, purlins, and rafters made a brown thicket of oak overhead. Here tenantry of all ages sat with their wives and families, and the servants were assisted in their ministrations by the sons and daughters of the owner's friends and neighbours. Christine lent a hand among the rest.

She was holding a plate in each hand towards a huge brown platter of baked rice-pudding, from which a footman was scooping a large spoonful, when a voice reached her ear over her shoulder: 'Allow me to hold them for you.'

Christine turned, and recognized in the speaker the nephew of the entertainer, a young man from London, whom she had already met on two or three occasions. She accepted the proffered help, and from that moment, whenever he passed her in their marchings to and fro during the remainder of the serving, he smiled acquaintance. When their work was done, he improved the few words into a conversation. He plainly had been attracted by her fairness.

Bellston was a self-assured young man, not particularly
good-looking, with more colour in his skin than even
Nicholas had. He had flushed a little in attracting her notice,
though the flush had nothing of nervousness in it – the air
with which it was accompanied making it curiously sugges-
tive of a flush of anger; and even when he laughed it was
difficult to banish that fancy.

The late autumn sunlight streamed in through the window
panes upon the heads and shoulders of the venerable patriarchs
of the hamlet, and upon the middle-aged, and upon the
young; upon men and women who had played out, or were to
play, tragedies or tragi-comedies in that nook of civilization
not less great, essentially, than those which, enacted on more
central arenas, fix the attention of the world. One of the party
was a cousin of Nicholas Long's, who sat with her husband
and children.

To make himself as locally harmonious as possible, Mr.
Bellston remarked to his companion on the scene –

'It does one's heart good,' he said, 'to see these simple
peasants enjoying themselves.'

'O Mr. Bellston!' exclaimed Christine; 'don't be to sure
about that word "simple"! You little think what they see and
meditate! Their reasonings and emotions are as complicated as
ours.'

She spoke with a vehemence which would have been hardly
present in her words but for her own relation to Nicholas.
The sense of that produced in her a nameless depression
thenceforward. The young man, however, still followed her
up.

'I am glad to hear you say it,' he returned warmly. 'I was
merely attuning myself to your mood, as I thought. The real
truth is that I know more of the Parthians, and Medes, and
dwellers in Mesopotamia – almost of any people, indeed –
than of the English rustics. Travel and exploration are my
profession, not the study of the British peasantry.'

Travel. There was sufficient coincidence between his
declaration and the course she had urged upon her lover, to
lend Bellston's account of himself a certain interest in Christine's ears. He might perhaps be able to tell her something that
would be useful to Nicholas, if their dream were carried out. A

door opened from the hall into the garden, and she somehow found herself outside, chatting with Mr. Bellston on this topic, till she thought that upon the whole she liked the young man. The garden being his uncle's, he took her round it with an air of proprietorship; and they went on amongst the Michaelmas daisies and chrysanthemums, and through a door to the fruit-garden. A green-house was open, and he went in and cut her a bunch of grapes.

'How daring of you! They are your uncle's.'

'O, he won't mind – I do anything here. A rough old buffer, isn't he?'

She was thinking of her Nic, and felt that, by comparison with her present acquaintance, the farmer more than held his own as a fine and intelligent fellow; but the harmony with her own existence in little things, which she found here, imparted an alien tinge to Nicholas just now. The latter, idealized by moonlight, or a thousand miles of distance, was altogether a more romantic object for a woman's dream than this smart new-lacquered man; but in the sun of afternoon, and amid a surrounding company, Mr. Bellston was a very tolerable companion.

When they re-entered the hall, Bellston entreated her to come with him up a spiral stair in the thickness of the wall, leading to a passage and gallery whence they could look down upon the scene below. The people had finished their feast, the newly-christened baby had been exhibited, and a few words having been spoken to them they began, amid a racketing of forms, to make for the greensward without, Nicholas's cousin and cousin's wife and cousin's children among the rest. While they were filing out, a voice was heard calling –

'Hullo! – here, Jim; where are you?' said Bellston's uncle. The young man descended, Christine following at leisure.

'Now will ye be a good fellow,' the Squire continued, 'and set them going outside in some dance or other that they know? I'm dog-tired, and I want to have a vew words with Mr Everard before we join 'em – hey, Everard? They are shy till somebody starts 'em; afterwards they'll keep gwine brisk enough.'

'Ay, that they wool,' said Squire Everard.

They followed to the lawn; and here it proved that James Bellston was as shy, or rather as averse, as any of the tenantry themselves, to acting the part of fugleman. Only the parish people had been at the feast, but outlying neighbours had now strolled in for a dance.

'They want "Speed the Plough,"' said Bellston, coming up breathless. 'It must be a country dance, I suppose? Now, Miss Everard, do have pity upon me. I am supposed to lead off; but really I know no more about speeding the plough than a child just born! Would you take one of the villagers? – just to start them, my uncle says. Suppose you take that handsome young farmer over there – I don't know his name, but I dare say you do – and I'll come on with one of the dairyman's daughters as a second couple.'

Christine turned in the direction signified and changed colour – though in the shade nobody noticed it. 'Oh, yes – I know him,' she said cooly. 'He is from near our own place – Mr. Nicholas Long.'

'That's capital – then you can easily make him stand as first couple with you. Now I must pick up mine.'

'I – I think I'll dance with you, Mr. Bellston,' she said with some trepidation. 'Because, you see,' she explained eagerly, 'I know the figure and you don't – so that I can help you; while Nicholas Long, I know, is familiar with the figure, and that will make two couples who know it – which is necessary, at least.'

Bellston showed his gratification by one of his angry pleasant flushes – he had hardly dared to ask for what she proffered freely; and having requested Nicholas to take the dairyman's daughter, led Christine in her place, Long promptly stepping up second with his charge. There were grim silent depths in Nic's character; a small deedy spark in his eye, as it caught Christine's was all that showed his consciousness of her. Then the fiddles began – the celebrated Mellstock fiddlers who, given free stripping, could play from sunset to dawn without turning a hair. The couples wheeled and swung, Nicholas taking Christine's hand in the course of business with the figure, when she waited for him to give it a little squeeze; but he did not.

Christine had the greatest difficulty in steering her partner through the maze, on account of his self-will, and when at last they reached the bottom of the long line, she was breathless with her hard labour. Resting here, she watched Nic and his lady; and, though she had decidedly cooled off in these later months, began to admire him anew. Nobody knew these dances like him, after all, or could do anything of this sort so well. His performance with the dairyman's daughter so won upon her, that when 'Speed the Plough' was over she contrived to speak to him.

'Nic, you are to dance with me next time.'

He said he would, and presently asked her in a formal public manner, lifting his hat gallantly. She showed a little backwardness, which he quite understood, and allowed him to lead her to the top, a row of enormous length appearing below them as if by magic as soon as they had taken their places. Truly the Squire was right when he said that they only wanted starting.

'What is it to be?' whispered Nicholas.

She turned to the band. 'The Honeymoon,' she said.

And then they trod the delightful last-century measure of that name, which if it had been ever danced better, was never danced with more zest. The perfect responsiveness which their tender acquaintance threw into the motions of Nicholas and his partner lent to their gyrations the fine adjustment of two interacting parts of a single machine. The excitement of the movement carried Christine back to the time – the unreflecting passionate time, about two years before – when she and Nic had been incipient lovers only; and it made her forget the carking anxieties, the vision of social breakers ahead, that had begun to take the gilding off her position now. Nicholas, on his part, had never ceased to be a lover; no personal worries had as yet made him conscious of any staleness, flatness, or unprofitableness of his admiration of Christine.

'Not quite so wildly, Nic,' she whispered. 'I don't object personally; but they'll notice us. How came you here?'

'I heard that you had driven over; and I set out – on purpose for this.'

'What – you have walked?'

'Yes. If I had waited for one of uncle's horses I should have been too late.'

'Five miles here and five back – ten miles on foot – merely to dance!'

'With you. What made you think of this old "Honeymoon" thing?'

'O! it came into my head when I saw you, as what would have been a reality with us if you had not been stupid about that licence, and had got it for a distant church.'

'Shall we try again?'

'No – I don't know. I'll think it over.'

The villagers admired their grace and skill, as the dancers themselves perceived; but they did not know what accompanied that admiration in one spot, at least.

'People who wonder they can foot it so featly together should know what some others think,' a waterman was saying to his neighbour. 'Then their wonder would be less.'

His comrade asked for information.

'Well – really I hardly believe it – but 'tis said they be man and wife. Yes sure – went to church and did the job a'most afore 'twas light one morning. But mind, not a word of this; for 'twould be the loss of a winter's work to me if I had spread such a report and it were not true.'

When the dance had ended she rejoined her own section of the company. Her father and Mr. Bellston the elder had now come out from the house, and were smoking in the background. Presently she found that her father was at her elbow.

'Christine, don't dance too often with young Long – as a mere matter of prudence, I mean, as volk might think it odd, he being one of our own neighbouring farmers. I should not mention this to 'ee if he were an ordinary young fellow; but being superior to the rest it behoves you to be careful.'

'Exactly, papa,' said Christine.

But the revived sense that she was deceiving him threw a damp over her spirits. 'But, after all,' she said to herself, 'he is a young man of Elsenford, handsome, able, and the soul of honour; and I am a young woman of the adjoining parish, who have been constantly thrown into communication with him. Is it not, by nature's rule, the most proper thing in the world that I should marry him, and is it not an absurd conventional regulation which says that such a union would be wrong?

It may be concluded that the strength of Christine's large-minded argument was rather an evidence of weakness than of strength in the passion it concerned, which had required neither argument nor reasoning of any kind for its maintenance when full and flush in its early days.

When driving home in the dark with her father she sank into pensive silence. She was thinking of Nicholas having to trudge on foot all those miles back after his exertions on the sward. Mr. Everard, arousing himself from a nap, said suddenly, 'I have something to mention to 'ee, by George – so I have, Chris! You probably know what it is?'

She expressed ignorance, wondering if her father had discovered anything of her secret.

'Well, according to *him* you know it. But I will tell 'ee. Perhaps you noticed young Jim Bellston walking me off down the lawn with him? – whether or no, we walked together a good while; and he informed me that he wanted to pay his addresses to 'ee. I naturally said that it depended upon yourself; and he replied that you were willing enough; you had given him particular encouragement – showing your preference for him by specially choosing him for your partner – hey? "In that case," says I, "go on and conquer – settle it with her – I have no objection." The poor fellow was very grateful, and in short, there we left the matter. He'll propose tomorrow.'

She saw now to her dismay what James Bellston had read as encouragement. 'He has mistaken me altogether,' she said. 'I had no idea of such a thing.'

'What, you won't have him?'

'Indeed, I cannot!'

'Chrissy,' said Mr. Everard with emphasis, 'there's *noo*body whom I should so like you to marry as that young man. He's a thoroughly clever fellow, and fairly well provided for. He's travelled all over the temperate zone; but he says that directly he marries he's going to give up all that, and be a regular stay-at-home. You would be nowhere safer than in his hands.'

'It is true,' she answered. 'He *is* a highly desirable match, and I *should* be well provided for, and probably very safe in his hands.'

'Then don't be skittish, and stand-to.'

She had spoken from her conscience and understanding, and not to please her father. As a reflecting woman she believed that

such a marriage would be a wise one. In great things
Nicholas was closest to her nature; in little things Bellston
seemed immeasurably nearer than Nic; and life was made up
of little things.

Altogether the firmament looked black for Nicholas Long,
notwithstanding her half-hour's ardour for him when she
saw him dancing with the dairyman's daughter. Most great
passions, movements, and beliefs – individual and national –
burst during their decline into a temporary irradiation, which
rivals their original splendour; and then they speedily become
extinct. Perhaps the dance had given the last flare-up to
Christine's love. It seemed to have improvidently consumed
for its immediate purpose all her ardour forwards, so that for
the future there was nothing left but frigidity.

Nicholas had certainly been very foolish about that licence!

IV

This laxity of emotional tone was further increased by an
incident, when, two days later, she kept an appointment
with Nicholas in the Sallows. The Sallows was an extension
of shrubberies and plantations along the banks of the Froom,
accessible from the lawn of Froom-Everard House only,
except by wading through the river at the waterfall or
elsewhere. Near the brink was a thicket of box in which a
trunk lay prostrate; this had been once or twice their trys-
ting-place, though it was by no means a safe one; and it was
here she sat awaiting him now.

The noise of the stream muffled any sound of footsteps,
and it was before she was aware of his approach that she
looked up and saw him wading across at the top of the
waterfall.

Noontide lights and dwarfed shadows always banished the
romantic aspect of her love for Nicholas. Moreover, something new had occured to disturb her; and if ever she had
regretted giving way to a tenderness for him – which perhaps
she had not done with any distinctness – she regretted it
now. Yet in the bottom of their hearts those two were
excellently paired, the very twin halves of a perfect whole;

and their love was pure. But at this hour surfaces showed garishly, and obscured the depths. Probably her regret appeared in her face.

He walked up to her without speaking, the water running from his boots; and, taking one of her hands in each of his own, looked narrowly into her eyes.

'Have you thought it over?'

'What?'

'Whether we shall try again; you remember saying you would at the dance?'

'Oh, I had forgoten that!'

'You are sorry we tried at all!' he said accusingly.

'I am not so sorry for the fact as for the rumours,' she said.

'Ah! rumours?'

'They say we are already married,'

'Who?'

'I cannot tell exactly. I heard some whispering to that effect. Somebody in the village told one of the servants, I believe. This man said that he was crossing the churchyard early on that unfortunate foggy morning, and heard voices in the chancel, and peeped through the window as well as the dim panes would let him; and there he saw you and me and Mr. Bealand, and so on; but thinking his surmises would be dangerous knowledge, he hastened on. And so the story got afloat. Then your aunt, too —'

'Good Lord! – what has she done?'

'The story was told her, and she said proudly, "O yes, it is true enough. I have seen the licence. But it is not to be known yet."'

'Seen the licence? How the —'

'Accidentally, I believe, when your coat was hanging somewhere.'

The information, coupled with the infelicitious word 'proudly,' caused Nicholas to flush with mortification. He knew that it was in his aunt's nature to make a brag of that sort; but worse than the brag was the fact that this was the first occasion on which Christine had deigned to show her consciousness that such a marriage would be a source of pride to his relatives – the only two he had in the world.

'You are sorry, then, even to be thought my wife, much less to be it.' He dropped her hand, which fell lifelessly.

'It is not sorry exactly, dear Nic. But I feel uncomfortable and vexed, that after screwing up my courage, my fidelity, to the point of going to church, you should have so muddled – managed the matter that it has ended in neither one thing nor the other. How can I meet acquaintances, when I don't know what they are thinking of me?'

'Then, dear Christine, let us mend the muddle. I'll go away for a few days and get another licence, and you can come to me.'

She shrank from this perceptibly. 'I cannot screw myself up to it a second time,' she said. 'I am sure I cannot! Besides, I promised Mr. Bealand. And yet how can I continue to see you after such a rumour? We shall be watched now, for certain.'

'Then don't see me.'

'I fear I must not for the present. Altogether —'

'What?'

'I am very depressed.'

These views were not very inspiriting to Nicholas, as he construed them. It may indeed have been possible that he construed them wrongly, and should have insisted upon her making the rumour true. Unfortunately, too, he had come to her in a hurry through brambles and briars, water and weed, and the shaggy wildness which hung about his appearance at this fine and correct time of day lent an impracticability to the look of him.

'You blame me – you repent your courses – you repent that you ever, ever owned anything to me!'

'No, Nicholas, I do not repent that,' she returned gently, though with firmness. 'But I think that you ought not to have got that licence without asking me first; and I also think that you ought to have known how it would be if you lived on here in your present position, and made no effort to better it. I can bear whatever comes, for social ruin is not personal ruin or even personal disgrace. But as a sensible, new-risen poet says, whom I have been reading this morning:–

The world and its ways have a certain worth:
And to press a point while these oppose

Were simple policy. Better wait.

As soon as you had got my promise, Nic, you should have gone away – yes – and made a name, and come back to claim me. That was my silly girlish dream about my hero.'

'Perhaps I can do as much yet! And would you have indeed liked better to live away from me for family reasons, than to run a risk in seeing me for affection's sake? O what a cold heart it has grown! If I had been a prince, and you a dairymaid, I'd have stood by you in the face of the world!'

She shook her head. 'Ah – you don't know what society is – you don't know.'

'Perhaps not. Who was that strange gentleman of about seven-and-twenty I saw at Mr. Bellston's christening feast?'

'Oh – that was his nephew James. Now he is a man who has seen an unusual extent of the world for his age. He is a great traveller, you know.'

'Indeed.'

'In fact an explorer. He is very entertaining.'

'No doubt.'

Nicholas received no shock of jealousy from her announcement. He knew her so well that he could see she was not in the least in love with Bellston. But he asked if Bellston were going to continue his explorations.

'Not if he settles in life. Otherwise he will, I suppose.'

'Perhaps I could be a great explorer, too, if I tried.'

'You could, I am sure.'

They sat apart, and not together; each looking afar off at vague objects, and not in each other's eyes. Thus the sad autumn afternoon waned, while the waterfall hissed sarcastically of the inevitableness of the unpleasant. Very different this from the time when they had first met there.

The nook was most picturesque; but it looked horridly common and stupid now. Their sentiment had set a colour hardly less visible than a material one on surrounding objects, as sentiment must where life is but thought. Nicholas was as devoted as ever to the fair Christine; but unhappily he too had moods and humours, and the division between them was not closed.

She had no sooner got indoors and sat down to her work-table than her father entered the drawing-room. She handed him his newspaper; he took it without a word, went and stood on the hearthrug, and flung the paper on the floor.

'Christine, what's the meaning of this terrible story? I was just on my way to look at the register.'

She looked at him without speech.

'You have married – Nicholas Long?'

'No father.'

'No? Can you say no in the face of such facts as I have been put in possession of?'

'Yes.'

'But – the note you wrote to the rector – and the going to church?'

She briefly explained that their attempt had failed.

'Ah! Then this is what the dancing meant, was it? By —, it makes me —. How long has this been going on, may I ask?'

'This what?'

'What, indeed! Why, making him your beau. Now listen to me. All's well that ends well; from this day, madam, this moment, he is to be nothing more to you. You are not to see him. Cut him adrift instantly! I only wish his volk were on my farm – out they should go, or I would know the reason why. However, you are to write him a letter to this effect at once.'

'How can I cut him adrift?'

'Why not? You must, my good maid!'

'Well, though I have not actually married him, I have solemnly sworn to be his wife when he comes home from abroad to claim me. It would be gross perjury not to fulfil my promise. Besides, no woman can go to church with a man to deliberately solemnize matrimony, and refuse him afterwards, if he does nothing wrong meanwhile.'

The uttered sound of her strong conviction seemed to kindle in Christine a livelier perception of all its bearings than she had known while it had lain unformulated in her mind. For when she had done speaking she fell down on her knees before her father, covered her face, and said, 'Please, please forgive me, papa! How *could* I do it without letting you know! I don't know, I don't know!'

When she looked up she found that, in the turmoil of his mind, her father was moving about the room. 'You are within an ace of ruining yourself, ruining me, ruining us all!' he said. 'You are nearly as bad as your brother, begad!'

'Perhaps I am – yes – perhaps I am!'

'That I should father such a harum-scarum brood!'

'It is very bad; but Nicholas —'

'He's a scoundrel!'

'He is *not* a scoundrel!' cried she, turning quickly. 'He's as good and worthy as you or I, or anybody bearing our name, or any nobleman in the kingdom, if you come to that! Only – only' – she could not continue the argument on those lines. 'Now, father, listen!' she sobbed; 'if you taunt me I'll go off and join him at his farm this very day, and marry him tomorrow, that's what I'll do!'

'I don't taant ye!'

'I wish to avoid unseemliness as much as you.'

She went away. When she came back a quarter of an hour later, thinking to find the room empty, he was standing there as before, never having apparently moved. His manner had quite changed. He seemed to take a resigned and entirely different view of circumstances.

'Christine, here's a paragraph in the paper hinting at a secret wedding, and I'm blazed if it don't point to you. Well, since this was to happen, I'll bear it, and not complain. All volk have crosses, and this is one of mine. Now, this is what I've got to say – I feel that you must carry out this attempt at marrying Nicholas Long. Faith, you must! The rumour will become a scandal if you don't – that's my view. I have tried to look at the brightest side of the case. Nicholas Long is a young man superior to most of his class, and fairly presentable. And he's not poor – at least his uncle is not. I believe the old muddler could buy me up any day. However, a farmer's wife you must be, as far as I can see. As you've made your bed, so ye must lie. Parents propose, and ungrateful children dispose. You shall marry him, and immediately.'

Christine hardly knew what to make of this. 'He is quite willing to wait, and so am I. We can wait for two or three years, and then he will be as worthy as —'

'You must marry him. And the sooner the better, if 'tis to be done at all. . . . And yet I did wish you could have been Jim Bellston's wife. I did wish it! But no.'

'I, too, wished it and do still, in one sense,' she returned gently. His moderation had won her out of her defiant mood, and she was willing to reason with him.

'You do?' he said surprised.

'I see that in a worldly sense my conduct with Mr. Long may be considered a mistake.'

'H'm – I am glad to hear that – after my death you may see it more clearly still; and you won't have long to wait to my reckoning.'

She fell into bitter repentance, and kissed him in her anguish. 'Don't say that!' she cried. 'Tell me what to do?'

'If you'll leave me for an hour or two I'll think. Drive to the market and back – the carriage is at the door – and I'll try to collect my senses. Dinner can be put back till you return.'

In a few minutes she was dressed, and the carriage bore her up the hill which divided the village and manor from the market-town.

V

A quarter of an hour brought her into the High Street, and for want of a more important errand she called at the harness-maker's for a dog-collar that she required.

It happened to be market-day, and Nicholas, having postponed the engagements which called him thither to keep the appointment with her in the Sallows, rushed off at the end of the afternoon to attend to them as well as he could. Arriving thus in a great hurry on account of the lateness of the hour, he still retained the wild, amphibious appearance which had marked him when he came up from the meadows to her side – an exceptional condition of things which had scarcely ever before occurred. When she crossed the pavement from the shop door, the shopman bowing and escorting her to the carriage, Nicholas chanced to be standing at the road-waggon office, talking to the master of the waggons. There were a good many people about, and those near paused and looked at her transit, in the full stroke of the level October sun, which went under the brims of their hats, and pierced through their button-holes. From the group she heard murmured the words: 'Mrs. Nicholas Long.'

The unexpected remark, not without distinct satire in its tone, took her so greatly by surprise that she was confounded. Nicholas was by this time nearer, though coming against the sun he had not yet perceived her. Influenced by her father's lecture, she felt angry with him for being there and causing this awkwardness. Her notice of him was therefore slight, supercilious perhaps, slurred over; and her vexation at his presence showed distinctly in her face as she sat down in her seat. Instead of catching his waiting eye, she positively turned her head away.

A moment after she was sorry she had treated him so; but he was gone.

Reaching home she found on her dressing-table a note from her father. The statement was brief:

I have considered and am of the same opinion. You must marry him. He can leave home at once and travel as proposed. I have written to him to this effect. I don't want any victuals, so don't wait dinner for me.

Nicholas was the wrong kind of man to be blind to Christine's mortification, though he did not know its entire cause. He had lately foreseen something of this sort as possible.

'It serves me right,' he thought, as he trotted homeward. 'It was absurd – wicked of me to lead her on so. The sacrifice would have been too great – too cruel!' And yet, though he thus took her part, he flushed with indignation every time he said to himself, 'She is ashamed of me!'

On the ridge which overlooked Froom-Everard he met a neighbour of his – a stock dealer – in his gig, and they drew rein and exchanged a few words. A part of the dealer's conversation had much meaning for Nicholas.

'I've had occasion to call on Squire Everard,' the former said; 'but he couldn't see me on account of being quite knocked up at some bad news he has heard.'

Nicholas rode on past Froom-Everard to Elsenford Farm, pondering. He had new and startling matter for thought as soon as he got there. The Squire's note had arrived. At first he could not credit its import; then he saw further, took in the tone of the letter, saw the writer's contempt behind the words, and understood that the letter was written as by a man hemmed into a corner. Christine was defiantly – insultingly – hurled at his head. He was accepted because he was so despised.

And yet with what respect he had treated her and hers! Now he was reminded of what an agricultural friend had said years ago, seeing the eyes of Nicholas fixed on Christine as on an angel when she passed: 'Better a little fire to warm 'ee than a great one to burn 'ee. No good can come of throwing your heart there.' He went into the mead, sat down, and asked himself four questions:

1.   How could she live near her acquaintance as his wife, even in his absence, without suffering martyrdom from the stings of their contempt?

2.   Would not this entail total estrangement between Christine and her family also, and her own consequent misery?

3.   Must not such isolation extinguish her affection for him?

4.   Supposing that her father rigged them out as colonists and sent them off to America, was not the effect of such exile upon one of her gentle nurture likely to be as the last?

In short, whatever they should embark in together would be cruelty to her, and his death would be a relief. It would, indeed, in one aspect be a relief to her now, if she were so ashamed of him as she had appeared to be that day. Were he dead, this little episode with him would fade away like a dream.

Mr Everard was a good-hearted man at bottom, but to take his enraged offer seriously was impossible. Obviously it was hotly made in his first bitterness at what he had heard. The least thing that he could do would be to go away and never trouble her more. To travel and learn and come back in two years, as mapped out in their first sanguine scheme, required a staunch heart on her side, if the necessary expenditure of time and money were to be afterwards justified; and it were folly to calculate on that when he had seen today that her heart was failing her already. To travel and disappear and not be heard of for many years would be a far more independent stroke, and it would leave her entirely unfettered. Perhaps he might rival in this kind the accomplished Mr. Bellston, of whose journeyings he had heard so much.

He sat and sat and the fog rose out of the river, enveloping him like a fleece; first his feet and knees, then his arms and body, and finally submerging his head. When he had come to a decision he went up again into the homestead. He would be independent, if he died for it, and he would free Christine. Exile was the only course. The first step was to inform his uncle of his determination.

Two days later Nicholas was on the same spot in the mead, at almost the same hour of eve. But there was no fog now; a blusterous autumn wind had ousted the still, golden days and misty nights; and he was going, full of purpose, in the opposite-direction. When he had last entered the mead he was an inhabitant of the Froom valley; in forty-eight hours he had severed himself from that spot as completely as if he had never belonged to it. All that appertained to him in the Froom valley now was circumscribed by the portmanteau in his hand.

In making his preparations for departure he had unconsciously held a faint, foolish hope that she would communicate with him and make up their estrangement in some soft womanly way. But she had given no signal, and it was too evident to him that her latest mood had grown to be her fixed one, proving how well founded had been his impulse to set her free.

He entered the Sallows, found his way in the dark to the garden-door of the house, slipped under it a note to tell her of his departure and explaining its true reason to be a consciousness of her growing feeling that he was an encumbrance and a humiliation. Of the direction of his journey and of the date of his return he said nothing.

His course now took him into the high road, which he pursued for some miles in a north-easterly direction, still spinning the thread of sad inferences, and asking himself why he should ever return. At daybreak he stood on the hill above Shottsford-Forum, and awaited a coach which passed about this time along that highway towards Melchester and London.

VI

Some fifteen years after the date of the foregoing incidents, a man who had dwelt in far countries, and viewed many cities, arrived at Roy-Town, a roadside hamlet on the old western turnpike road, not five miles from Froom-Everard, and put up at the Buck's Head, an isolated inn at that spot. He was still barely of middle age, but it could be seen that a haze of grey was settling upon the locks of his hair, and that his face had lost colour and curve, as if by exposure to bleaching climates and strange atmospheres, or from ailments incidental thereto. He seemed to observe little around him, by reason of the intrusion of his musings upon the scene. In truth Nicholas Long was just now the creature of old hopes and fears consequent upon his arrival – this man who once had not cared if his name were blotted out from that district. The evening light showed wistful lines which he could not smooth away by the worlding's gloss of nonchalance that he had learnt to fling over his face.

The Buck's Head was a somewhat unusual place for a man of this sort to choose as a house of sojourn in preference to some Casterbridge inn four miles further on. Before he left home it had been a lively old tavern at which High-flyers, and Heralds, and Tally-hoes had changed horses on their stages up and down the country; but now the house was rather cavernous and chilly, the stable-roofs were hollow-backed, the landlord was asthmatic and the traffic gone.

He arrived in the afternoon, and when he had sent back the fly and was having a nondescript meal, he put a question to the waiting-maid with a mien of indifference.

'Squire Everard, of Froom-Everard Manor, has been dead some years, I believe?'

She replied in the affirmative.

'And are any of the family left there still?'

'O no, bless you, sir! They sold the place years ago – Squire Everard's son did – and went away. I've never heard where they went to. They came quite to nothing.'

'Never heard anything of the young lady – the Squire's daughter?'

'No. You see 'twas before I came to these parts.'

When the waitress left the room, Nicholas pushed aside his plate and gazed out of the window. He was not going over into the Froom Valley altogether on Christine's account, but she had greatly animated his motive in coming that way. Anyhow he would push on there now that he was so near, and not ask questions here where he was liable to be wrongly informed. The fundamental inquiry he had not ventured to make – whether Christine had married before the family went away. He had abstained because of an absurd dread of extinguishing hopeful surmise. That the Everards had left their old home was bad enough intelligence for one day.

Rising from the table he put on his hat and went out, ascending towards the upland which divided this district from his native vale. The first familiar feature that met his eye was a little spot on the distant sky – a clump of trees standing on a barrow which surmounted a yet more remote upland – a point where, in his childhood, he had believed people could stand and see America. He reached the further verge of the plateau on which he had entered. Ah, there was the valley – a greenish-grey stretch of colour – still looking placid and serene, as though it had not much missed him. If Christine was no longer there, why should he pause over it this evening? His uncle and aunt were dead, and tomorrow would be soon enough to inquire for remoter relatives. Thus, disinclined to go further, he turned to retrace his way to the inn.

In the backward path he now perceived the figure of a woman, who had been walking at a distance behind him; and as she drew nearer he began to be startled. Surely, despite the variations introduced into that figure by changing years, its ground-lines were those of Christine?

Nicholas had been sentimental enough to write to Christine immediately on landing at Southampton a day or two before this, addressing his letter at a venture to the old house, and merely telling her that he planned to reach the Roy-Town inn on the present afternoon. The news of the scattering of the Everards had dissipated his hope of hearing of her; but here she was.

So they met – there, alone, on the open down by a pond, just as if the meeting had been carefully arranged.

She threw up her veil. She was still beautiful, though the years had touched her; a little more matronly – much more homely. Or was it only that he was much less homely now – a man of the world – the sense of homeliness being relative? Her face had grown to be pre-eminently of the sort that would be called interesting. Her habiliments were of a demure and sober cast, though she was one who had used to dress so airily and so gaily. Years had laid on a few shadows too in this.

'I received your letter,' she said, when the momentary embarrassment of their first approach had passed. 'And I thought I would walk across the hills today, as it was fine. I have just called at the inn, and they told me you were out. I was now on my way homeward.'

He hardly listened to this, though he intently gazed at her. 'Christine,' he said, 'one word. Are you free?'

'I – I am in a certain sense,' she replied, colouring.

The announcement had a magical effect. The intervening time between past and present closed up for him, and moved by an impulse which he had combated for fifteen years, he seized her two hands and drew her towards him.

She started back, and became almost a mere acquaintance. 'I have to tell you,' she gasped, 'that I have – been married.'

Nicholas's rose-coloured dream was immediately toned down to a greyish tinge.

'I did not marry till many years after you had left,' she continued in the humble tones of one confessing to a crime. 'Oh Nic,' she cried reproachfully, 'how could you stay away so long?'

'Whom did you marry?'

'Mr. Bellston.'

'I – ought to have expected it.' He was going to add, 'And is he dead?' but he checked himself. Her dress unmistakably suggested widowhood; and she had said she was free.

'I must now hasten home,' said she. 'I felt that, considering my shortcomings at our parting so many years ago, I owed you the initiative now.'

'There is some of your old generosity in that. I'll walk with you, if I may. Where are you living, Christine?'

'In the same house, but not on the old conditions. I have part of it on lease; the farmer now tenanting the premises found the whole more than he wanted, and the owner allowed me to keep what rooms I chose. I am poor now, you know, Nicholas, and almost friendless. My brother sold the Froom-Everard estate when it came to him, and the person who bought it turned our home into a farm-house. Till my father's death my husband and I lived in the manor-house with him so that I have never lived away from the spot.'

She was poor. That, and the change of name, sufficiently accounted for the inn-servant's ignorance of her continued existence within the walls of her old home.

It was growing dusk, and he still walked with her. A woman's head arose from the declivity before them, and as she drew nearer, Christine asked him to go back. 'This is the wife of the farmer who shares the house,' she said. 'She is accustomed to come out and meet me whenever I walk far and am benighted. I am obliged to walk everywhere now.'

The farmer's wife, seeing that Christine was not alone, paused in her advance, and Nicholas said, 'Dear Christine, if your are obliged to do these things, I am not, and what wealth I can command you may command likewise. They say rolling stones gather no moss; but they gather dross sometimes. I was one of the pioneers to the gold-fields, you know, and made a sufficient fortune there for my wants. What is more, I kept it. When I had done this I was coming home, but hearing of my uncle's death I changed my plan, travelled, speculated, and increased my fortune. Now, before we part: you remember you stood with me at the altar once, and therefore I speak with less preparation than I should otherwise use. Before we part then I ask, shall another again intrude between us? Or shall we complete the union we began?'

She trembled – just as she had done at that very minute of standing with him in the church, to which he had recalled her mind. 'I will not enter into that now, dear Nicholas,' she replied. 'There will be more to talk of and consider first – more to explain, which it would have spoiled this meeting to have entered into now.'

'Yes, yes; but –'

'Further than the brief answer I first gave, Nic, don't press me tonight. I still have the old affection for you, or I should not have sought you. Let that suffice for the moment.'

'Very well, dear one. And when shall I call to see you?'

'I will write and fix an hour. I will tell you everything of my history then.'

And thus they parted, Nicholas feeling that he had not come here fruitlessly. When she and her companion were out of sight he retraced his steps to Roy-Town, where he made himself as comfortable as he could in the deserted old inn of his boyhood's days. He missed her companionship this evening more than he had done at any time during the whole fifteen years; and it was as though instead of separation there had been constant communion with her throughout that period. The tones of her voice had stirred his heart in a nook which had lain stagnant ever since he last heard them. They recalled the woman to whom he had once lifted his eyes as to a goddess. Her announcement that she had been another's came as a little shock to him, and he did not now lift his eyes to her in precisely the same way as he had lifted them at first. But he forgave her for marrying Bellston; what could he expect after fifteen years?

He slept at Roy-Town that night, and in the morning there was a short note from her, repeating more emphatically her statement of the previous evening – that she wished to inform him clearly of her circumstances, and to calmly consider with him the position in which she was placed. Would he call upon her on Sunday afternoon, when she was sure to be alone?

'Nic,' she wrote on, 'what a cosmopolite you are! I expected to find my old yeoman still; but I was quite awed in the presence of such a citizen of the world. Did I seem rusty and unpractised? Ah – you seemed so once to me!'

Tender playful words; the old Christine was in them. She said Sunday afternoon, and it was now only Saturday morning. He wished she had said today; that short revival of her image had vitalized to sudden heat feelings that had almost been stilled. Whatever she might have to explain as to her position – and it was awkwardly narrowed, no doubt – he could not give her up. Miss Everard or Mrs. Bellston, what mattered it? – she was the same Christine.

He did not go outside the inn all Saturday. He had no wish to see or do anything but to await the coming interview. So he smoked, and read the local newspaper of the previous week, and stowed himself in the chimney-corner. In the evening he felt that he could remain indoors no longer, and the moon being near the full, he started from the inn on foot in the same direction as that of yesterday, with the view of contemplating the old village and its precincts, and hovering round her house under the cloak of night.

With a stout stick in his hand he climbed over the five miles of upland in a comparatively short space of time. Nicholas had seen many strange lands and trodden many strange ways since he last walked that path, but as he trudged he seemed wonderfully like his old self, and had not the slightest difficulty in finding the way. In descending to the meads the streams perplexed him a little, some of the old foot-bridges having been removed; but he ultimately got across the larger water-courses, and pushed on to the village, avoiding her residence for the moment, lest she should encounter him, and think he had not respected the time of her appointment.

He found his way to the churchyard, and first ascertained where lay the two relations he had left alive at his departure; then he observed the gravestones of other inhabitants with whom he had been well acquainted, till by degrees he seemed to be in the society of all the elder Froom-Everard population, as he had known the place. Side by side as they had lived in his day here were they now. They had moved house in mass.

But no tomb of Mr. Bellston was visible, though, as he had lived at the manor-house, it would have been natural to find it here. In truth Nicholas was more anxious to discover that than anything being curious to know how long he had been dead. Seeing from the glimmer of a light in the church that somebody was there cleaning for Sunday he entered, and looked round upon the walls as well as he could. But there was no monument to her husband, though one had been erected to the Squire.

Nicholas addressed the young man who was sweeping. 'I don't see any monument or tomb to the late Mr. Bellston?'

'O no, sir; you won't see that,' said the young man drily.

'Why, pray?'

'Because he's not buried here. He's not Christian-buried anywhere, as far as we know. In short, perhaps he's not buried at all; and between ourselves, perhaps he's alive.'

Nicholas sank an inch shorter. 'Ah.' he answered.

'Then you don't know the peculiar circumstances, sir?'

'I am a stranger here – as to late years.'

'Mr. Bellston was a traveller – an explorer – it was his calling; you may have heard his name as such?'

'I remember.' Nicholas recalled the fact that this very bent of Mr. Bellston's was the incentive to his own roaming.

'Well, when he married he came and lived here with his wife and his wife's father, and said he would travel no more. But after a time he got weary of biding quiet here, and weary of her – he was not a good husband to the young lady by any means – and he betook himself again to his old trick of roving – with her money. Away he went quite out of the realm of human foot, into the bowels of Asia, and never was heard of more. He was murdered, it is said, but nobody knows; though as that was nine years ago he's dead enough in principle, if not in corporation. His widow lives quite humble, for between her husband and her brother she's left in very lean pasturage.'

Nicholas went back to the Buck's Head without hovering round her dwelling. This then was the explanation which she had wanted to make. Not dead, but missing. How could he have expected that the first fair promise of happiness held out to him would remain untarnished? She had said that she was free; and legally she was free, no doubt. Moreover, from her tone and manner he felt himself justified in concluding that she would be willing to run the risk of a union with him, in the improbability of her husband's existence. Even if that husband lived, his return was not a likely event, to judge from his character. A man who could spend her money on his own personal adventures would not be anxious to disturb her poverty after such a lapse of time.

Well, the prospect was not so unclouded as it had seemed. But could he, even now, give up Christine?

VII

Two months more brought the year nearly to a close, and found Nicholas Long tenant of a spacious house in the market-town nearest to Froom-Everard. A man of means, genial character, and a bachelor, he was an object of great interest to his neighbours, and to his neighbours' wives and daughters. But he took little note of this, and had made it his business to go twice a week, no matter what the weather, to the now farmhouse at Froom-Everard, a wing of which had been retained as the refuge of Christine. He always walked, to give no trouble in putting up a horse to a housekeeper whose staff was limited.

The two had put their heads together on the situation, had gone to a solicitor, had balanced possibilities, and had resolved to make the plunge of matrimony. 'Nothing venture, nothing have,' Christine had said, with some of her old audacity.

With almost gratuitous honesty they had let their intentions be widely known. Christine, it is true, had rather shrunk from publicity at first; but Nicholas argued that their boldness in this respect would have good results. With his friends he held that there was not the slightest probability of her being other than a widow, and a challenge to the missing man now, followed by no response, would stultify any unpleasant remarks which might be thrown at her after their union. To this end a paragraph was inserted in the Wessex papers, announcing that their marriage was proposed to be celebrated on such and such a day in December.

His periodic walks along the south side of the valley to visit her were among the happiest experiences of his life. The yellow leaves falling around him in the foreground, the well-watered meads on the left hand, and the woman he loved awaiting him at the back of the scene, promised a future of much serenity, as far as human judgement could foresee. On arriving, he would sit with her in the 'parlour' of the wing she retained, her general sitting-room, where the only relics of her early surroundings were an old clock from the other end of the house, and her own piano. Before it was quite dark they would stand, hand in hand, loking out of the window across the flat turf to the dark clump of trees which hid further view from their eyes.

'Do you wish you were still mistress here, dear?' he once said.

'Not at all,' said she cheerfully. 'I have a good enough room, and a good enough fire, and a good enough friend. Besides, my latter days as mistress of the house were not happy ones, and they spoilt the place for me. It was a punishment for my faithlessness. Nic, you do forgive me? Really you do?'

The twenty-third of December, the eve of the wedding-day, had arrived at last in the train of such uneventful ones as these. Nicholas had arranged to visit her that day a little later than usual, and see that everything was ready with her for the morrow's event and her removal to his house; for he had begun to look after her domestic affairs, and to lighten as much as possible the duties of her housekeeping.

He was to come to an early supper, which she had arranged to take the place of a wedding-breakfast next day – the latter not being feasible in her present situation. An hour or so after dark the wife of the farmer who lived in the other part of the house entered Christine's parlour to lay the cloth.

'What with getting the ham skinned, and the black pud-dings hotted up,' she said, 'it will take me all my time before he's here, if I begin this minute.'

'I'll lay the table myself,' said Christine, jumping up. 'Do you attend to the cooking.'

'Thank you, ma'am. And perhaps 'tis no matter seeing that it is the last night you'll have to do such work. I knew this sort of life wouldn't last long for 'ee, being born to better things.'

'It has lasted rather long, Mrs. Wake. And if he had not found me out it would have lasted all my days.'

'But he did find you out.'

'He did. And I'll lay the cloth immediately.'

Mrs. Wake went back to the kitchen, and Christine began to bustle about. She greatly enjoyed preparing this table for Nicholas and herself with her own hands. She took artistic pleasure in adjusting each article to its position, as if half an inch error were a point of high importance. Finally she placed the two candles where they were to stand, and sat down by the fire.

Mrs. Wake re-entered and regarded the effect. 'Why not have another candle or two, ma'am?' she said. ''Twould make it livelier. Say four.'

'Very well,' said Christine, and four candles were lighted. 'Really,' she added, surveying them, 'I have been so long accustomed to little economies that they look quite extravagant.'

'Ah, you'll soon think nothing of forty in his grand new house! Shall I bring in supper directly he comes, ma'am?'

'No, not for half an hour; and, Mrs. Wake, you and Betsy are busy in the kitchen, I know; so when he knocks don't disturb yourselves; I can let him in.'

She was again left alone, and, as it still wanted some time to Nicholas's appointment, she stood by the fire, looking at herself in the glass over the mantel. Reflectively raising a lock of her hair just above her temple she uncovered a small scar. That scar had a history. The terrible temper of her late husband – those sudden moods of irascibility which had made even his friendly excitements look like anger – had once caused him to set that mark upon her with the bezel of a ring he wore. He declared that the whole thing was an accident. She was a woman, and kept her own opinion.

Christine then turned her back to the glass and scanned the table and the candles, shining one at each corner like types of the four Evangelists, and thought they looked too assuming – too confident. She glanced up at the clock, which stood also in this room, there not being space enough for it in the passage. It was nearly seven, and she expected Nicholas at half-past. She liked the company of this venerable article in her lonely life: its tickings and whizzings were a sort of conversation. It now began to strike the hour. At the end something grated slightly. Then, without any warning, the clock inclined forward and fell at full length upon the floor.

The crash brought the farmer's wife rushing into the room. Christine had well-nigh sprung out of her shoes. Mrs. Wake's enquiry what had happened was answered by the evidence of her own eyes.

'How did it occur?' she said.

'I cannot say; it was not firmly fixed. I suppose. Dear me, how sorry I am! My dear father's hallclock! And now I suppose it is ruined.'

Assisted by Mrs. Wake, she lifted the clock. Every inch of glass was, of course, shattered but very little harm besides appeared to be done. They propped it up temporarily, though it would not go again.

Christine had soon recovered her composure, but she saw that Mrs. Wake was gloomy. 'What does it mean, Mrs. Wake?' she said. 'Is it ominous?'

'It is a sign of a violent death in the family.'

'Don't talk of it. I don't believe such things; and don't mention it to Mr. Long when he comes. *He's* not in the family yet, you know.'

'O no, it cannot refer to him,' said Mrs. Wake musingly.

'Some remote cousin, perhaps,' observed Christine, no less willing to humour her than to get rid of a shapeless dread which the incident had caused in her own mind. 'And – supper is almost ready, Mrs. Wake?'

'In three-quarters of an hour.'

Mrs. Wake left the room, and Christine sat on. Though it still wanted fifteen minutes to the hour at which Nicholas had promised to be there, she began to grow impatient. After the accustomed ticking the dead silence was oppressive. But she had not to wait so long as she had expected; steps were heard approaching the door, and there was a knock.

Christine was already there to open it. The entrance had no lamp, but it was not particularly dark out of doors. She could see the outline of a man, and cried cheerfully, 'You are early; it is very good of you.'

'I beg pardon. It is not Mr. Bellston himself – only a messenger with his bag and great-coat. But he will be here soon.'

The voice was not the voice of Nicholas, and the intelligence was strange. 'I – I don't understand. Mr. Bellston?' she faintly replied.

'Yes, ma'am. A gentleman – a stranger to me – gave me these things at Casterbridge station to bring on here, and told me to say that Mr. Bellston had arrived there, and is detained for half-an-hour, but will be here in the course of the evening.'

She sank into a chair. The porter put a small battered portmanteau on the floor, the coat on a chair, and looking into the room at the spread table said, 'If you are disappointed, ma'am, that your husband (as I s'pose he is) is not come, I can assure you he'll soon be here. He's stopped to get a shave, to my thinking, seeing he wanted it. What he said was that I could tell you he had heard the news in Ireland, and would have come sooner, his hand being forced; but was hindered crossing by the weather, having took passage in a sailing vessel. What news he meant he didn't say.'

'Ah, yes,' she faltered. It was plain that the man knew nothing of her intended remarriage.

Mechanically rising and giving him a shilling, she answered to his 'good-night,' and he withdrew, the beat of his footsteps lessening in the distance. She was alone; but in what a solitude.

Christine stood in the middle of the hall, just as the man had left her, in the gloomy silence of the stopped clock within the adjoining room, till she aroused herself, and turning to the portmanteau and great-coat brought them to the light of the candles, and examined them. The portmanteau bore painted upon it the initials 'J.B.' in white letters – the well-known initials of her husband.

She examined the great-coat. In the breast-pocket was an empty spirit flask, which she firmly fancied she recognized as the one she had filled many times for him when he was living at home with her.

She turned desultorily hither and thither, until she heard another tread without, and there came a second knocking at the door. She did not respond to it; and Nicholas – for it was he – thinking that he was not heard by reason of a concentration on tomorrow's proceedings, opened the door softly, and came on to the door of her room, which stood unclosed, just as it had been left by the Casterbridge porter.

Nicholas uttered a blithe greeting, cast his eye round the parlour, which with its tall candles, blazing fire, snow-white cloth, and prettily-spread table, formed a cheerful spectacle enough for a man who had been walking in the dark for an hour.

'My bride – almost, at last!' he cried, encircling her with his arms.

Instead of responding, her figure became limp, frigid, heavy; her head fell back, and he found that she had fainted.

It was natural, he thought. She had had many little worrying matters to attend to, and but slight assistance. He ought

to have seen more effectually to her affairs; the closeness of the
event had over-excited her. Nicholas kissed her unconscious
face – more than once, little thinking what news it was that
had changed its aspect. Loth to call Mrs. Wake, he carried
Christine to a couch and laid her down. This had the effect of
reviving her. Nicholas bent and whispered in her ear, 'Lie
quiet, dearest, no hurry; and dream, dream, dream of happy
days. It is only I. You will soon be better.' He held her by the
hand.

'No, no, no!' she said, with a stare. 'O, how can this be?'

Nicholas was alarmed and perplexed, but the disclosure was
not long delayed. When she had sat up, and by degrees made
the stunning event know to him, he stood as if transfixed.

'Ah – is it so?' said he. Then, becoming quite meek, 'And
why was he so cruel as to – delay his return till now?'

She dutifully recited the explanation her husband had given
her through the messenger; but her mechanical manner of
telling it showed how much she doubted its truth. It was too
unlikely that his arrival at such a dramatic moment should not
be a contrived surprise, quite of a piece with his previous
dealings towards her.

'But perhaps it may be true – and he may have become kind
now – not as he used to be,' she faltered. 'Yes, perhaps,
Nicholas, he is an altered man – we'll hope he is. I suppose I
ought not to have listened to my legal advisers, and assumed
his death so surely? Anyhow, I am roughly received back into
– the right way!'

Nicholas burst out bitterly: 'O what too, too honest fools
we were! – to so court daylight upon our intention by putting
that announcement in the papers! Why could we not have
married privately, and gone away, so that he would never
have known what had become of you, even if he had
returned? Christine, he has done it to. . . . But I'll say no
more. Of course we – might fly now.'

'No, no; we might not,' said she hastily.

'Very well. But this is hard to bear! "When I looked for
good then evil came unto me, and when I waited for light
there came darkness." So once said a sorely tried man in the
land of Uz, and so say I now! . . . I wonder if he is almost
here at this moment?'

She told him she supposed Bellston was approaching by the path across the fields, having sent on his great-coat, which he would not want walking.

'And is this meal laid for him, or for me?'

'It was laid for you.'

'And it will be eaten by him?'

'Yes.'

'Christine, are you *sure* that he is come, or have you been sleeping over the fire and dreaming it?'

She pointed anew to the portmanteau with the initials 'J.B.', and to the coat beside it.

'Well, good-bye – good-bye! Curse that parson for not marrying us fifteen years ago!'

It is unnecessary to dwell further upon that parting. There are scenes wherein the words spoken do not even approximate to the level of the mental communion between the actors. Suffice it to say that part they did, and quickly; and Nicholas, more dead than alive, went out of the house homewards.

Why had he ever come back? During his absence he had not cared for Christine as he cared now. If he had been younger he might have felt tempted to descend into the meads instead of keeping along their edge. The Froom was down there, and he knew of quiet pools in that stream to which death would come easily. But he was too old to put an end to himself for such a reason as love; and another thought, too, kept him from seriously contemplating any desperate act. His affection for her was strongly protective, and in the event of her requiring a friend's support in future troubles there was none but himself left in the world to afford it. So he walked on.

Meanwhile Christine had resigned herself to circumstances. A resolve to continue worthy of her history and of her family lent her heroism and dignity. She called Mrs. Wake, and explained to that worthy woman as much of what had occurred as she deemed necessary. Mrs. Wake was too amazed to reply; she retreated slowly, her lips parted; till at the door she said with a dry mouth, 'And the beautiful supper, ma'am?'

'Serve it when he comes.'

'When Mr. Bellston – yes, ma'am, I will.' She still stood gazing, as if she could hardly take in the order.

'That will do, Mrs. Wake. I am much obliged to you for all your kindness.' And Christine was left alone again, and then she wept.

She sat down and waited. That awful silence of the stopped clock began anew, but she did not mind it now. She was listening for a footfall in a state of mental tensity which almost took away from her the power of motion. It seemed to her that the natural interval for her husband's journey thither must have expired; but she was not sure, and waited on.

Mrs. Wake again came in. 'You have not rung for supper –'

'He is not yet come, Mrs. Wake. If you want to go to bed, bring in the supper and set it on the table. It will be nearly as good cold. Leave the door unbarred.'

Mrs. Wake did as was suggested, made up the fire, and went away. Shortly afterwards Christine heard her retire to her chamber. But Christine still sat on, and still her husband postponed his entry.

She aroused herself once or twice to freshen the fire, but was ignorant how the night was going. Her watch was upstairs and she did not make the effort to go up to consult it. In her seat she continued; and still the supper waited, and still he did not come.

At length she was so nearly persuaded that the arrival of his things must have been a dream after all, that she again went over to them, felt them, and examined them. His they unquestionably were; and their forwarding by the porter had been quite natural. She sighed and sat down again.

Presently she fell into a doze, and when she again became conscious she found that the four candles had burnt into their sockets and gone out. The fire still emitted a feeble shine. Christine did not take the trouble to get more candles, but stirred the fire and sat on.

After a long period she heard a creaking of the chamber floor and stairs at the other end of the house, and knew that the farmer's family were getting up. By-and-by Mrs. Wake entered the room, candle in hand, bouncing open the door in her morning manner, obviously without any expectation of finding a person there.

'Lord-a-mercy! What, sitting here again, ma'am?'

'Yes, I am sitting here still.'

'You've been there ever since last night?'

'Yes.'

'Then —'

'He's not come.'

'Well, he won't come at this time o' morning,' said the farmer's wife. 'Do 'ee get on to bed, ma'am. You must be shrammed to death!'

It occurred to Christine now that possibly her husband had thought better of obtruding himself upon her company within an hour of revealing his existence to her, and had decided to pay a more formal visit next day. She therefore adopted Mrs. Wake's suggestion and retired.

VIII

Nicholas had gone straight home, neither speaking to nor seeing a soul. From that hour a change seemed to come over him. He had ever possessed a full share of self-consciousness; he had been readily piqued, had shown an unusual dread of being personally obtrusive. But now his sense of self, as an individual provoking opinion, appeared to leave him. When, therefore, after a day or two of seclusion, he came forth again, and the few acquaintances he had formed in the town condoled with him on what had happened, and pitied his haggard looks, he did not shrink from their regard as he would have done formerly, but took their sympathy as it would have been accepted by a child.

It reached his ears that Bellston had not appeared on the evening of his arrival at any hotel in the town or neighbourhood, or entered his wife's house at all. 'That's a part of his cruelty,' thought Nicholas. And when two or three days had passed, and still no account came to him of Bellston having joined her, he ventured to set out from Froom-Everard.

Christine was so shaken that she was obliged to receive him as she lay on a sofa, beside the square table which was to have borne their evening feast. She fixed her eyes wistfully upon him, and smiled a sad smile.

'He has not come?' said Nicholas under his breath.

'He has not.'

Then Nicholas sat beside her, and they talked on general topics merely like saddened old friends. But they could not keep away the subject of Bellston, their voices dropping as it forced its way in. Christine, no less than Nicholas, knowing her husband's character, inferred that, having stopped her game, as he would have phrased it, he was taking things leisurely, and, finding nothing very attractive in her limited mode of living, was meaning to return to her only when he had nothing better to do.

The bolt which laid low their hopes had struck so recently that they could hardly look each other in the face when speaking that day. But when a week or two had passed, and all the horizon still remained as vacant of Bellston as before, Nicholas and she could talk of the event with calm wonderment. Why had he come, to go again like this?

And then there set in a period of resigned surmise, during which

> So like, so very like, was day to day,

that to tell of one of them is to tell of all. Nicholas would arrive between three and four in the afternoon, a faint trepidation influencing his walk as he neared her door. He would knock; she would always reply in person, having watched for him from the window. Then he would whisper –

'He has not come?'

'He has not,' she would say.

Nicholas would enter then, and she, being ready bonneted, they would walk into the Sallows together as far as to the spot which they had frequently made their place of appointment in their youthful days. A plank bridge, which Bellston had caused to be thrown over the stream during his residence with her in the manor-house, was now again removed, and all was just the same as in Nicholas's time, when he had been accustomed to wade across on the edge of the cascade and come up to her like a merman from the deep. Here on the felled trunk, which still lay rotting in its old place, they would now sit, gazing at the descending sheet of water, with its never-ending sarcastic hiss at their baffled attempts to make themselves one flesh. Returning to the house they would sit down together to tea, after which, and the confidential chat that accompanied it, he walked home by the declining light. This proceeding became as periodic as an astronomical recurrence. Twice a week he came – all through that winter, all through the spring following, through the summer, through the autumn, the next winter, the next year, and the next, till an appreciable span of human life had passed by. Bellston still tarried.

Years and years Nic walked that way, at this interval of three days, from his house in the neighbouring town; and in every instance the aforesaid order of things was customary; and still on his arrival the form of words went on –

'He has not come?'

'He has not.'

So they grew older. The dim shape of that third one stood continually between them; they could not displace it; neither, on the other hand, could it effectually part them. They were in close communion, yet not indissolubly united; lovers, yet never growing cured of love. By the time that the fifth year of Nic's visiting had arrived, on about the five-hundredth occasion of his presence at her tea-table, he noticed that the bleaching process which had begun upon his own locks was also spreading to hers. He told her so, and they laughed. Yet she was in good health: a condition of suspense, which would have half-killed a man, had been endured by her without complaint, and even with composure.

One day, when these years of abeyance had numbered seven, they had strolled as usual as far as the waterfall, whose faint roar formed a sort of calling voice sufficient in the circumstances to direct their listlessness. Pausing there, he looked up at her face and said, 'Why should we not try again Christine? We are legally at liberty to do so now. Nothing venture nothing have.'

But she would not. Perhaps a little primness of idea was by this time ousting the native daring of Christine. 'What he has done once he can do twice,' she said. 'He is not dead, and if we were to marry he would say we had "forced his hand," as he said before, and duly reappear.'

Some years after, when Christine was about fifty, and Nicholas fifty-three, a new trouble of a minor kind arrived. He found an inconvenience in traversing the distance between their two houses, particularly in damp weather, the years he had spent in trying climates abroad having sown the seeds of rheumatism, which made a journey undesirable on inclement days, even in a carriage. He told her of this new difficulty, as he did of everything.

'If you could live nearer,' suggested she.

Unluckily there was no house near. But Nicholas, though not a millionaire, was a man of means; he obtained a small piece of ground on lease at the nearest spot to her home that it could be so obtained, which was on the opposite brink of the Froom, this river forming the boundary of the Froom-Everard manor; and here he built a cottage large enough for his wants. This took time, and when he got into it he found its situation a great comfort to him. He was not more than five hundred yards from her now, and gained a new pleasure in feeling that all sounds which greeted his ears, in the day or in the night, also fell upon hers – the caw of a particular rook, the voice of a neighbouring nightingale, the whistle of a local breeze, or the purl of the fall in the meadows, whose rush was a material rendering of time's ceaseless scour over themselves, wearing them away without uniting them.

Christine's missing husband was taking shape as a myth among the surrounding residents; but he was still believed in as corporeally imminent by Christine herself, and also, in a milder degree, by Nicholas. For a curious unconsciousness of the long lapse of time since his revelation of himself seemed to affect the pair. There had been no passing events to serve as chronological milestones, and the evening on which she had kept supper waiting for him still loomed out with startling nearness in their retrospects.

In the seventeenth pensive year of this their parallel march towards the common bourne, a labourer came in a hurry one day to Nicholas's house and brought strange tidings. The present owner of Froom-Everard – a non-resident – had been improving his property in sundry ways, and one of these was by dredging the stream which, in the course of years, had become choked with mud and weeds in its passage through the Sallows. The process necessitated a reconstruction of the waterfall. When the river had been pumped dry for this purpose, the skeleton of a man had been found jammed among the piles supporting the edge of the fall. Every particle of his flesh and clothing had been eaten by fishes or abraded to nothing by the water, but the relics of a gold watch remained, and on the inside of the case was engraved the name of the maker of her husband's watch, which she well remembered.

Nicholas, deeply agitated, hastened down to the place and examined the remains attentively, afterwards going across to Christine, and breaking the discovery to her. She would not come to view the skeleton, which lay extended on the grass, not a finger or toe-bone missing, so neatly had the aquatic operators done their work. Conjecture was directed to the question how Bellston had got there; and conjecture alone could give an explanation.

It was supposed that, on his way to call upon her, he had taken a short cut through the grounds, with which he was naturally very familiar, and coming to the fall under the trees had expected to find there the plank which, during his occupancy of the premises with Christine and her father, he had placed there for crossing into the meads on the other side instead of wading across as Nicholas had done. Before discovering its removal he had probably overbalanced himself, and was thus precipitated into the cascade, the piles beneath the descending current wedging him between them like the prongs of a pitchfork, and effectually preventing the rising of his body, over which the weeds grew. Such was the reasonable supposition concerning the discovery; but proof was never forthcoming.

'To think,' said Nicholas, when the remains had been decently interred, and he was again sitting with Christine – though not beside the waterfall – 'to think how we visited him! How we sat over him, hours and hours, gazing at him, bewailing our fate, when all the time he was ironically hissing at us from the spot, in an unknown tongue, that we could marry if we chose!'

She echoed the sentiment with a sigh.

'I have strange fancies,' she said. 'I suppose it *must* have been my husband who came back, and not some other man.'

Nicholas felt that there was little doubt. 'Besides – the skeleton,' he said.

'Yes. . . . If it could not have been another person's – but no, of course it was he.'

'You might have married me on the day we had fixed, and there would have been no impediment. You would now have been seventeen years my wife, and we might have had tall sons and daughters.'

'It might have been so,' she murmured.

'Well – is it still better late than never?'

The question was one which had become complicated by the increasing years of each. Their wills were somewhat enfeebled now, their hearts sickened of tender enterprise by hope too long deferred. Having postponed the consideration of their course till a year after the interment of Bellston, each seemed less disposed than formerly to take it up again.

'Is it worth while, after so many years?' she said to him. 'We are fairly happy as we are – perhaps happier than we should be in any other relation, seeing what old people we have grown. The weight is gone from our lives: the shadow no longer divides us: then let us be joyful together as we are, dearest Nic, in the days of our vanity; and

With mirth and laughter let old wrinkles come.'

He fell in with these views of hers to some extent. But occasionally he ventured to urge her to reconsider the case, though he spoke not with the fervour of his earlier years.

Autumn, 1887

ALICIA'S DIARY

I – SHE MISSES HER SISTER

July 7. – I wander about the house in a mood of unutterable sadness, for my dear sister Caroline has left home today with my mother, and I shall not see them again for several weeks. They have accepted a long-standing invitation to visit some old friends of ours, the Marlets, who live at Versailles for cheapness – my mother thinking that it will be for the good of Caroline to see a little of France and Paris. But I don't quite like her going. I fear she may lose some of that childlike simplicity and gentleness which so characterize her, and have been nourished by the seclusion of our life here. Her solicitude about her pony before starting was quite touching, and she made me promise to visit it daily, and see that it came to no harm.

Caroline gone abroad, and I left here! It is the reverse of an ordinary situation, for good or ill-luck has mostly ordained that I should be the absent one. Mother will be quite tired out by the young enthusiasm of Caroline. She will demand to be taken everywhere – to Paris continually, of course; to all the stock shrines of history's devotees; to palaces and prisons; to kings' tombs and queens' tombs; to cemeteries and picture-galleries, and royal hunting forests. My poor mother, having gone over most of this ground many times before, will perhaps not find the perambulation so exhilarating as will Caroline herself. I wish I could have gone with them. I would not have minded having my legs walked off to please Caroline. But this regret is absurd: I could not, of course, leave my father with not a soul in the house to attend to the calls of the parishioners or to pour out his tea.

July 15. – A letter from Caroline today. It is very strange that she tells me nothing which I expected her to tell – only trivial details. She seems dazzled by the brilliancy of Paris –

which no doubt appears still more brilliant to her from the fact of her only being able to obtain occasional glimpses of it. She would see that Paris, too, has a seamy side if you live there. I was not aware that the Marlets knew so many people. If as mother has said, they went to reside at Versailles for reasons of economy, they will not effect much in that direction while they make a practice of entertaining all the acquaintances who happen to be in their neighbourhood. They do not confine their hospitalities to English people, either. I wonder who this M. de la Feste is, in whom Caroline says my mother is so much interested.

July 18. – Another letter from Caroline. I have learnt from this epistle, that M. Charles de la Feste is 'only one of the many friends of the Marlets'; that though a Frenchman by birth and now again temporarily at Versailles, he has lived in England many many years; that he is a talented landscape and marine painter, and has exhibited at the *Salon*, and I think in London. His style and subjects are considered somewhat peculiar in Paris – rather English than Continental. I have not as yet learnt his age, or his condition, married or single. From the tone and nature of her remarks about him he sometimes seems to be a middle-aged family man, sometimes, quite the reverse. From his nomadic habits I should say the latter is the most likely. He has travelled and seen a great deal, she tells me, and knows more about English literature than she knows herself.

July 21. – Letter from Caroline. Query: Is 'a friend of ours and the Marlets,' of whom she now anonymously and mysteriously speaks, the same personage as the 'M. de la Feste' of her former letters? He must be the same, I think, from his pursuits. If so, whence this sudden change of tone? . . . I have been lost in thought for at least a quarter of an hour since writing the preceding sentence. Suppose my dear sister is falling in love with this young man – there is no longer any doubt about his age; what a very awkward, risky thing for her! I do hope that my mother has an eye on these proceedings. But, then, poor mother never sees the drift of anything: she is in truth less of a mother to Caroline than I am. If I were there, how jealously I would watch him, and ascertain his designs!

I am of a stronger nature than Caroline. How I have supported her in the past through her little troubles and great griefs! Is she agitated at the presence of this, to her, new and strange feeling? But I am assuming her to be desperately in love, when I have no proof of anything of the kind. He may be merely a casual friend, of whom I shall hear no more.

July 24. – Then he *is* a bachelor, as I suspected. 'If M. de la Feste ever marries he will,' etc. So she writes. They are getting into close quarters, obviously. Also, 'Something to keep my hair smooth, which M. de la Feste told me he had found useful for the tips of his moustache.' Very naïvely related this; and with how much unconsciousness of the intimacy between them that the remark reveals! But my mother – what can she be doing? Does she know of this? And if so, why does she not allude to it in her letters to my father? . . . I have been to look at Caroline's pony, in obedience to her reiterated request that I would not miss a day in seeing that she was well cared for. Anxious as Caroline was about this pony of hers before starting, she now never mentioned the poor animal once in her letters. The image of her pet suffers from displacement.

August 3. – Caroline's forgetfulness of her pony has naturally enough extended to me, her sister. It is ten days since she last wrote, and but for a note from my mother I should not know if she were dead or alive.

II – NEWS INTERESTING AND SERIOUS

August 5. – A cloud of letters. A letter from Caroline, another from mother; also one from each to my father.

The probability to which all the intelligence from my sister has pointed of late turns out to be a fact. There is an engagement, or almost an engagement, announced between my dear Caroline and M. de la Feste – to Caroline's sublime happiness, and my mother's entire satisfaction; as well as to that of the Marlets. They and my mother seem to know all about the young man – which is more that I do, though a little extended information about him, considering that I am Caroline's elder sister, would not have been amiss. I half feel with my father, who is much surprised, and, I am sure, not altogether satisfied, that he should not have been consulted at all before matters reached such a definite stage, though he is too amiable to say so openly. I don't quite say that a good thing should have been hindered for the sake of our opinion, if it is a good thing; but the announcement comes very suddenly. It must have been foreseen by my mother for some time that this upshot was probable, and Caroline might have told me more distinctly that M. de la Feste was her lover, instead of alluding so mysteriously to him as only a friend of the Marlets, and lately dropping his name altogether. My father, without exactly objecting to him as a Frenchman, 'wishes he were of English or some other reasonable nationality for one's son-in-law,' but I tell him that the demarcations of races, kingdoms, and creeds, are wearing down every day, that patriotism is a sort of vice, and that the character of the individual is all we need think about in this case. I wonder, if in the event of their marriage, he will continue to live at Versailles, or if he will come to England.

August 7. – A supplemental letter from Caroline, answering, by anticipation, some of the aforesaid queries. She tells me that 'Charles,' though he makes Versailles his present home, is by no means bound by his profession to continue there; that he will live just where she wishes, provided it be not too far from some centre of thought, art, and civilization. My mother and herself both think that the marriage should not take place till next year. He exhibits landscapes and canal scenery every year, she says; so I suppose he is popular, and that his income is sufficient to keep them in comfort. If not, I do not see why my father could not settle something more on them than he had intended, and diminish by a little what he had proposed for me, whilst it was imagined that I should be the first to stand in need of such.

'Of engaging manner, attractive appearance, and virtuous character,' is the reply I receive from her in answer to my request for a personal description. That is vague enough, and I would rather have had one definite fact of complexion, voice, deed, or opinion. But of course she has no eye now for material qualities; she cannot see him as he is. She sees him irradiated with glories such as never appertained and never will appertain to any man, foreign, English, or Colonial. To think that Caroline, two years my junior, and so childlike as to be five years my junior in nature, should be engaged to be married before me. But that is what happens in families more often than we are apt to remember.

August 16. – Interesting news today. Charles, she says, has pleaded that their marriage may just as well be this year as next; and he seems to have nearly converted my mother to the same way of thinking. I do not myself see any reason for delay, beyond the standing one of my father having as yet had no opportunity of forming an opinion upon the man, the time, or anything. However, he takes his lot very quietly, and they are coming home to talk the question over with us; Caroline having decided not to make any positive arrangements for this change of state till she has seen me. Subject to my own and my father's approval, she says, they are inclined to settle the date of the wedding for November, three months from the present time, that it shall take place here in the village, that I, of course, shall be bridesmaid, and many other particulars. She draws an artless picture of the probable effect upon the minds of the villagers of this romantic performance in the chancel of our old church, in which she is to be chief actor – the foreign gentleman dropping down like a god from the skies, picking her up, and triumphantly carrying her off. Her only grief will be separation from me, but this is to be assuaged by my going and staying with her for long months at a time. This simple prattle is very sweet to me, my dear sister, but I cannot help feeling sad at the occasion of it. In the nature of things it is obvious that I shall never be to you again what I hitherto have been: your guide, counsellor, and most familiar friend.

M. de la Feste does certainly seem to be all that one could desire as protector to a sensitive fragile child like Caroline, and for that I am thankful. Still, I must remember that I see him as yet only through her eyes. For her sake I am intensely anxious to meet him, and scrutinise him through and through, and learn what the man is really made of who is to have such a treasure in his keeping. The engagement has certainly been formed a little precipitately; I quite agree with my father in that: still, good and happy marriages have been made in a hurry before now, and mother seems well satisfied.

August 20. – A terrible announcement came this morning; and we are in deep trouble. I have been quite unable to steady my thoughts on anything today till now – half-past eleven at night – and I only attempt writing these notes because I am too restless to remain idle, and there is nothing but waiting and waiting left for me to do. Mother has been taken dangerously ill at Versailles: they were within a day or two of starting; but all thought of leaving must now be postponed, for she cannot possibly be moved in her present state. I don't like the sound of hæmorrhage at all in a woman of her full habit, and Caroline and the Marlets have not exaggerated their accounts I am certain. On the receipt of the letter my father instantly decided to go to her, and I have been occupied all day in getting him off, for as he calculates on being absent several days, there have been many matters for him to arrange before setting out – the chief being to find some one who will do duty for him next Sunday – a quest of no small difficulty at such short notice; but at last poor old feeble Mr. Dugdale has agreed to attempt it, with Mr. Highman, the Scripture reader, to assist him in the lessons.

I fain would have gone with father to escape the irksome anxiety of awaiting here; but somebody had to stay, and I could best be spared. George has driven him to the station to meet the last train by which he will catch the midnight boat, and reach Havre some time in the morning. He hates the sea, and a night passage in particular. I hope he will get there without mishap of any kind; but I feel anxious for him, stay-at-home as he is, and unable to cope with any difficulty. Such an errand, too; the journey will be sad enough at best. I almost think I ought to have been the one to go to her.

August 21. – I nearly fell asleep of heaviness of spirit last night over my writing. My father must have reached Paris by this time; and now here comes a letter. . . .

Later. – The letter was to express an earnest hope that my father had set out. My poor mother is sinking, they fear. What will become of Caroline? O, how I wish I could see my mother; why could not both have gone?

Later. – I get up from my chair, and walk from window to window, and then come and write a line. I cannot even divine how poor Caroline's marriage is to be carried out if mother dies. I pray that father may have got there in time to talk to her and receive some directions from her about Caroline and M. de la Feste – a man whom neither my father nor I have seen. I, who might be useful in this emergency, am doomed to stay here, waiting in suspense.

August 23. – A letter from my father containing the sad news that my mother's spirit has flown. Poor little Caroline is heartbroken – she was always more my mother's pet than I was. It is some comfort to know that my father arrived in time to hear from her own lips her strongly expressed wish that Caroline's marriage should be solemnized as soon as possible. M. de la Feste seems to have been a great favourite of my dear mother's; and I suppose it now becomes almost a sacred duty of my father to accept him as a son-in-law without criticism.

III – HER GLOOM LIGHTENS A LITTLE

September 10. – I have inserted nothing in my diary for more than a fortnight. Events have been altogether too sad for me to have the spirit to put them on paper. And yet there comes a time when the act of recording one's trouble is recognized as a welcome method of dwelling upon it. . . .

My dear mother has been brought home and buried here in the parish. It was not so much her own wish that this should be done as my father's, who particularly desired that she should lie in the family vault beside his first wife. I saw them side by side before the vault was closed – two womem beloved by one man. As I stood, and Caroline by my side, I fell into a sort of dream, and had an odd fancy that Caroline and I might be also beloved of one, and lie like these together – an impossibility, of course, being sisters. When I awoke from my reverie Caroline took my hand and said it was time to leave.

September 14. – The wedding is indefinitely postponed. Caroline is like a girl awakening in the middle of a somnambulistic experience, and does not realize where she is, or how she stands. She walks about silently, and I cannot tell her thoughts, as I used to do. It was her own doing to write to M.

de la Feste and tell him that the wedding could not possibly take place this autumn as originally planned. There is something depressing in this long postponement if she is to marry him at all; and yet I do not see how it could be avoided.

October 20. – I have had so much to occupy me in consoling Caroline that I have been continually overlooking my diary. Her life was much nearer to my mother's than mine was. She has never, as I, lived away from home long enough to become self-dependent, and hence in her first loss, and all that it involved, she dropped like a rain-beaten lily. But she is of a nature whose wounds soon heal, even though they may be deep, and the supreme poignancy of her sorrow has already passed.

My father is of opinion that the wedding should not be delayed too long. While at Versailles he made the acquaintance of M. de la Feste, and though they had but a short and hurried communion with each other, he was much impressed by M. de la Feste's disposition and conduct, and is strongly in favour of his suit. It is odd that Caroline's betrothed should influence in his favour all who come near him. His portrait, which dear Caroline has shown me, exhibits him to be of a physique that partly accounts for this: but there must be something more than mere appearance, and it is probably some sort of glamour or fascinating power – the quality which prevented Caroline from describing him to me with any accuracy of detail. At the same time, I see from the photograph that his face and head are remarkably well formed; and though the contours of his mouth are hidden by his moustache, his arched brows show well the romantic disposition of a true lover and painter of Nature. I think that the owner of such a face as this must be tender and sympathetic and true.

October 30. – As my sister's grief for her mother becomes more and more calmed, her love for M. de la Feste begins to reassume its former absorbing command of her. She thinks of him incessantly, and writes whole treatises to him by way of letters. Her blank disappointment at his announcement of his inability to pay us a visit quite so soon as he had promised, was quite tragic. I, too, am disappointed, for I wanted to see and estimate him. But having arranged to go to Holland to seize some aerial effects for his pictures, which are only to be obtained at this time of the autumn, he is obliged to postpone his journey this way, which is now to be made early in the new year. I think myself that he ought to have come at all sacrifices, considering Caroline's recent loss, the sad postponement of what she was looking forward to, and her single-minded affection for him. Still, who knows; his professional success is important. Moreover, she is cheerful, and hopeful, and the delay will soon be overpast.

IV – SHE BEHOLDS THE ATTRACTIVE STRANGER

February 16. – We have had such a dull life here all the winter that I have found nothing important enough to set down, and broke off my journal accordingly. I resume it now to make an entry on the subject of dear Caroline's future. It seems that she was too grieved, immediately after the loss of our mother, to answer definitely the question of M. de la Feste how long the postponement was to be; then, afterwards, it was agreed that the matter should be discussed on his autumn visit; but as he did not come, it has remained in abeyance till this week, when Caroline, with the greatest simplicity and confidence, has written to him without any further pressure on his part, and told him that she is quite ready to fix the time, and will do so as soon as he arrives to see her. She is a little frightened now, lest it should seem forward in her to have revived the subject of her own accord; but she may assume that his question has been waiting on for an answer ever since, and that she has, therefore, acted only within her promise. In truth, the secret at the bottom of it all is that she is somewhat saddened because he has not latterly reminded her of the pause in their affairs – that, in short, his original impatience to possess her is not now found to animate him so obviously. I suppose that he loves her as much as ever; indeed, I am sure he must do so, seeing how lovable she is. It is mostly thus with all men when women are out of their sight; they grow negligent. Caroline must have patience, and remember that a man of his genius has many and important calls upon his time. In justice to her I must add that she does remember it fairly well, and has as much patience as any girl ever had in the circumstances. He

hopes to come at the beginning of April at latest. Well, when
he comes we shall see him.

April 5. – I think that what M. de la Feste writes is
reasonable enough, though Caroline looks heartsick about it.
It is hardly worth while for him to cross all the way to
England and back just now, while the sea is so turbulent,
seeing that he will be obliged, in any event, to come in May,
when he has to be in London for professional purposes, at
which time he can take us easily on his way both coming and
going. When Caroline becomes his wife she will be more
practical, no doubt; but she is such a child as yet and there is
no contenting her with reasons. However, the time will pass
quickly, there being so much to do in preparing a trousseau
for her, which must now be put in hand in order that we may
have plenty of leisure to get it ready. On no account must
Caroline be married in half-mourning: I am sure that mother,
could she know, would not wish it, and it is odd that Caroline
should be so intractably persistent on this point, when she is
usually so yielding.

April 30. – This month has flown on swallow's wings. We
are in a great state of excitement – I as much as she – I cannot
quite tell why. He is really coming in ten days, he says.

May 9. Four p.m. – I am so agitated I can scarcely write, and
yet am particularly impelled to do so before leaving my room.
It is the unexpected shape of an expected event which has
caused my absurd excitement, which proves me almost as
much a school-girl as Caroline.

M. de la Feste was not, as we understood, to have come till
tomorrow; but he is here – just arrived. All household
directions have devolved upon me, for my father, not thinking M. de la Feste would appear before us for another four-
and-twenty hours, left home before post time to attend a
distant consecration; and hence Caroline and I were in no
small excitement when Charles's letter was opened, and we
read that he had been unexpectedly favoured in the dispatch of
his studio work, and would follow his letter in a few hours.
We sent the covered carriage to meet the train indicated, and
waited like two newly strung harps for the first sound of the
returning wheels. At last we heard them on the gravel; and the
question arose who was to receive him. It was, strictly

speaking, my duty; but I felt timid; I could not help shirking it, and insisted that Caroline should go down. She did not, however, go near the door as she usually does when anybody is expected, but waited palpitating in the drawing-room. He little thought when he saw the silent hall, and the apparently deserted house, how that house was at the very same moment alive and throbbing with interest under the surface. I stood at the back of the upper landing, where nobody could see me from downstairs, and heard him walk across the hall – a lighter step than my father's – and heard him then go into the drawing-room, and the servant shut the door behind him and go away.

What a pretty lover's meeting they must have had in there all to themselves! Caroline's sweet face looking up from her black gown – how it must have touched him. I know she wept very much, for I heard her: and her eyes will be red after-wards, and no wonder, poor dear, though she is no doubt happy. I can imagine what she is telling him while I write this – her fears lest anything should have happened to prevent his coming after all – gentle, smiling reproaches for his long delay; and things of that sort. His two portmanteaus are at this moment crossing the landing on the way to his room. I wonder if I ought to go down.

A little later. – I have seen him! It was not at all in the way that I intended to encounter him, and I am vexed. Just after his portmanteaus were brought up I went out from my room to descend, when, at the moment of stepping towards the first stair, my eyes were caught by an object in the hall below, and I paused for an instant, till I saw that it was a bundle of canvas and sticks, composing a sketching tent and easel. At the same nick of time the drawing-room door opened and the affianced pair came out. They were saying they would go into the garden; and he waited a moment while she put on her hat. My idea was to let them pass on without seeing me, since they seemed not to want my company, but I had got too far on the landing to retreat; he looked up, and stood staring at me – engrossed in a dream-like fixity. Thereupon I, too, instead of advancing as I ought to have done, stood moonstruck and awkward, and before I could gather my weak senses suf-ficiently to descend, she had called him, and they went out by the garden door together. I then thought of following them, but have changed my mind, and come here to jot down these few lines. It is all I am fit for. . . .

He is even more handsome than I expected. I was right in feeling he must have an attraction beyond that of form: it appeared even in that momentary glance. How happy Caroline ought to be. But I must, of course, go down to be ready with tea in the drawing-room by the time they come indoors.

11 p.m. – I have made the acquaintance of M. de la Feste; and I seem to be another woman from the effect of it. I cannot describe why this should be so, but conversation with him seems to expand the view, and open the heart, and raise one as upon stilts to wider prospects. He has a good intellectual forehead, perfect eyebrows, dark hair and eyes, an animated manner, and a persuasive voice. His voice is soft in quality – too soft for a man, perhaps; and yet on second thoughts I would not have it less so. We have been talking of his art; I had no notion that art demanded such sacrifices or such tender devotion; or that there were two roads for choice within its precincts, the road of vulgar money-making, and the road of high aims and consequent inappreciation for many long years by the public. That he has adopted the latter need not be said to those who understand him. It is a blessing for Caroline that she has been chosen by such a man, and she ought not to lament at postponements and delays, since they have arisen unavoidably. Whether he finds hers a sufficiently rich nature, intellectually and emotionally, for his own, I know not, but he seems occasionally to be disappointed at her simple views of things. Does he really feel such love for her at this moment as he no doubt believes himself to be feeling, and as he no doubt hopes to feel for the remainder of his life towards her?

It was a curious thing he told me when we were left for a few minutes alone; that Caroline had alluded so slightly to me in her conversation and letters that he had not realized my presence in the house here at all. But, of course, it was only natural that she should write and talk most about herself. I suppose it was on account of the fact of his being taken in some measure unawares, that I caught him on two or three occasions regarding me fixedly in a way that disquieted me somewhat, having been lately in so little society; till my glance aroused him from his reverie, and he looked elsewhere in some confusion. It was fortunate that he did so, and thus failed to notice my own. It shows that he, too, is not particularly a society person.

May 10. – Have had another interesting conversation with M. de la Feste on schools of landscape painting in the drawing-room after dinner this evening – my father having fallen asleep, and left nobody but Caroline and myself for Charles to talk to. I did not mean to say so much to him, and had taken a volume of *Modern Painters* from the bookcase to occupy myself with, while leaving the two lovers to themselves; but he would include me in his audience, and I was obliged to lay the book aside. However, I insisted on keeping Caroline in the conversation, though her views on pictorial art were only too charmingly crude and primitive.

Tomorrow, if fine, we are all three going to Wherryborne Wood, where Charles will give us practical illustrations of the principles of coloring that he has enumerated tonight. I am determined not to occupy his attention to the exclusion of Caroline, and my plan is that when we are in the dense part of the wood I will lag behind, and slip away, and leave them to return by themselves. I suppose the reason of his attentiveness to me lies in his simply wishing to win the good opinion of one who is so closely united to Caroline, and so likely to influence her good opinion of him.

May 11. Late. – I cannot sleep, and in desperation have lit my candle and taken up my pen. My restlessness is occasioned by what has occured today, which at first I did not mean to write down, or trust to any heart but my own. We went to Wherryborne Wood – Caroline, Charles and I, as we had intended – and walked all three along the green track through the midst, Charles in the middle between Caroline and myself. Presently I found that, as usual, he and I were the only talkers, Caroline amusing herself by observing birds and squirrels as she walked docilely alongside her betrothed. Having noticed this I dropped behind at the first opportunity and slipped among the trees, in a direction in which I knew I should find another path that would take me home. Upon this track I by and by emerged, and walked along it in silent thought till, at a bend, I suddenly encountered M. de la Feste standing stock still and smiling thoughtfully at me.

'Where is Caroline?' said I.

'Only a little way off,' says he. 'When we missed you from behind us we thought you might have mistaken the direction we had followed, so she has gone one way to find you and I have come this way.'

We then went back to find Caroline, but could not discover her anywhere, and the upshot was that he and I were wandering about the woods alone for more than an hour. On reaching home we found she had given us up after searching a little while, and arrived there some time before. I should not be so disturbed by the incident if I had not perceived that, during her absence from us, he did not make any earnest effort to rediscover her; and in answer to my repeated expressions of wonder as to whither she could have wandered he only said, 'Oh, she's quite safe; she told me she knew the way home from any part of this wood. Let us go on with our talk. I assure you I value this privilege of being with one I so much admire more than you imagine;' and other things of that kind. I was so foolish as to show a little perturbation – I cannot tell why I did not control myself; and I think he noticed that I was not cool. Caroline has, with her simple good faith, thought nothing of the occurrence; yet altogether I am not satisfied.

V – HER SITUATION IS A TRYING ONE

May 15. – The more I think of it day after day, the more convinced I am that my suspicions are true. He is too interested in me – well, in plain words, loves me; or, not to degrade that phrase, has a wild passion for me; and his affection for Caroline is that towards a sister only. That is the distressing truth; how it has come about I cannot tell, and it wears upon me.

A hundred little circumstances have revealed this to me, and the longer I dwell upon it the more agitating does the consideration become. Heaven only can help me out of the terrible difficulty in which this places me. I have done nothing to encourage him to be faithless to her. I have studiously kept

out of his way; have persistently refused to be a third in their
interviews. Yet all to no purpose. Some fatality has seemed to
rule, ever since he came to the house, that this disastrous
inversion of things should arise. If I had only foreseen the
possibility of it before he arrived, how gladly would I have
departed on some visit or other to the meanest friend to hinder
such an apparent treachery. But I blindly welcomed him –
indeed, made myself particularly agreeable to him for her
sake.

There is no possibility of my suspicions being wrong; not
until they have reached absolute certainty have I dared even to
admit the truth to myself. His conduct today would have
proved them true had I entertained no previous apprehen-
sions. Some photographs of myself came for me by post,
and they were handed round at the breakfast table and
criticised. I put them temporarily on a side table, and did not
remember them until an hour afterwards when I was in my
own room. On going to fetch them I discovered him standing
at the table with his back towards the door bending over the
photographs, one of which he raised to his lips.

The witnessing this act so frightened me that I crept away to
escape observation. It was the climax to a series of slight and
significant actions all tending to the same conclusion. The
question for me now is, what am I to do? To go away is what
first occurs to me, but what reason can I give Caroline and my
father for such a step; besides, it might precipitate some sort of
catastrophe by driving Charles to desperation. For the present, therefore, I have decided that I can only wait, though his
contiguity is strangely disturbing to me now, and I hardly
retain strength of mind to encounter him. How will the
distressing complication end?

May 19. – And so it has come! My mere avoidance of him
has precipitated the worst issue – a declaration. I had occasion
to go into the kitchen garden to gather some of the double
ragged-robins which grew in a corner there. Almost as soon
as I had entered I heard footsteps without. The door opened
and shut, and I turned to behold him just inside it. As the
garden is closed by four walls and the gardener was absent, the
spot ensured absolute privacy. He came along the path by the
asparagus-bed, and overtook me.

'You know why I come, Alicia?' said he, in a tremulous voice.

I said nothing, and hung my head, for by his tone I did know.

'Yes,' he went on, 'it is you I love; my sentiment towards your sister is one of affection too, but protective, tutelary affection – no more. Say what you will I cannot help it. I mistook my feeling for her, and I know how much I am to blame for my want of self-knowledge. I have fought against this discovery night and day; but it cannot be concealed. Why did I ever see you, since I could not see you till I had committed myself? At the moment my eyes beheld you on that day of my arrival, I said, "This is the woman for whom my manhood has waited." Ever since an unaccountable fascination has riveted my heart to you. Answer one word!'

'O, M. de la Feste!' I burst out. What I said more I cannot remember, but I suppose that the misery I was in showed pretty plainly, for he said, 'Something must be done to let her know; perhaps I have mistaken her affection, too; but all depends upon what you feel.'

'I cannot tell what I feel,' said I, 'except that this seems terrible treachery; and every moment that I stay with you here makes it worse! . . . Try to keep faith with her – her young heart is tender; believe me there is no mistake in the quality of her love for you. Would there were! This would kill her if she knew it!'

He sighed heavily. 'She ought never to be my wife,' he said. 'Leaving my own happiness out of the question, it would be a cruelty to her to unite her to me.'

I said I could not hear such words from him, and begged him in tears to go away; he obeyed, and I heard the garden door shut behind him. What is to be the end of the announcement, and the fate of Caroline?

May 20. – I put a good deal on paper yesterday, and yet not all. I was, in truth, hoping against hope, against conviction, against too conscious self-judgment. I scarcely dare own the truth now, yet it relieves my aching heart to set it down. Yes, I love him – that is the dreadful fact, and I can no longer parry, evade, or deny it to myself, though to the rest of the world it can never be owned. I love Caroline's betrothed, and he loves me. It is no yesterday's passion, cultivated by our converse; it came at first sight, independently of my will; and my talk with him yesterday made rather against it than for it, but, alas, did not quench it. God forgive us both for this terrible treachery.

May 25. – All is vague; our courses shapeless. He comes and goes, being occupied, ostensibly at least, with sketching in his tent in the wood. Whether he and she see each other privately I cannot tell, but I rather think they do not; that she sadly awaits him, and he does not appear. Not a sign from him that my repulse has done him any good, or that he will endeavour to keep faith with her. O, if I only had the compulsion of a god, and she the self-sacrifice of a martyr!

May 31. – It has all ended – or rather this act of the sad drama has ended – in nothing. He has left us. No day for the fulfilment of the engagement with Caroline is named, my father not being the man to press any one on such a matter, or, indeed, to interfere in any way. We two girls are, in fact, quite defenceless in a case of this kind; lovers may come when they choose, and desert when they choose; poor father is too urbane to utter a word of remonstrance or inquiry. Moreover, as the approved of my dead mother, M. de la Feste has a sort of autocratic power with my father, who holds it unkind to her memory to have an opinion about him. I, feeling it my duty, asked M. de la Feste at the last moment about the engagement, in a voice I could not keep firm.

'Since the death of your mother all has been indefinite – all!' he said gloomily. That was the whole. Possibly, Wherryborne Rectory may see him no more.

June 7. – M. de la Feste has written – one letter to her, one to me. Hers could not have been very warm, for she did not brighten on reading it. Mine was an ordinary note of friendship, filling an ordinary sheet of paper, which I handed over to Caroline when I had finished looking it through. But there was a scrap of paper in the bottom of the envelope, which I dared not show any one. This scrap is his real letter: I scanned it alone in my room, trembling, hot and cold by turns. He tells me he is very wretched; that he deplores what has happened, but was helpless. Why did I let him see me, if only to make him faithless. Alas, alas!

June 21. – My dear Caroline has lost appetite, spirits, health. Hope deferred maketh the heart sick. His letters to her grow colder – if indeed he has written more than one. He has refrained from writing again to me – he knows it is no use. Altogether the situation that he and she and I are in is melancholy in the extreme. Why are human hearts so perverse?

VI – HER INGENUITY INSTIGATES HER

September 19. – Three months of anxious care – till at length I have taken the extreme step of writing to him. Our chief distress has been caused by the state of poor Caroline, who, after sinking by degrees into such extreme weakness as to make it doubtful if she can ever recover full vigour, has today been taken much worse. Her position is very critical. The doctor says plainly that she is dying of a broken heart – and that even the removal of the cause may not now restore her. Ought I to have written to Charles sooner? But how could I when she forbade me? It was her pride only which instigated her, and I should not have obeyed.

Sept. 26. – Charles has arrived and has seen her. He is shocked, conscience-stricken, remorseful. I have told him that he can do no good beyond cheering her by his presence. I do not know what he thinks of proposing to her if she gets better, but he says little to her at present: indeed he dares not: his words agitate her dangerously.

Sept. 28. – After a struggle between duty and selfishness, such as I pray to Heaven I may never have to undergo again, I have asked him for pity's sake to make her his wife, here and now, as she lies. I said to him that the poor child would not trouble him long; and such a solemnization would soothe her last hours as nothing else could do. He said that he would willingly do so, and had thought of it himself; but for one forbidding reason: in the event of her death as his wife he can never marry me, her sister, according to our laws. I started at his words. He went on: 'On the other hand, if I were sure that immediate marriage with me would save her life, I would not refuse, for possibly I might after a while, and out of sight of you, make myself fairly content with one of so sweet a disposition as hers; but if, as is probable, neither my marrying her nor any other act can avail to save her life, by so doing I lose both her and you.' I could not answer him.

Sept. 29. – He continued firm in his reasons for refusal till this morning, and then I became possessed with an idea, which I at once propounded to him. It was that he should at least consent to a *form* of marriage with Caroline, in consideration of her love; a form which need not be a legal union, but one which would satisfy her sick and enfeebled soul. Such things have been done, and the sentiment of feeling herself his would inexpressibly comfort her mind, I am sure. Then, if she is taken from us, I should not have lost the power of becoming his lawful wife at some future day, if indeed should be deemed expedient; if, on the other hand, she lives, he can on her recovery inform her of the incompleteness of their marriage contract, the ceremony can be repeated, and I can, and I am sure willingly would, avoid troubling them with my presence till grey hairs and wrinkles made his unfortunate passion for me a thing of the past. I put all this before him; but he demurred.

Sept. 30. – I have urged him again. He says he will consider. It is not time to mince matters, and as a further inducement I have offered to enter into a solemn engagement to marry him myself a year after her death.

Sept. 30. Later. – An agitating interview. He says he will agree to whatever I propose, the three possibilities and our contingent acts being recorded as follows: First, in the event of dear Caroline being taken from us, I marry him on the expiration of a year: Second, in the forlorn chance of her recovery I take upon myself the responsibility of explaining to Caroline the true nature of the ceremony he has gone through with her, that it was done at my suggestion to make her happy at once, before a special licence could be obtained, and that a public ceremony at church is awaiting her: Third, in the unlikely event of her cooling, and refusing to repeat the ceremony with him, I leave England, join him abroad, and there wed him, agreeing not to live in England again until Caroline has either married another or regards her attachment to Charles as a bygone matter. I have thought over these conditions, and have agreed to them all as they stand.

11 p.m. – I do not much like this scheme, after all. For one thing, I have just sounded my father on it before parting with him for the night, my impression having been that he would see no objection. But he says he could on no account countenance any such unreal proceeding; however good our intentions, and even though the poor girl were dying, it would not be right. So I sadly seek my pillow.

October 1. – I am sure my father is wrong in his view. Why is it not right, if it would be balm to Caroline's wounded soul, and if a real ceremony is absolutley refused by Charles – moreover is hardly practicable in the difficulty of getting a special licence, if he were agreed? My father does not know, or will not believe, that Caroline's attachemnt has been the cause of her hopeless condition. But that it is so, and that the form of words would give her inexpressible happiness, I know well; for I whispered tentatively in her ear on such marriages, and the effect was great. Henceforth my father cannot be taken into confidence on the subject of Caroline. He does not understand her.

12 o'clock noon. – I have taken advantage of my father's absence today to confide my secret notion to a thoughtful young man, who called here this morning to speak to my father. He is the Mr. Theophilus Highman, of whom I have already had occasion to speak – a Scripture reader in the next town, and is soon going to be ordained. I told him the pitiable case, and my remedy. He says ardently that he will assist me – would do anything for me (he is, in truth, an admirer of mine); he sees no wrong in such an act of charity. He is coming again to the house this afternoon before my father returns, to carry out the idea. I have spoken to Charles, who promises to be ready. I must now break the news to Caroline.

11 o'clock p.m. – I have been in too much excitement till now to set down the result. We have accomplished our plan; and though I feel like a guilty sinner, I am glad. My father, of course is not to be informed as yet. Caroline has had a seraphic expression upon her wasted, transparent face ever since. I should hardly be surprised if it really saved her life even now, and rendered a legitimate union necessary between them. In that case my father can be informed of the whole proceeding, and in the face of such wonderful success cannot disapprove.

Meanwhile poor Charles has not lost the possibility of taking unworthy me to fill her place should she —. But I cannot contemplate that alternative unmoved, and will not write it. Charles left for the South of Europe immediately after the ceremony. He was in a high-strung, throbbing, almost wild state of mind at first, but grew calmer under my exhortations. I had to pay the penalty of receiving a farewell kiss from him, which I much regret, considering its meaning; but he took me so unexpectedly, and in a moment was gone.

Oct. 6. – She certainly is better, and even when she found that Charles had been suddenly obliged to leave, she received the news quite cheerfully. The doctor says that her apparent improvement may be delusive; but I think our impressing upon her the necessity of keeping what has occurred a secret from papa, and everybody, helps to give her a zest for life.

Oct. 8. – She is still mending. I am glad to have saved her – my only sister – if I have done so; though I shall now never become Charles's wife.

VIII – A SURPRISE AWAITS HER

Feb. 5. – Writing has been absolutely impossible for a long while; but I now reach a stage at which it seems possible to jot down a line. Caroline's recovery, extending over four months, has been very engrossing; at first slow, latterly rapid. But a fearful complication of affairs attends it!

> O what a tangled web we weave
> When first we practise to deceive!

Charles has written reproachfully to me from Venice, where he is. He says how can he fulfil in the real what he has enacted in the counterfeit, while he still loves me? Yet how, on the other hand, can he leave it unfulfilled? All this time I have not told her, and up to this minute she believes that he has indeed taken her for better, for worse, till death them do part. It is a harassing position for me, and all three. In the awful approach of death, one's judgment loses its balance, and we do anything to meet the exigencies of the moment, with a single eye to the one who excites our sympathy, and from whom we seem on the brink of being separated for ever.

Had he really married her at that time all would be settled now. But he took too much thought; she might have died, and then he had his reason. If indeed it had turned out so, I should now be perhaps a sad woman; but not a tempest-tossed one. . . . The possibility of his claiming me after all is what lies at the root of my agitation. Everything hangs by a thread. Suppose I tell her the marriage was a mockery; suppose she is indignant with me and with him for the deception – and then? Otherwise, suppose she is not indignant but forgives all; he is bound to marry her; and honour constrains me to urge him thereto, in spite of what he protests, and to smooth the way to this issue by my method of informing her. I have meant to tell her the last month – ever since she has been strong enough to bear such tidings; but I have been without the power – the moral force. Surely I must write, and get him to come and assist me.

March 14. – She continually wonders why he does not come, the five months of his enforced absence having expired; and still more she wonders why he does not write oftener. His last letter was cold, she says, and she fears he regrets his marriage, which he may only have celebrated with her for pity's sake, thinking she was sure to die. It makes one's heart bleed to hear her hovering thus so near the truth, and yet never discerning its actual shape.

A minor trouble besets met, too, in the person of the young Scripture reader, whose conscience pricks him for the part he played. Surely I am punished if ever woman were, for a too ingenious perversion of her better judgment!

April 2. – She is practically well. The faint pink revives in her cheek, though it is not quite so full as heretofore. But she still wonders what she can have done to offend 'her dear husband,' and I have been obliged to tell the smallest part of the truth – an unimportant fragment of the whole, in fact, I said that I feared for the moment he might regret the precipitancy of the act, which her illness caused, his affairs not having been quite sufficiently advanced for marriage just then, though he will doubtless come to her as soon as he has a home ready. Meanwhile I have written to him, peremptorily, to come and relieve me in this awful dilemma. He will find no note of love in that.

April 10. – To my alarm the letter I lately addressed to him at Venice, where he is staying, as well as the last one she sent him, have received no reply. She thinks he is ill. I do not quite think that, but I wish we could hear from him. Perhaps the peremptoriness of my words had offended him; it grieves me to think it possible. *I* offend him! But too much of this. I *must* tell her the truth, or she may in her ignorance commit herself to some course or other that may be ruinously compromising. She said plaintively just now that if he could see her, and know how occupied with him and him alone is her every waking hour, she is sure he would forgive her the wicked presumption of becoming his wife. Very sweet all that, and touching. I could not conceal my tears.

April 15. – The house is in confusion; my father is angry and distressed, and I am distracted. Caroline has disappeared – gone away secretly. I cannot help thinking that I know where she is gone to. How guilty I seem, and how innocent she! O that I had told her before now!

1 o'clock. – No trace of her as yet. We find also that the little waiting-maid we have here in training has disappeared with Caroline, and there is not much doubt that Caroline, fearing to travel alone, had induced this girl to go with her as companion. I am almost sure she has started in desperation to find him, and that Venice is her goal. Why should she run away, if not to join her husband, as she thinks him? Now that I consider, there have been indications of this wish in her for days, as in birds of passage there lurk signs of their incipient intention; and yet I did not think she would have taken such an extreme step, unaided, and without consulting me. I can only jot down the bare facts – I have no time for reflections. But fancy Caroline travelling across the continent of Europe with a chit of a girl, who will be more of a charge than an assistance! They will be a mark for every marauder who encounters them.

Evening: 8 o'clock. – Yes, it is as I surmised. She has gone to join him. A note posted by her in Budmouth Regis at daybreak has reached me this afternoon – thanks to the fortunate chance of one of the servants calling for letters in town today, or I should not have got it until tomorrow. She merely asserts her determination of going to him, and has started privately, that nothing may hinder her; stating nothing about her route. That such a gentle thing should suddenly become so calmly resolute quite surprises me. Alas, he may have left Venice – she may not find him for weeks – may not at all.

My father, on learning the facts, bade me at once have everything ready by nine this evening, in time to drive to the train that meets the night steam-boat. This I have done, and there being an hour to spare before we start, I relieve the suspense of waiting by taking up my pen. He says overtake her we must, and calls Charles the hardest of names. He believes, of course, that she is merely an infatuated girl rushing off to meet her lover; and how can the wretched I tell him that she is more, and in a sense better than that – yet not sufficiently more and better to make this flight to Charles anything but a still greater danger to her than a mere lover's impulse. We shall go by way of Paris, and we think we may overtake her there. I hear my father walking restlessly up and down the hall, and can write no more.

VIII – SHE TRAVELS IN PURSUIT

April 16. Evening, Paris, Hôtel —. – There is no overtaking her at this place; but she had been here, as I thought, no other hotel in Paris being known to her. We go on tomorrow morning.

April 18. Venice. – A morning of adventures and emotions which leave me sick and weary, and yet unable to sleep, though I have lain down on the sofa of my room for more than an hour in the attempt. I therefore make up my diary to date in a hurried fashion, for the sake of the riddance it affords to ideas which otherwise remain suspended hotly in the brain.

We arrived here this morning in broad sunlight, which lit up the sea-girt buildings as we approached so that they seemed like a city of cork floating raft-like on the smooth, blue deep. But I only glanced from the carriage window at the lovely scene, and we were soon across the intervening water and inside the railway station. When we got to the front steps the row of black gondolas and the shouts of the gondoliers so bewildered my father that he was understood to require two gondolas instead of one with two oars, and so I found him in one and myself in another. We got this righted after a while, and were rowed at once to the hotel on the Riva degli Schiavoni where M. de la Feste had been staying when we last heard from him, the way being down the Grand Canal for some distance, under the Rialto, and then by narrow canals which eventually brought us under the Bridge of Sighs – harmonious to our moods! – and out again into open water. The scene was purity itself as to colour, but it was cruel that I should behold it for the first time under such circumstances.

As soon as we entered the hotel, which is an old-fashioned place, like most places here, where people are taken *en pension* as well as the ordinary way, I rushed to the framed list of visitors hanging in the hall, and in a moment I saw Charles's names upon it among the rest. But she was our chief thought. I turned to the hall porter, and – knowing that she would have travelled as 'Madame de la Feste' – I asked for her under that name, without my father hearing. (He, poor soul, was making confused inquiries outside the door about 'an English lady,' as if there were not a score of English ladies at hand.)

'She has just come,' said the porter. 'Madame came by the very early train this morning, when Monsieur was asleep, and she requested us not to disturb him. She is now in her room.'

Whether Caroline had seen us from the window, or overheard me, I do not know, but at that moment I heard footsteps on the bare marble stairs, and she appeared in person descending.

'Caroline!' I exclaimed, 'why have you done this?' and rushed up to her.

She did not answer; but looked down to hide her emotion, which she conquered after the lapse of a few seconds, putting on a practical tone that belied her.

'I am just going to my husband,' she said. 'I have not yet seen him. I have not been here long.' She condescended to give no further reason for her movements, and made as if to move on. I implored her to come into a private room where I could speak to her in confidence, but she objected. However, the dining-room close at hand, was quite empty at this hour, and I got her inside and closed the door. I do not know how I began my explanation, or how I ended it, but I told her briefly and brokenly enough that the marriage was not real.

'Not real?' she said vacantly.

'It is not,' said I. 'You will find that it is all as I say.'

She could not believe my meaning even then. 'Not his wife?' she cried. 'It is impossible. What am I, then?'

I added more details and reiterated the reason for my conduct as well as I could; but Heaven knows how very difficult I found it to feel a jot more justification for it in my own mind than she did in hers.

The revulsion of feeling, as soon as she really comprehended all, was most distressing. After her grief had in some measure spent itself she turned against both him and me.

'Why should have I been deceived like this?' she demanded, with a bitter haughtiness of which I had not deemed such a tractable creature capable. 'Do you suppose that *anything* could justify such an impositon? What, O what a snare you have spread for me!'

I murmured, 'Your life seemed to require it,' but she did not hear me. She sank down in a chair, covered her face, and then my father came in. 'O, here you are!' he said. 'I could not find you. And Caroline!'

'And were *you*, papa, a party to this strange deed of kindness?'

'To what?' said he.

Then out it all came, and for the first time he was made acquainted with the fact that the scheme for soothing her illness, which I had sounded him upon, had been really carried out. In a moment he sided with Caroline. My repeated assurance that my motive was good availed less than nothing. In a minute of two Caroline arose and went abruptly out of the room, and my father followed her, leaving me alone to my reflections.

I was so bent upon finding Charles immediately that I did not notice whither they went. The servants told me that M. de la Feste was just outside smoking, and one of them went to look for him, I following; but before we had gone many steps he came out of the hotel behind me. I expected him to be amazed; but he showed no surprise at seeing me, though he showed another kind of feeling to an extent which dismayed me. I may have revealed something similar; but I struggled hard against all emotion, and as soon as I could I told him she had come. He simply said 'Yes' in a low voice.

'You know it, Charles?' said I.

'I have just learnt it,' he said.

'O, Charles,' I went on, 'having delayed completing your marriage with her till now, I fear – it has become a serious position for us. Why did you not reply to our letters?'

'I was purposing to reply in person: I did not know how to address her on the point – how to address you. But what has become of her?'

'She has gone off with my father,' said I; 'indignant with you, and scorning me.'

He was silent: and I suggested that we should follow them, pointing out the direction which I fancied their gondola had taken. As the one we got into was doubly manned we soon came in view of their two figures ahead of us, while they were not likely to observe us, our boat having the 'felze' on, while theirs was uncovered. They shot into a narrow canal just beyond the Giardino Reale, and by the time we were floating up between its slimy walls we saw them getting out of their gondola at the steps which lead up near the end of the Via 22 Marzo. When we reached the same spot they were walking up and down the Via in consultation. Getting out he stood on the lower steps watching them. I watched him. He seemed to fall into a reverie.

'Will you not go and speak to her?' said I at length.

He assented, and went forward. Still he did not hasten to join them, but, screened by a projecting window, observed their musing converse. At last he looked back at me; whereupon I pointed forward, and he in obedience stepped out, and met them face to face. Caroline flushed hot, bowed haughtily to him, turned away, and taking my father's arm violently, led him off before he had had time to use his own judgment. They disappeard into a narrow *calle* or alley, leading to the back of the buildings on the Grand Canal.

M. de la Feste came slowly back; as he stepped in beside me I realized my position so vividly that my heart might almost have been heard to beat. The third condition had arisen – the least expected by either of us. She had refused him; he was free to claim me.

We returned in the boat together. He seemed quite absorbed till we had turned the angle into the Grand Canal, when he broke the silence. 'She spoke very bitterly to you in the *salle-à-manger*,' he said. 'I do not think she was quite warranted in speaking so to you, who had nursed her so tenderly.'

'O, but I think she was,' I answered. 'It was there I told her what had been done; she did not know till then.'

'She was very dignified – very striking,' he murmured 'You were more.'

'But how do you know what passed between us,' said I. He then told me that he had seen and heard all. The dining- room was divided by folding-doors from an inner portion, and he had been sitting in the latter part when we entered the outer, so that our words were distinctly audible.

'But, dear Alicia,' he went on, 'I was more impressed by the affection of your apology to her than by anything else. And do you know that now the conditions have arisen which give me liberty to consider you my affianced?' I had been expecting this, but yet was not prepared. I stammered out that we would not discuss it then.

'Why not?' said he. 'Do you know that we may marry here and now? She has cast off both you and me.'

'It cannot be,' said I, firmly. 'She has not been fairly asked to be your wife in fact – to repeat the service lawfully; and until that has been done it would be grievous sin in me to accept you.'

I had not noticed where the gondoliers were rowing us. I suppose he had given them some direction unheard by me, for as I resigned myself in despairing indolence to the motion of the gondola, I perceived that it was taking us up the Canal, and, turning into a side opening near the Palazzo Grimani, drew up at some steps near the end of a large church.

'Where are we?' said I.

'It is the Church of the Frari,' he replied. 'We might be married there. At any rate, let us go inside and grow calm, and decide what to do.'

When we had entered I found that whether a place to marry

in or not, it was one to depress. The word which Venice speaks most constantly – decay – was in a sense accentuated here. The whole large fabric itself seeming sinking into an earth which was not solid enough to bear it. Cobwebbed cracks zigzagged the walls, and similar webs clouded the window-panes. A sickly-sweet smell pervaded the aisle. After walking about with him a little while in embarrassing silences, divided only by his cursory explanations of the monuments and other objects, and almost fearing he might produce a marriage licence, I went to a door in the south transept which opened into the sacristy.

I glanced through it, towards the small altar at the upper end. The place was empty save of one figure; and she was kneeling here in front of the beautiful altarpiece by Bellini. Beautiful though it was she seemed not to see it. She was weeping and praying as though her heart was broken. She was my sister Caroline. I beckoned to Charles, and he came to my side, and looked through the door with me.

'Speak to her.' said I. 'She will forgive you.'

I gently pushed him through the doorway, and went back into the transept, down the nave, and onward to the west door. There I saw my father, to whom I spoke. He answered severely that having first obtained comfortable quarters in a *pension* on the Grand Canal, he had gone back to the hotel on the Riva degli Schiavoni to find me; but that I was not there. He was now waiting for Caroline, to accompany her back to the *pension*, at which she had requested to be left to herself as much as possible till she could regain some composure.

I told him that it was useless to dwell on what was past, that I no doubt had erred, that the remedy lay in the future and their marriage. In this he quite agreed with me, and on my informing him that M. de la Feste was at that moment with Caroline in the sacristy, he assented to my proposal that we should leave them to themselves, and return together to await them at the *pension*, where he had also engaged a room for me. This we did, and going up to the chamber he had chosen for me, which overlooked the Canal, I leant from the window to watch for the gondola that should contain Charles and my sister.

They were not long in coming. I recognised them by the colour of her sunshade as soon as they turned the bend on my right hand. They were side by side of necessity, but there was no conversation between them, and I thought that she looked flushed and he pale. When they were rowed in to the steps of our house he handed her up. I fancied she might have refused his assistance, but she did not. Soon I heard her pass my door, and wishing to know the result of their interview I went downstairs, seeing that the gondola had not put off with him. He was turning from the door, but not towards the water, intending apparently to walk home by way of the *calle* which led into the Via 22 Marzo.

'Has she forgiven you?' said I.

'I have not asked her, he said.

'But you are bound to do so,' I told him.

He paused, and then said, 'Alicia, let us understand each other. Do you mean to tell me, once for all, that if your sister is willing to become my wife you absolutely make way for her, and will not entertain any thought of what I suggested to you any more?'

'I do tell you so,' said I with dry lips. 'you belong to her – how can I do otherwise?'

'Yes; it is so; it is purely a question of honour,' he returned. 'Very well then, honour shall be my word, and not my love. I will put the question to her frankly; if she says yes, the marriage shall be. But not here. It shall be at your own house in England.'

'When?' said I.

'I will accompany her there,' he replied, 'and it shall be within a week of her return. I have nothing to gain by delay. But I will not answer for the consequences.'

'What do you mean?' said I. He made no reply, went away, and I came back to my room.

IX – SHE WITNESSES THE END

April 20. Milan, 10.30 p.m. – We are thus far on our way homeward. I, being decidedly *de trop*, travel apart from the rest as much as I can. Having dined at the hotel here, I went out by myself, regardless of the proprieties, for I could not stay in. I walked at a leisurely pace along the Via Allesandro

Manzoni till my eye was caught by the grand Galleria Vittorio Emanuele, and I entered under the high glass arcades till I reached the central octagon, where I sat down on one of a group of chairs placed there. Becoming accustomed to the stream of promenaders, I soon observed, seated on the chairs opposite, Caroline and Charles. This was the first occasion on which I had seen them *en tête à tête* since my conversation with him. She soon caught sight of me; averted her eyes; then, apparently abondoning herself to an impulse, she jumped up from her seat and came across to me. We had not spoken to each other since the meeting in Venice.

'Alicia,' she said, sitting down by my side, 'Charles asks me to forgive you, and I do forgive you.'

I pressed her hand, with tears in my eyes, and said, 'And do you forgive him?'

'Yes,' said she, shyly.

'And what's the result?' said I.

'We are to be married directly we reach home.'

This was almost the whole of our conversation; she walked home with me, Charles following a little way behind, though she kept turning her head, as if anxious that he should overtake us. 'Honour and not love' seemed to ring in my ears. So matters stand. Caroline is again happy.

April 25. – We have reached home, Charles with us. Events are now moving in silent speed, almost with velocity, indeed; and I sometimes feel oppressed by the strange and preternatural ease which seems to accompany their flow. Charles is staying at the neighbouring town; he is only waiting for the marriage licence; when obtained he is to come here, be quietly married to her, and carry her off. It is rather resignation than content which sits on his face; but he has not spoken a word more to me on the the burning subject, or deviated one hair's breadth from the course he laid down. They may be happy in time to come: I hope so. But I cannot shake off depression.

May 6. – Eve of the wedding. Caroline is serenely happy, though not blithe. But there is nothing to excite anxiety about her. I wish I could say the same of him. He comes and goes like a ghost, and yet nobody seems to observe this strangeness in his mien. I could not help being here for the ceremony; but my absence would have resulted in less disquiet on his part, I believe.

However, I may be wrong in attributing causes: my father simply says that Charles and Caroline have as good a chance of being happy as other people. Well, tomorrow settles all.

May 7. – They are married: we have just returned from church. Charles looked so pale this morning that my father asked him if he was ill. He said, 'No: only a slight headache;' and we started for the church. There was no hitch or hindrance; and the thing is done.

4 p.m. – They ought to have set out on their journey by this time; but there is an unaccountable delay. Charles went out half-an-hour ago, and has not yet returned. Caroline is waiting in the hall; but I am dreadfully afraid they will miss the train. I suppose the trifling hindrance is of no account; and yet I am full of misgivings. . . .

Sept. 14. – Four months have passed; *only* four months! it seems like years. Can it be that only seventeen weeks ago I set on this paper the fact of their marriage? I am now an aged woman by comparison!

On that never to be forgotten day we waited and waited, and Charles did not return. At six o'clock, when poor little Caroline had gone back to her room in a state of suspense impossible to describe, a man who worked in the water-meadows came to the house and asked for my father. He had an interview with him in the study. My father then rang his bell, and sent for me. I went down; and I then learnt the fatal news. Charles was no more. The waterman had been going to shut down the hatches of a weir in the meads when he saw a hat on the edge of the pool below, floating round and round in the eddy, and looking into the pool saw something strange at the bottom. He knew what it meant, and lowering the hatches so that the water was still, could distinctly see the body. It is needless to write particulars that were in the newspapers at the time. Charles was brought to the house, but he was dead.

We all feared for Caroline; and she suffered much; but strange to say, her suffering was purely of the nature of deep grief which found relief in sobbing and tears. It came out at the inquest that Charles had been accustomed to cross the meads to give an occasional halfcrown to an old man who lived on the opposite hill, who had once been a landscape painter in an humble way till he lost his eyesight; and

it was assumed that he had gone thither for the same purpose today, and to bid him farewell. On this information
the coroner's jury found that his death had been caused by
misadventure; and everybody believes to this hour that he was
drowned while crossing the weir to relieve the old man.
Except one: she believes in no accident. After the stunning
effect of the first news, I thought it strange that he should have
chosen to go on such an errand at the last moment, and to go
personally, when there was so little time to spare since any gift
could have been so easily sent by another hand. Further
reflection has convinced me that this step out of life was as
much a part of the day's plan as was the wedding in the church
hard by. They were the two halves of his complete intention
when he gave me on the Grand Canal that assurance which I
shall never forget: 'Very well, then; honour shall be my word,
not love. If she says "Yes," the marriage shall be.'

   I do not know why I should have made this entry at this
particular time; but it has occurred to me to do it – to
complete, in a measure, that part of my desultory chronicle
which relates to the love-story of my sister and Charles. She
lives on meekly in her grief, and will probably outlive it; while
I – but never mind me.

X – SHE ADDS A NOTE LONG AFTER

Five years later. – I have lighted upon this old diary, which it
has interested me to look over, containing, as it does, records
of the time when life shone more warmly in my eye than it
does now. I am impelled to add one sentence to round off its
record of the past. About a year ago my sister Caroline, after a
persistent wooing, accepted the hand and heart of Theophilus
Higham, once the blushing young Scripture reader who
assisted at the substitute for a marriage I planned, and now the
fully-ordained curate of the next parish. His penitence for the
part he played ended in love. We have all now made atone-
ment for our sins against her: may she be deceived no more.

1887

THE GRAVE BY THE HANDPOST

I never pass through Chalk-Newton without turning to regard the neighbouring upland, at a point where a lane crosses the lone straight highway dividing this from the next parish; a sight which does not fail to recall the event that once happened there; and, though it may seem superfluous, at this date, to disinter more memories of village history, the whispers of that spot may claim to bc preserved.

It was on a dark, yet mild and exceptionally dry evening at Christmas-time (according to the testimony of William Dewy of Mellstock, Michael Mail, and others), that the choir of Chalk-Newton – a large parish situate about half-way between the towns of Ivel and Casterbridge, and now a railway station – left their homes just before midnight to repeat their annual harmonies under the windows of the local population. The band of instrumentalists and singers was one of the largest in the county; and, unlike the smaller and finer Mellstock string-band, which eschewed all but the catgut, it included brass and reed performers at full Sunday services, and reached all across the west gallery.

On this night there were two or three violins, two 'cellos, a tenor viol, double bass, hautboy, clarionets, serpent, and seven singers. It was, however, not the choir's labours, but what its members chanced to witness, that particularly marked the occasion.

They had pursued their rounds for many years without meeting with any incident of an unusual kind, but tonight, according to the assertions of several, there prevailed, to begin with, an exceptionally solemn and thoughtful mood among two or three of the oldest in the band, as if they were thinking they might be joined by the phantoms of dead friends who had been of their number in earlier years, and now were mute in the churchyard under flattening mounds – friends who had shown greater zest for melody in their time than was shown in this; or that some past voice of a semi-transparent figure might quaver from some bedroom window its acknowledgment of their nocturnal greeting, instead of a familiar living neighbour. Whether this were fact or fancy, the younger members of the choir met together with their customary thoughtlessness and buoyancy. When they had gathered by the stone stump of the cross in the middle of the village, near the White Horse Inn, which they made their starting point, someone observed that they were full early, that it was not yet twelve o'clock. The local waits of those days mostly refrained from sounding a note before Christmas morning had astronomically arrived, and not caring to return to their beer, they decided to begin with some outlying cottages in Sidlinch Lane, where the people had no clocks, and would not know whether it were night or morning. In that direction they accordingly went; and as they ascended to higher ground their attention was attracted by a light beyond the houses, quite at the top of the lane.

The road from Chalk-Newton to Broad Sidlinch is about two miles long and in the middle of its course, where it passes over the ridge dividing the two villages, it crosses at right angles, as has been stated, the lonely monotonous old highway know as Long Ash Lane, which runs, straight as a surveyor's line, many miles north and south of this spot, on the foundation of a Roman road, and has often been mentioned in these narratives. Though now quite deserted and grass-grown, at the beginning of the century it was well kept and frequented by traffic. The glimmering light appeared to come from the precise point where the roads intersected.

'I think I know what that mid mean!' one of the group remarked.

They stood a few moments, discussing the probability of the light having origin in an event of which rumours had reached them, and resolved to go up the hill.

Approaching the high land their conjectures were strengthened. Long Ash Lane cut athwart them, right and left; and they saw that at the junction of the four ways, under the handpost, a grave was dug, into which, as the choir drew nigh, a corpse had just been thrown by the four Sidlinch men employed for the purpose. The cart and horse which had brought the body thither stood silently by.

The singers and musicians from Chalk-Newton halted, and looked on while the gravediggers shovelled in and trod down the earth, till, the hole being filled, the latter threw down their spades into the cart, and prepared to depart.

'Who mid ye be a-burying there?' asked Lot Swanhills in a raised voice. 'Not the sergeant?'

The Sidlinch men had been so deeply engrossed in their task that they had not noticed the lanterns of the Chalk-Newton choir till now.

'What – be you the Newton carol-singers?' returned the representative of Sidlinch.

'Ay, sure. Can it be that it is old Sergeant Holway you've a-buried there?'

''Tis so. You've heard about it, then?'

The choir knew no particulars – only that he had shot himself in his apple-closet on the previous Sunday. 'Nobody seem'th to know what 'a did it for, 'a b'lieve? Leastwise, we don't know at Chalk-Newton,' continued Lot.

'O yes. It all came out at the inquest.'

The singers drew close, and the Sidlinch men, pausing to rest after their labours, told the story. 'It was all owing to that son of his, poor old man. It broke his heart.'

'But the son is a soldier, surely; now with his regiment in the East Indies?'

'Ay. And it have been rough with the army over there lately. 'Twas a pity his father persuaded him to go. But Luke shouldn't have twyted the sergeant o't, since 'a did it for the best.'

The circumstances, in brief, were these: The sergeant who had come to this lamentable end, father of the young soldier who had gone with his regiment to the East, had been singularly comfortable in his military experiences, these having ended long before the outbreak of the great war with France. On his discharge, after duly serving his time, he had returned to his native village, and married, and taken kindly to domestic life. But the war in which England next involved herself had cost him many frettings that age and infirmity prevented him from being ever again an active unit of the army. When his only son grew to young manhood, and the question arose of his going out in life, the lad expressed his wish to be a mechanic. But his father advised enthusiastically for the army.

'Trade is coming to nothing in these days,' he said. 'And if the war with the French lasts, as it will, trade will be still worse. The army, Luke – that's the thing for 'ee. 'Twas the making of me, and 'twill be the making of you. I hadn't half such a chance as you'll have in these splendid hotter times.'

Luke demurred, for he was a home-keeping, peace-loving youth. But, putting respectful trust in his father's judgment, he at length gave way, and enlisted in the —d Foot. In the course of a few weeks he was sent out to India to his regiment, which had distinguished itself in the East under General Wellesley.

But Luke was unlucky. News came home indirectly that he lay sick out there; and then on one recent day when his father was out walking, the old man had received tidings that a letter awaited him at Casterbridge. The sergeant sent a special messenger the whole nine miles, and the letter was paid for and brought home; but though, as he had guessed, it came from Luke, its contents were of an unexpected tenor.

The letter had been written during a time of deep depression. Luke said that his life was a burden and a slavery, and bitterly reproached his father for advising him to embark on a career for which he felt unsuited. He found himself suffering fatigues and illnesses without gaining glory, and engaged in a cause which he did not understand or appreciate. If it had not been for his father's bad advice he, Luke, would now have been working comfortably at a trade in the village that he had never wished to leave.

After reading the letter the sergeant advanced a few steps till he was quite out of sight of everybody, and then sat down on the bank by the wayside.

When he arose half-an-hour later he looked withered and broken and from that day his natural spirits left him. Wounded to the quick by his son's sarcastic stings, he indulged in liquor more and more frequently. His wife had died some years before this date, and the sergeant lived alone in the house which had been hers. One morning in the

December under notice the report of a gun had been heard on his premises, and on entering the neighbours found him in a dying state. He had shot himself with an old firelock that he used for scaring birds; and from what he had said the day before, and the arrangements he had made for his decease, there was no doubt that his end had been deliberately planned, as a consequence of the despondency into which he had been thrown by his son's letter. The coroner's jury returned a verdict of *felo de se*.

'Here's his son's letter,' said one of the Sidlinch men. ''Twas found in his father's pocket. You can see by the state o't how many times he read it over. Howsomever, the Lord's will be done, since it must, whether or no.'

The grave was filled up and levelled, no mound being shaped over it. The Sidlinch men then bade the Chalk-Newton choir good-night, and departed with the cart in which they had brought the sergeant's body to the hill. When their tread had died away from the ear, and the wind swept over the isolated grave with its customary siffle of indifference, Lot Swanhills turned and spoke to old Richard Toller, the hautboy player.

''Tis hard upon a man, and he a wold sojer, to serve en so, Richard. Not that the sergeant was ever in a battle bigger than would go into a half-acre paddock, that's true. Still his soul ought to hae as good a chance as another man's all the same, hey?'

Richard replied that he was quite of the same opinion. 'What d'ye say to lifting up a carrel over his grave, as 'tis Christmas, and no hurry to begin down in parish, and 'twouldn't take up ten minutes, and not a soul up here to say us nay, or know anything about it?'

Lot nodded assent. 'The man ought to hae his chances,' he repeated.

'Ye may as well spet upon his grave, for all the good we shall do en by what we lift up, now he's got so far,' said Notton, the clarinet man and professed sceptic of the choir. 'But I'm agreed if the rest be.'

They thereupon placed themselves in a semicircle by the newly stirred earth, and roused the dull air with the well-known Number Sixteen of their collection, which Lot gave out as being the one he thought best suited to the occasion and the mood:–

> He comes' the pri'-soners to' re-lease',
> In Sa'-tan's bon'-dage held'.

'Jown it – we've never played to a dead man afore', said Ezra Cattstock, when, having concluded the last verse, they stood reflecting for a breath or two. 'But it do seem more merciful than to go away and leave en, as they t'other fellers have done.'

'Now backalong to Newton, and by the time we get overright the pa'son's 'twill be half after twelve,' said the leader.

They had not, however, done more than gather up their instruments when the wind brought to their notice the noise of a vehicle rapidly driven up the same lane from Sidlinch which the gravediggers had lately retraced. To avoid being run over when moving on, they waited till the benighted traveller, whoever he might be, should pass them where they stood in the wider area of the Cross.

In half a minute the light of the lanterns fell upon a hired fly, drawn by a steaming and jaded horse. It reached the handpost, when a voice from the inside cried, 'Stop here!' The driver pulled rein. The carriage door was opened from within, and there leapt out a private soldier in the uniform of some line regiment. He looked around, and was apparently surprised to see the musicians standing there.

'Have you buried a man here?' he asked.

'No. We bain't Sidlinch folk, thank God; we be Newton choir. Though a man is just buried here, that's true; and we've raised a carrel over the poor mortal's natomy. What – do my eyes see before me young Luke Holway, that went wi' his regiment to the East Indies, or do I see his spirit straight from the battlefield? Be you the son that wrote the letter –.'

'Don't – don't ask me. The funeral is over, then?'

'There wer no funeral, in a Christen manner of speaking. But's buried, sure enough. You must have met the men going back in the empty cart.'

'Like a dog in a ditch, and all through me!'

He remained silent, looking at the grave, and they could not help pitying him. 'My friends,' he said, 'I understand better now. You have, I suppose, in neighbourly charity, sung peace to his soul? I thank you, from my heart, for your kind pity. Yes; I am Sergeant Holway's miserable son – I'm the son who has brought about his father's death, as truly as if I had done it with my own hand.'

'No, no. Don't ye take on so, young man. He'd been naturally low for a good while, off and on, so we hear.'

'We were out in the East when I wrote to him. Everything had seemed to go wrong with me. Just after my letter had gone we were ordered home. That's how it is you see me here. As soon as we got into barracks at Casterbridge I heard o' this – . . . Damn me! I'll dare to follow my father, and make away with myself too. It is the only thing left to do!'

'Don't ye be rash, Luke Holway, I say again; but try to make amends by your future life. And maybe your father will smile a smile down from heaven upon 'ee for 't.'

He shook his head. 'I don't know about that!' he answered bitterly.

'Try and be worthy of your father at his best. 'Tis not too late.'

'D'ye think not? I fancy it is! . . . Well, I'll turn it over. Thank you for your good counsel. I'll live for one thing, at any rate. I'll move father's body to a decent Christian churchyard, if I do it with my own hands. I can't save his life, but I can give him an honourable grave. He shan't lie in this accursed place!'

'Ay, as our pa'son says, 'tis a barbarous custom they keep up at Sidlinch, and ought to be done away wi'. The man a' old soldier, too. You see, our pa'son is not like yours at Sidlinch.'

'He says it is barbarous, does he? So it is!' cried the soldier. 'Now hearken, my friends.' Then he proceeded to inquire if they would increase his indebtedness to them by undertaking the removal, privately, of the body of the suicide to the churchyard, not of Sidlinch, a parish he now hated, but of Chalk-Newton. He would give them all he possessed to do it.

Lot asked Ezra Cattstock what he thought of it.

Cattstock, the 'cello player, who was also the sexton, demurred, and advised the young soldier to sound the rector about it first. ''Mid be he would object, and yet 'a mid'nt. The pa'son o' Sidlinch is a hard man, I own ye, and 'a said if folk will kill theirselves in hot blood they must take the consequences. But ours don't think like that at all, and might allow it.'

'What's his name?'

'The honourable and reverent Mr. Oldham, brother to Lord Wessex. But you needn't be afeard o' en on that account. He'll talk to 'ee like a common man, if so be you haven't had enough drink to gie 'ee bad breath.'

'O, the same as formerly. I'll ask him. Thank you. And that duty done –'

'What then?'

'There's war in Spain. I hear our next move is there. I'll try to show myself to be what my father wished me. I don't suppose I shall – but I'll try in my feeble way. That much I swear – here over his body. So help me God.'

Luke smacked his palm against the white hand-post with such force that it shook. 'Yes, there's war in Spain; and another chance for me to be worthy of father.'

So the matter ended that night. That the private acted in one thing as he had vowed to do soon became apparent, for during the Christmas week the rector came into the churchyard when Cattstock was there, and asked him to find a spot that would be suitable for the purpose of such an interment, adding that he had slightly known the late sergeant, and was not aware of any law which forbade him to assent to the removal, the letter of the rule having been observed. But as he did not wish to seem moved by opposition to his neighbour at Sidlinch, he had stipulated that the act of charity should be carried out at night, and as privately as possible, and that the grave should be in an obcure part of the enclosure. 'You had better see the young man about it at once,' added the rector.

But before Ezra had done anything Luke came down to his house. His furlough had been cut short, owing to new developments of the war in the Peninsula, and being obliged to go back to his regiment immediately, he was compelled to leave the exhumation and reinterment to his friends. Everything was paid for, and he implored them all to see it carried out forthwith.

With this the soldier left. The next day Ezra, on thinking the matter over, again went across to the rectory, struck with sudden misgiving. He had remembered that the sergeant had been buried without a coffin, and he was not sure that a stake had not been driven through him. The business would be more troublesome than they had at first supposed.

'Yes, indeed!' murmured the rector. 'I am afraid it is not feasible after all.'

The next event was the arrival of a headstone by carrier from the nearest town; to be left at Mr. Ezra Cattstock's; all expenses paid. The sexton and the carrier deposited the stone in the former's outhouse; and Ezra, left alone, put on his spectacles and read the brief and simple inscription:–

HERE LYETH THE BODY OF SAMUEL HOLWAY, LATE SERGEANT IN HIS MAJESTY'S —D REGIMENT OF FOOT, WHO DEPARTED THIS LIFE DECEMBER THE 20TH, 180–. ERECTED BY L.H.
'I AM NOT WORTHY TO BE CALLED THY SON.'

Ezra again called at the riverside rectory. 'The stone is come, sir. But I'm afeard we can't do it nohow.'

'I should like to oblige him,' said the gentlemanly old incumbent. 'And I would forego all fees willingly. Still, if you and the others don't think you can carry it out, I am in doubt what to say.'

'Well, sir; I've made inquiry of a Sidlinch woman as to his burial, and what I thought seems true. They buried en wi' a new six-foot hurdle-saul drough's body, from the sheep-pen up in North Ewelease though they won't own to it now. And the question is, Is the moving worth while, considering the awkwardness?'

'Have you heard anything more of the young man?'

Ezra had only heard that he had embarked that week for Spain with the rest of the regiment. 'And if he's as desperate as 'a seemed, we shall never see him here in England again.'

'It is an awkward case,' said the rector.

Ezra talked it over with the choir; one of whom suggested that the stone might be erected at the cross-roads. This was regarded as impracticable. Another said that it might be set up in the churchyard without removing the body; but this was seen to be dishonest. So nothing was done.

The headstone remained in Ezra's outhouse till, growing tired of seeing it there, he put it away among the bushes at the bottom of his garden. The subject was sometimes revived among them, but it always ended with: 'considering how 'a was buried, we can hardly make a job o't.'

There was always the consciousness that Luke would never come back, an impression strengthened by the disasters which were rumoured to have befallen the army in Spain. This tended to make their inertness permanent. The headstone grew green as it lay on its back under Ezra's bushes; then a tree by the river was blown down, and, falling across the stone, cracked it in three pieces. Ultimately the pieces became buried in the leaves and mould.

Luke had not been born a Chalk-Newton man, and he had no relations left in Sidlinch, so that no tidings of him reached either village throughout the war. But after Waterloo and the fall of Napoleon there arrived at Sidlinch one day an English sergeant-major covered with stripes and, as it turned out, rich in glory. Foreign service had so totally changed Luke Holway that it was not until he told his name that the inhabitants recognized him as the sergeant's only son.

He had served with unswerving effectiveness through the Peninsular campaigns under Wellington; had fought at Busaco, Fuentes d'Onore, Ciudad Rodrigo, Badajoz, Salamanca, Vittoria, Quatre Bras, and Waterloo; and had now returned to enjoy a more than earned pension and repose in his native district.

He hardly stayed in Sidlinch longer than to take a meal on his arrival. The same evening he started on foot over the hill to Chalk-Newton, passing the handpost, and saying as he glanced at the spot, 'Thank God: he's not there!' Nightfall was approaching when he reachd the latter village; but he made straight for the churchyard. On his entering it there remained light enough to discern the headstones by, and these be narrowly scanned. But though he searched the front part by the road, and the back part by the river, what he sought he could not find – the grave of Sergeant Holway, and a memorial bearing the inscription: 'I AM NOT WORTHY TO BE CALLED THY SON.'

He left the churchyard and made inquiries. The honourable

and reverend old rector was dead, and so were many of the choir; but by degrees the sergeant-major learnt that his father still lay at the cross-roads in Long Ash Lane.

Luke pursued his way moodily homewards, to do which, in the natural course, he would be compelled to repass the spot, there being no other road between the two villages. But he could not now go by that place, vociferous with reproaches in his father's tones; and he got over the hedge and wandered deviously through the ploughed fields to avoid the scene. Through many a fight and fatigue Luke had been sustained by the thought that he was restoring the family honour and making noble amends. Yet his father lay still in degradation. It was rather a sentiment than a fact that his father's body had been made to suffer for his own misdeeds; but to his super-sensitiveness it seemed that his efforts to retrieve his character and to propitiate the shade of the insulted one had ended in failure.

He endeavoured, however, to shake off his lethargy, and, not liking the associations of Sidlinch, hired a small cottage at Chalk-Newton which had long been empty. Here he lived alone, becoming quite a hermit, and allowing no woman to enter the house.

The Christmas after taking up his abode herein he was sitting in the chimney corner by himself, when he heard faint notes in the distance, and soon a melody burst forth immediately outside his own window. It came from the carol-singers, as usual; and though many of the old hands, Ezra and Lot included, had gone to their rest, the same old carols were still played out of the same old books. There resounded through the sergeant-major's window-shutters the familiar lines that the deceased choir had rendered over his father's grave:—

> He comes' the pri'-soners to' re-lease',
>   In Sa'-tan's bon'-dage held'.

When they had finished they went on to another house, leaving him to silence and loneliness as before.

The candle wanted snuffing, but he did not snuff it, and he sat on till it had burnt down into the socket and made waves of shadow on the ceiling.

The Christmas cheerfulness of next morning was broken at breakfast-time by tragic intelligence which went down the village like wind. Sergeant-Major Holway had been found shot through the head by his own hand at the cross-roads in Long Ash Lane where his father lay buried.

On the table in the cottage he had left a piece of paper, on which he had written his wish that he might be buried at the Cross beside his father. But the paper was accidentally swept to the floor, and overlooked till after his funeral, which took place in the ordinary way in the churchyard.

Christmas 1897

ENTER A DRAGOON

I lately had a melancholy experience (said the gentleman who is answerable for the truth of this story). It was that of going over a doomed house with whose outside aspect I had long been familiar – a house, that is, which by reason of age and dilapidation was to be pulled down during the following week. Some of the thatch, brown and rotten as the gills of old mushrooms, had, indeed, been removed before I walked over the building. Seeing that it was only a very small house – which is usually called a 'cottage-residence' – situated in a remote hamlet, and that it was not more than a hundred years old, if so much, I was led to think in my progress through the hollow rooms, with their cracked walls and sloping floors, what an exceptional number of abrupt family incidents had taken place therein – to reckon only those which had come to my own knowledge. And no doubt there were many more of which I had never heard.

It stood at the top of a garden stretching down to the lane or street that ran through a hermit-group of dwellings in Mell-stock parish. From a green gate at the lower entrance, over which the thorn hedge had been shaped to an arch by constant clippings, a gravel path ascended between the box edges of once trim raspberry, strawberry, and vegetable plots, towards the front door. This was in colour an ancient and bleached green that could be rubbed off with the finger, and it bore a small long-featured brass knocker covered with verdigris in its crevices. For some years before this eve of demolition the homestead had degenerated, and been divided into two tene-ments to serve as cottages for farm labourers; but in its prime it had indisputable claim to be considered neat, pretty, and genteel.

The variety of incidents above alluded to was mainly owing to the nature of the tenure, whereby the place had been occupied by families not quite of the kind customary in such

spots – people whose circumstances, position, or antecedents
were more or less of a critical happy-go-lucky cast. And of
these residents the family whose term comprised the story I
wish to relate was that of Mr. Jacob Paddock the market-
gardener, who dwelt there for some years with his wife and
grown-up daughter.

I

An evident commotion was agitating the premises, which
jerked busy sounds across the front plot, resembling those of a
disturbed hive. If a member of the household appeared at the
door it was with a countenance of abstraction and concern.

Evening began to bend over the scene; and the other
inhabitants of the hamlet came out to draw water, their
common well being in the public road opposite the garden and
house of the Paddocks. Having wound up their bucketsfull
respectively they lingered, and spoke significantly together.
From their words any casual listener might have gathered
information of what had occurred.

The woodman who lived nearest the site of the story told
most of the tale. Selina, the daughter of the Paddocks opposite,
had been surprised that afternoon by receiving a letter from her
once intended husband, then a corporal, but now a sergeant-
major of dragoons, whom she had hitherto supposed to be one
of the slain in the Battle of the Alma two or three years before.

'She picked up wi'en against her father's wish, as we know,
and before he got his stripes,' their informant continued. 'Not
but that the man was as hearty a feller as you'd meet this side o'
London. But Jacob, you see, wished her to do better, and one
can understand it. However, she was determined to stick to
him at that time; and for what happened she was not much to
blame, so near as they were to matrimony when the war broke
out and spoiled all.'

'Even the very pig had been killed for the wedding,' said a
woman, 'and the barrel o' beer ordered in. O, the man meant
honourable enough. But to be off in two days to fight in a
foreign country – 'twas natural of her father to say they should
wait till he got back.'

'And he never came,' murmured one in the shade.

'The war ended but her man never turned up again. She was not sure he was killed, but was too proud, or too timid, to go and hunt for him.'

'One reason why her father forgave her when he found out how matters stood was, as he said plain at the time, that he liked the man, and could see that he meant to act straight. So the old folks made the best of what they couldn't mend, and kept her there with 'em, when some wouldn't. Time has proved seemingly that he did mean to act straight, now that he has writ to her that he's coming. She'd stuck to him all through the time, 'tis my belief, if t'other hadn't come along.'

'At the time of the courtship,' resumed the woodman, 'the regiment was quartered in Casterbridge barracks, and he and she got acquainted by his calling to buy a penn'orth of rath-ripes off that tree yonder in her father's orchard – though 'twas said he seed *her* over hedge as well as the apples. He declared 'twas a kind of apple he much fancied; and he called for a penn'orth every day till the tree was cleared. It ended in his calling for her.'

'Twas a thousand pities they didn't jine up at once and ha' done wi' it.'

'Well; better late than never, if so be he'll have her now. But, Lord, she'd that faith in 'en that she'd no more belief that he was alive, when a' didn't come, than that the undermost man in our churchyard was alive. She'd never have thought of another but for that – O no!'

''Tis awkward, altogether, for her now.'

'Still she hadn't married wi' the new man. Though to be sure she would have committed it next week, even the licence being got, they say, for she'd have no banns this time, the first being so unfortunate.'

'Perhaps the sergeant-major will think he's released, and go as he came.'

'O, not as I reckon. Soldiers bain't particular, and she's a tidy piece o' furniture still. What will happen is that she'll have her soldier, and break off with the master-wheelwright, licence or no – daze me if she won't.'

In the progress of these desultory conjectures the form of another neighbour arose in the gloom. She nodded to the people at the well, who replied 'G'd night, Mrs. Stone,' as she passed through Mr Paddock's gate towards his door. She was an intimate friend of the latter's household, and the group followed her with their eyes up the path and past the windows, which were now lighted up by candles inside.

II

Mrs Stone paused at the door, knocked, and was admitted by Selina's mother, who took her visitor at once into the parlour on the left hand, where a table was partly spread for supper. On the 'beaufet' against the wall stood probably the only object which would have attracted the eye of a local stranger in an otherwise ordinarily furnished room, a great plum-cake guarded as if it were a curiosity by a glass shade of the kind seen in museums – square, with a wooden back like those enclosing stuffed specimens of rare feather or fur. This was the mummy of the cake intended in earlier days for the wedding-feast of Selina and the soldier, which had been religiously and lovingly preserved by the former as a testimony to her intentional respectability in spite of an untoward subsequent circumstance, which will be mentioned. This relic was now as dry as a brick, and seemed to belong to a pre-existent civilization. Till quite recently, Selina had been in the habit of pausing before it daily, and recalling the accident whose consequences had thrown a shadow over her life ever since – that of which the water-drawers had spoken – the sudden news one morning that the Route had come for the —th Dragoons, two days only being the interval before departure; the hurried consultation as to what should be done, the second time of asking being past but not the third; and the decision that it would be unwise to solemnize matrimony in such haphazard circumstances, even if it were possible, which was doubtful.

Before the fire the young woman in question was now seated on a low stool, in the stillness of reverie, and a toddling boy played about the floor around her.

'Ah, Mrs. Stone!' said Selina, rising slowly. 'How kind of you to come in. You'll bide to supper? Mother has told you the strange news, of course?'

'No. But I heard it outside, that is, that you'd had a letter from Mr. Clark – Sergeant-Major Clark, as they say he is now – and that he's coming to make it up with 'ee.'

'Yes; coming tonight – all the way from the north of England where he's quartered. I don't know whether I'm happy or – frightened at it. Of course I always believed that if he was alive he'd come and keep his solemn vow to me. But when it is printed that a man is killed – what can you think?'

'It *was* printed?'

'Why, yes. After the Battle of the Alma the book of the names of the killed and wounded was nailed up against Casterbridge Town Hall door. 'Twas on a Saturday, and I walked there o'purpose to read and see for myself, for I'd heard that his name was down. There was a crowd of people round the book, looking for the names of relations; and I can mind that when they saw me they made way for me – knowing that we'd been just going to be married – and that, as you may say, I belonged to him. Well, I reached up my arm, and turned over the farrels of the book, and under the "killed" I read his surname, but instead of "John" they'd printed "James," and I thought 'twas a mistake, and that it must be he. Who could have guessed there were two nearly of one name in one regiment.'

'Well – he's coming to finish the wedding of 'ee as may be said; so never mind, my dear. All's well that ends well.'

'That's what he seems to say. But then he has not heard yet about Mr. Miller; and that's what rather terrifies me. Luckily my marriage with him next week was to have been by licence, and not banns, as in John's case; and it was not so well known on that account. Still, I don't know what to think.'

'Everything seems to come just 'twixt cup and lip with 'ee, don't it now, Miss Paddock. Two weddings broke off – 'tis odd! How came you to accept Mr. Miller, my dear?'

'He's been so good and faithful! Not minding about the child at all; for he knew the rights of the story. He's dearly fond o' Johnny, you know – just as if 'twere his own – isn't he, my duck? Do Mr. Miller love you or don't he?'

'Iss! An' I love Mr. Miller,' said the toddler.

'Well, you see, Mrs. Stone, he said he'd make me a comfortable home; and thinking 'twould be a good thing for

Johnny, Mr. Miller being so much better off than me, I agreed at last, just as a widow might – which is what I have always felt myself, ever since I saw what I thought was John's name printed there. I hope John will forgive me!'

'So he will forgive 'ee, since 'twas no manner of wrong to him. He ought to have sent 'ee a line, saying 'twas another man.'

Selina's mother entered. 'We've not known of this an hour, Mrs. Stone,' she said. 'The letter was brought up from Lower Mellstock Post-office by one of the school children, only this afternoon. Mr. Miller was coming here this very night to settle about the wedding doings. Hark! Is that your father? Or is it Mr. Miller already come?'

The footsteps entered the porch; there was a brushing on the mat, and the door of the room sprung back to disclose a rubicund man about thirty years of age, of thriving master-mechanic appearance and obviously comfortable temper. On seeing the child, and before taking any notice whatever of the elders, the comer made a noise like the crowing of a cock and flapped his arms as if they were wings, a method of entry which had the unqualified admiration of Johnny.

'Yes – it is he,' said Selina constrainedly advancing.

'What – were you all talking about me, my dear?' said the genial young man when he had finished his crowing and resumed human manners. 'Why what's the matter,' he went on. 'You look struck all of a heap.' Mr. Miller spread an aspect of concern over his own face, and drew a chair up to the fire.

'O mother, would you tell Mr. Miller, if he don't know?'

'*Mister* Miller! and going to be married in six days!' he interposed.

'Ah – he don't know it yet!' murmured Mrs. Paddock.

'Know what?'

'Well – John Clark – now Sergeant-Major Clark – wasn't shot at Alma after all. 'Twas another of almost the same name.'

'Now that's interesting! There were several cases like that.'

'And he's home again; and he's coming here tonight to see her.'

'Whatever shall I say, that he may not be offended with what I've done?' interposed Selina.

'But why should it matter if he be?'

'O! I must agree to be his wife if he forgives me – of course I must.'

'Must! But why not say nay, Selina, even if he do forgive 'ee?'

'O no! How can I without being wicked? You were very very kind, Mr. Miller, to ask me to have you; no other man would have done it after what had happened; and I agreed, even though I did not feel half so warm as I ought. Yet it was entirely owing to my believing him in the grave, as I knew that if he were not he would carry out his promise; and this shows that I was right in trusting him.'

'Yes. . . . He must be a goodish sort of fellow,' said Mr. Miller, for a moment so impressed with the excellently faithful conduct of the sergeant-major of dragoons that he disregarded its effect upon his own position. He sighed slowly and added, 'Well, Selina, 'tis for you to say. I love you, and I love the boy; and there's my chinney-corner and sticks o' furniture ready for 'ee both.'

'Yes, I know! But I mustn't hear it any more now,' murmured Selina quickly. 'John will be here soon. I hope he'll see how it all was when I tell him. If so be I could have written it to him it would have been better.'

'You think he doesn't know a single word about our having been on the brink o't. But perhaps it's the other way – he's heard of it and that may have brought him.'

'Ah – perhaps he has!' she said brightening. 'And already forgives me.'

'If not, speak out straight and fair, and tell him exactly how it fell out. If he's a man he'll see it.'

'O he's a man true enough. But I really do think I shan't have to tell him at all, since you've put it to me that way!'

As it was now Johnny's bedtime he was carried upstairs, and when Selina came down again her mother observed with some anxiety, 'I fancy Mr. Clark must be here soon if he's coming; and that being so, perhaps Mr. Miller wouldn't mind – wishing us good-night! since you are so determined to stick to your sergeant-major.' A little bitterness bubbled amid the closing words. 'It would be less awkward, Mr. Miller not being here – if he will allow me to say it.'

'To be sure; to be sure,' the master-wheelwright exclaimed

with instant conviction, rising alertly from his chair. 'Lord bless my soul,' he said, taking up his hat and stick, 'and we to have been married in six days! But Selina – you're right. You do belong to the child's father since he's alive. I'll try to make the best of it.'

Before the generous miller had got further there came a knock to the door accompanied by the noise of wheels.

'I thought I heard something driving up!' said Mrs Paddock.

They heard Mr. Paddock, who had been smoking in the room opposite, rise and go to the door, and in a moment a voice familiar enough to Selina was audibly saying, 'At last I am here again – not without many interruptions! How is it with 'ee, Mr. Paddock? And how is she? Thought never to see me again, I suppose?' A step with a clink of spurs in it struck upon the entry floor.

'Danged if I bain't catched!' murmured Mr. Miller, forgetting company-speech. 'Never mind – I may as well meet him here as elsewhere; and I should like to see the chap, and make friends with en, as he seems one o' the right sort.' He returned to the fireplace just as the sergeant-major was ushered in.

III

He was a good specimen of the long-service soldier of those days; a not unhandsome man, with a certain undemonstrative dignity, which some might have said to be partly owing to the stiffness of his uniform about his neck, the high stock being still worn. He was much stouter than when Selina had parted from him. Although she had not meant to be demonstrative she ran across to him directly she saw him, and he held her in his arms and kissed her.

Then in much agitation she whispered something to him, at which he seemed to be much surprised.

'He's just put to bed,' she continued. 'You can go up and see him. I knew you'd come if you were alive! But I had quite gi'd you up for dead. You've been home in England ever since the war ended?'

'Yes, dear.'

'Why didn't you come sooner?'

'That's just what I ask myself! Why was I such a sappy as not to hurry here the first day I set foot on shore! Well, who'd have thought it – you are as pretty as ever!'

He relinquished her to peep upstairs a little way, where, by looking through the ballusters, he could see Johnny's cot just within an open door. On his stepping down again Mr. Miller was preparing to depart.

'Now, what's this? I am sorry to see anybody going the moment I've come,' expostulated the sergeant-major. 'I though we might make an evening of it. There's a nine gallon cask o' "Phœnix" beer outside in the trap, and a ham, and half a rawmil' cheese; for I thought you might be short o' forage in a lonely place like this; and it struck me we might like to ask in a neighbour or two. But perhaps it would be taking a liberty?'

'O no, not at all,' said Mr. Paddock, who was now in the room, in a judicial manner. 'Very thoughtful of 'ee, only 'twas not necessary, for we had just laid in an extry stock of eatables and drinkables in preparation for the coming event.'

''Twas very kind, upon my heart', said the soldier, 'to think me worth such a jocund preparation, since you could only have got my letter this morning.'

Selina gazed at her father to stop him, and exchanged embarrassed glances with Miller. Contrary to her hopes Sergeant-Major Clark plainly did not know that the preparations referred to were for something quite other than his own visit.

The movement of the horse outside, and the impatient tapping of a whip-handle upon the vehicle reminded them that Clark's driver was still in waiting. The provisions were brought into the house, and the cart dismissed. Miller, with very little pressure indeed, accepted an invitation to supper, and a few neighbours were induced to come in to make up a cheerful party.

During the laying of the meal, and throughout its continuance, Selina, who sat beside her first intended husband, tried frequently to break the news to him of her engagement to the other – now terminated so suddenly, and so happily for her heart, and her sense of womanly virtue. But the talk ran entirely upon the late war; and though fortified by half a horn

of the strong ale brought by the sergeant-major she decided
that she might have a better opportunity when supper was
over of revealing the situation to him in private.

Having supped, Clark leaned back at ease in his chair and
looked around. 'We used sometimes to have a dance in that
other room after supper, Selina dear, I recollect. We used to
clear out all the furniture into this room before beginning.
Have you kept up such goings on?'

'No, not at all!' said his sweetheart, sadly.

'We were not unlikely to revive it in a few days,' said Mr.
Paddock. 'But, howsomever, there's seemingly many a slip,
as the saying is.'

'Yes, I'll tell John all about that by and by!' interposed
Selina; at which, perceiving that the secret which he did not
like keeping was to be kept even yet, her father held his
tongue with some show of testiness.

The subject of a dance having been broached, to put the
thought in practice was the feeling of all. Soon after the
tables and chairs were borne from the opposite room to this
by zealous hands, and two of the villagers sent home for a
fiddle and tambourine, when the majority began to tread a
measure well known in that secluded vale. Selina naturally
danced with the sergeant-major, not altogether to her
father's satisfaction, and to the real uneasiness of her mother,
both of whom would have preferred a postponement of
festivities till the rashly anticipated relationship between their
daughter and Clark in the past had been made fact by the
church's ordinances. They did not, however, express a positive objection, Mr. Paddock remembering, with
self-reproach, that it was owing to his original strongly
expressed disapproval of Selina's being a soldier's wife that
the wedding had been delayed, and finally hindered – with
worse consequences than were expected; and ever since the
misadventure brought about by his government he had
allowed events to steer their own courses.

'My tails will surely catch in your spurs, John!' murmured
the daughter of the house, as she whirled around upon his arm
with the rapt soul and look of a somnambulist. 'I didn't know
we should dance, or I would have put on my other frock.'

'I'll take care, my love. We've danced here before. Do you

think your father objects to me now? I've risen in rank. I fancy he's still a little against me.'

'He has repented, times enough.'

'And so have I! If I had married you then 'twould have saved many a misfortune. I have sometimes thought it might have been possible to rush the ceremony through somehow before I left; though we were only in the second asking, were we? And even if I had come back straight here when we returned from the Crimea, and married you then, how much happier I should have been!'

'Dear John, to say that! Why didn't you?'

'O – dilatoriness and want of thought, and a fear of facing your father after so long. I was in hospital a great while, you know. But how familiar the place seems again! What's that I saw on the beaufet in the other room? It never used to be there. A sort of withered corpse of a cake – not an old bride-cake surely?'

'Yes, John, ours. 'Tis the very one that was made for our wedding three years ago.'

'Sakes alive! Why, time shuts up together, and all between then and now seems not to have been! What became of that wedding-gown that they were making in this room, I remember – a bluish, whitish, frothy thing?'

'I have that too.'

'Really! . . . Why, Selina —.'

'Yes!'

'Why not put it on now?'

'Wouldn't it seem —. And yet, O how I should like to! It would remind them all, if we told them what it was, how we really meant to be married on that bygone day!' Her eyes were again laden with wet.

'Yes. . . . The pity that we didn't – the pity!' Moody mournfulness seemed to hold silent awhile one not naturally taciturn. 'Well – will you? he said.

'I will – the next dance, if mother don't mind.'

Accordingly, just before the next figure was formed, Selina disappeared, and speedily came downstairs in a creased and box-worn, but still airy and pretty, muslin gown, which was indeed the very one that had been meant to grace her as a bride three years before.

'It is dreadfully old-fashioned,' she apologized.

'Not at all. What a grand thought of mine! Now, let's to't again.'

She explained to some of them as he led her to the second dance, what the frock had been meant for, and that she had put it on at his request. And again athwart and around the room they went.

'You seem the bride!' he said.

'But I couldn't wear this gown to be married in now!' she replied, ecstatically, 'or I shouldn't have put it on and made it dusty. It is really too old-fashioned, and so folded and fretted out, you can't think. That was with my taking it out so many times to look at. I have never put it on – never – till now!'

'Selina, I am thinking of giving up the army. Will you emigrate with me to New Zealand? I've an uncle out there doing well, and he'd soon help me to making a larger income. The English army is glorious, but it ain't altogether enriching.'

'Of course, anywhere that you decide upon. Is it healthy there for Johnny?'

'A lovely climate. And I shall never be happy in England. . . . Aha!' he concluded again, with a bitterness of unexpected strength, 'would to Heaven I had come straight back here!'

As the dance brought round one neighbour after another the re-united pair were thrown into juxtaposition with Bob Heartall among the rest who had been called in; one whose chronic expression was that he carried inside him a joke on the point of bursting with its own vastness. He took occasion now to let out a little of its quality, shaking his head at Selina as he addressed her in an undertone –

'This is a bit of a topper to the bridegroom ho! ho! 'Twill teach en the liberty you'll expect when you've married en!'

'What does he mean by a "topper,"' the sergeant-major asked, who, not being of local extraction, despised the venerable local language, and also seemed to suppose 'bridegroom' to be an anticipatory name for himself. 'I only hope I shall never be worse treated than you've treated me tonight!'

Selina looked frightened. 'He didn't mean you, dear,' she said as they moved on. 'We thought perhaps you knew what had happened owing to your coming just at this time. Had you – heard anything about – what I intended?'

'Not a breath – how should I – away up in Yorkshire? It was by the merest accident that I came just at this date to make peace with you for my delay.'

'I was engaged to be married to Mr. Bartholomew Miller. That's what it is! I would have let 'ee know by letter, but there was no time, only hearing from 'ee this afternoon. . . . You won't desert me for it, will you, John? Because, as you know, I quite supposed you dead, and – and –' Her eyes were full of tears of trepidation, and he might have felt a sob heaving within her.

IV

The soldier was silent during two or three double bars of the tune. 'When were you to have been married to the said Mr. Bartholomew Miller?' he inquired.

'Quite soon.'

'How soon?'

'Next week – O yes – just the same as it was with you and me. There's a strange fate of interruption hanging over me, I sometimes think! He had bought the licence, which I preferred so that it mightn't be like – ours. But it made no difference to the fate of it.'

'Had bought the licence! The devil!'

'Don't be angry, dear John. I didn't know!'

'No, no, I'm not angry.'

'It was so kind of him, considering!'

'Yes. . . . I see, of course, how natural your action was – never thinking of seeing me any more! Is it the Mr. Miller who is in this dance?'

'Yes.'

Clark glanced round upon Bartholomew and was silent again for some little while, and she stole a look at him, to find that he seemed changed. 'John, you look ill!' she almost sobbed. ''Tisn't me, is it?'

'O dear, no. Though I hadn't somehow, expected it. I can't find fault with you for a moment – and I don't. . . . This is a deuce of a long dance, don't you think? We've been at it twenty minutes if a second, and the figure doesn't allow one much rest. I'm quite out of breath.'

'They like them so dreadfully long here. Shall we drop out? Or I'll stop the fiddler.'

'O no, no, I think I can finish. But although I look healthy enough I have never been so strong as I formerly was, since that long illness I had in the hospital at Scutari.'

'And I knew nothing about it!'

'You couldn't, dear, as I didn't write. What a fool I have been altogether!' He gave a twitch, as of one in pain. 'I won't dance again when this one is over. The fact is I have travelled a long way today, and it seems to have knocked me up a bit.'

There could be no doubt that the sergeant-major was unwell, and Selina made herself miserable by still believing that her story was the cause of his ailment. Suddenly he said in a changed voice, and she perceived that he was paler than ever:

'I must sit down.'

Letting go her waist he went quickly to the other room. She followed, and found him in the nearest chair, his face bent down upon his hands and arms, which were resting on the table.

'What's the matter?' said her father, who sat there dozing by the fire.

'John isn't well. . . . We are going to New Zealand when we are married, father . A lovely country! . . . John, would you like something to drink?'

'A drop o' that Schiedam of old Owlett's that's under stairs, perhaps,' suggested her father. 'Not that nowadays 'tis much better than licensed liquor.'

'John,' she said, putting her face close to his and pressing his arm. 'Will you have a drop of spirits or something?'

He did not reply, and Selina observed that his ear and the side of his face were quite white. Convinced that his illness was serious, a growing dismay seized hold of her. The dance ended; her mother came in, and learning what had happened, looked narrowly at the sergeant-major.

'We must not let him lie like that, lift him up,' she said. 'Let him rest in the window-bench on some cushions.'

They unfolded his arms and hands as they lay clasped upon the table, and on lifting his head found his features to bear the very impress of death itself. Bartholomew Miller, who had now come in, assisted Mr. Paddock to make a comfortable couch in the window-seat, where they stretched out Clark upon his back.

Still he seemed unconscious. 'We must get a doctor,' said Selina. 'O, my dear John, how is it you be taken like this?'

'My impression is that he's dead!' murmured Mr. Paddock. 'He don't breathe enough to move a tomtit's feather.'

There were plenty to volunteer to go for a doctor, but as it would be at least an hour before he could get there the case seemed somewhat hopeless. The dancing-party ended as unceremoniously as it had begun; but the guests lingered round the premises till the doctor should arrive. When he did come the sergeant-major's extremities were already cold, and there was no doubt that death had overtaken him almost at the moment that he had sat down.

The medical practitioner quite refused to accept the unhappy Selina's theory that her revelation had in any way induced Clark's sudden collapse. Both he and the coroner afterwards, who found the immediate cause to be heart-failure, held that such a supposition was unwarranted by facts. They asserted that a long day's journey, a hurried drive, and then an exhausting dance, were sufficient for such a result upon a heart enfeebled by fatty degeneration after the privations of a Crimean winter and other trying experiences, the coincidence of the sad event with any disclosure of hers being a pure accident.

This conclusion, however, did not dislodge Selina's opinion that the shock of her statement had been the immediate stroke which had felled a constitution so undermined.

V

At this date the Casterbridge Barracks were cavalry quarters, their adaptation to artillery having been effected some years later. It had been owing to the fact that the —th Dragoons, in which John Clark had served, happened to be lying there that Selina made his acquaintance. At the time of his death the barracks were occupied by the Scots Greys, but when the pathetic circumstances of the sergeant-major's end became known in the town the officers of the Greys offered the services of their fine reed and brass band, that he might have a funeral marked by due military honours. His body was accordingly removed to the barracks, and carried thence to the churchyard in the Durnover quarter on the following afternoon, one of the Grey's most ancient and docile chargers being blacked up to represent Clark's horse on the occasion.

Everybody pitied Selina, whose story was well known. She followed the corpse as the only mourner, Clark having been without relations in this part of the country, and a communication with his regiment having brought none from a distance. She sat in a little shabby brown-black mourning carriage, squeezing herself up in a corner to be as much as possible out of sight during the slow and dramatic march through the town to the tune from *Saul*. When the interment had taken place, the volleys being fired, and the return journey begun, it was with something like a shock that she found the military escort to be moving at a quick march to the lively strains of 'Off she goes!' as if all care for the sergeant-major was expected to be ended with the late discharge of the carbines. It was, by chance, the very tune to which they had been footing when he died, and unable to bear its notes, she hastily told her driver to drop behind. The band and military party diminished up the High Street, and Selina turned over Swan bridge and homeward to Mellstock.

Then recommenced for her a life whose incidents were precisely of a suit with those which had preceded the soldier's return; but how different in her appreciation of them! Her narrow miss of the recovered respectability they had hoped for from that tardy event worked upon her parents as an irritant, and after the first week or two of her mourning her life with them grew almost insupportable. She had impulsively taken to herself the weeds of a widow, for such she seemed to herself to be, and clothed little Johnny in sables likewise. This assumption of a moral relationship to the deceased, which she asserted to be only not a legal one by two most unexpected accidents, led the old people to indulge in sarcasm at her expense whenever they beheld her attire, though all the while it cost them more pain to utter than it gave her to hear it. Having become accustomed by her residence at home to the business carried on by her father, she surprised them one day by going off with the child to Chalk-Newton, in the direction of the town of Ivell, and opening a miniature fruit and vegetable shop, attending Ivell market with her produce. Her business grew somewhat larger, and it was soon sufficient to enable her to support herself and the boy in comfort. She called herself 'Mrs John Clark' from the day of leaving home, and painted the name on her signboard – no man forbidding her.

By degrees the pain of her state was forgotten in her new circumstances, and getting to be generally accepted as the widow of a sergeant-major of dragoons – an assumption which her modest and mournful demeanour seemed to substantiate – her life became a placid one, her mind being nourished by the melancholy luxury of dreaming what might have been her future in New Zealand with John, if he had only lived to take her there. Her only travels now were a journey to Ivell on market-days, and once a fortnight to the churchyard in which Clark lay, there to tend, with Johnny's assistance, as widows are wont to do, the flowers she had planted upon his grave.

On a day about eighteen months after his unexpected decease, Selina was surprised in her lodging over her little shop by a visit from Bartholomew Miller. He had called on her once or twice before, on which occasions he had used without a word of comment the name by which she was known.

'I've come this time,' he said, 'less because I was in this direction than to ask you, Mrs. Clark, what you mid well guess. I've come o' purpose, in short.'

She smiled.

"'Tis to ask me again to marry you?'

'Yes, of course. You see, his coming back for 'ee proved what I always believed of 'ee, though others didn't. There's nobody but would be glad to welcome you to our parish again, now you've showed your independence and acted up to your trust in his promise. Well, my dear, will you come?'

'I'd rather bide as Mrs. Clark, I think,' she answered. 'I am not ashamed of my position at all; for I am John's widow in the eyes of Heaven.'

'I quite agree – that's why I've come. Still, you won't like to be always straining at this shop-keeping and market-standing; and 'twould be better for Johnny if you had nothing to do but tend him.'

He here touched the only weak spot in Selina's resistance to his proposal – the good of the boy. To promote that there were other men she might have married off hand without loving them if they had asked her to; but though she had known the worthy speaker from her youth, she could not for the moment fancy herself happy as Mrs. Miller.

He paused awhile. 'I ought to tell 'ee, Mrs. Clark,' he said by and by, 'that marrying is getting to be a pressing question with me. Not on my own account at all. The truth is, that mother is growing old, and I am away from home a good deal, so that it is almost necessary there should be another person in the house with her besides me. That's the practical consideration which forces me to think of taking a wife, apart from my wish to take you; and you know there's nobody in the world I care for so much.'

She said something about there being far better women than she, and other natural commonplaces; but assured him she was most grateful to him for feeling what he felt, as indeed she sincerely was. However, Selina would not consent to be the useful third person in his comfortable home – at any rate just then. He went away, after taking tea with her, without discerning much hope for him in her goodbye.

VI

After that evening she saw and heard nothing of him for a great while. Her fortnightly journeys to the sergeant-major's grave were continued, whenever weather did not hinder them; and Mr. Miller must have known, she thought, of this custom of hers. But though the churchyard was not nearly so far from his homestead as was her shop at Chalk-Newton, he never appeared in the accidental way that lovers use.

An explanation was forthcoming in the shape of a letter from her mother, who casually mentioned that Mr. Bartholomew Miller had gone away to the other side of Shottsford-Forum to be married to a thriving dairyman's daughter that he knew there. His chief motive, it was reported, had been less one of love than a wish to provide a companion for his aged mother.

Selina was practical enough to know that she had lost a good and possibly the only opportunity of settling in life after what had happened, and for a moment she regretted her independence. But she became calm on reflection, and to fortify herself in her course started that afternoon to tend the sergeant-major's grave, in which she took the same sober pleasure as at first.

On reaching the churchyard and turning the corner towards the spot as usual, she was surprised to perceive another woman, also apparently a respectable widow, and with a tiny boy by her side, bending over Clark's turf, and spudding up with the point of her umbrella some ivy-roots that Selina had reverently planted there to form an evergreen mantle over the mound.

'What are you digging up my ivy for!' cried Selina, rushing forward so excitedly that Johnny tumbled over a grave with the force of the tug she gave his hand in her sudden start.

'Your ivy?' said the respectable woman.

'Why yes! I planted it there – on my husband's grave.'

'*Your* husband's!'

'Yes. The late Sergeant-Major Clark. Anyhow, as good as my husband, for he was just going to be.'

'Indeed. But who may be my husband, if not he? I am the only Mrs. John Clark, widow of the late Sergeant-Major of Dragoons, and this is his only son and heir.'

'How can that be?' faltered Selina, her throat seeming to stick together as she just began to perceive its possibility. 'He had been – going to marry me twice – and we were going to New Zealand.'

'Ah! – I remember about you,' returned the legitimate widow calmly and not unkindly. 'You must be Selina; he spoke of you now and then, and said that his relations with you would always be a weight on his conscience. Well; the history of my life with him is soon told. When he came back from the Crimea he became acquainted with me at my home in the north, and we were married within a month of first knowing each other. Unfortunately, after living together a few months, we could not agree; and after a particularly sharp quarrel, in which perhaps, I was most in the wrong – as I don't mind owning here by his graveside – he went away from me, declaring he would buy his discharge and emigrate to New Zealand, and never come back to me any more. The next thing I heard was that he had died suddenly at Mellstock at some low carouse; and as he had left me in such anger to live no more with me, I wouldn't come down to his funeral, or do anything in relation to him. 'Twas temper, I know, but that was the fact. Even if we had parted friends it would have been a serious expense to travel three hundred miles to get there, for one who wasn't left so very well off. . . . I am sorry I pulled up your ivy-roots; but that common sort of ivy is considered a weed in my part of the country.'

December 1899

A TRYST AT AN ANCIENT EARTHWORK

At one's every step forward it rises higher against the south sky, with an obtrusive personality that compels the senses to regard it and consider. The eyes may bend in another direction, but never without the consciousness of its heavy, high-shouldered presence at its point of vantage. Across the intervening levels the gale races in a straight line from the fort, as if breathed out of it hitherward. With the shifting of the clouds the faces of the steeps vary in colour and in shade, broad lights appearing where mist and vagueness had prevailed, dissolving in their turn into melancholy gray, which spreads over and eclipses the luminous bluffs. In this so-thought immutable spectacle all is change.

Out of the invisible marine region on the other side birds soar suddenly into the air, and hang over the summits of the heights with the indifference of long familiarity. Their forms are white against the tawny concave of cloud, and the curves they exhibit in their floating signify that they are sea-gulls which have journeyed inland from expected stress of weather. As the birds rise behind the fort, so do the clouds rise behind the birds, almost as it seems, stroking with their bagging bosoms the uppermost flyers.

The profile of the whole stupendous ruin, as seen at a distance of a mile eastward, is cleanly cut as that walls of earth. The towering closeness of these on each hand, their impenetrability, and their ponderousness, are felt as a physical pressure. The way is now up the second of them, which stands steeper and higher than the first. To turn aside, as did Christian's companion from such a Hill of Difficulty, is the more natural tendency; but the way to the interior is upward. There is, of course, an entrance to the fortress; but that lies far off on the other side. It might possibly have been the wiser course to seek for easier ingress there.

However, being here, I ascend the second acclivity. The

grass stems – the grey beard of the hill – sway in a mass close
to my stooping face. The dead heads of these various grasses –
fescues, fox-tails, and ryes – bob and twitch as if pulled by a
string underground. From a few thistles a whistling proceeds;
and even the moss speaks, in its humble way, under the stress
of the blast.

That the summit of the second line of defence has been
gained is suddenly made known by a contrasting wind from a
new quarter, coming over with the curve of a cascade. These
novel gusts raise a sound from the whole camp or castle,
playing upon it bodily as upon a harp. It is with the same
difficulty that a foothold can be preserved under their sweep.
Looking aloft for a moment I perceive that the sky is much
more overcast than it has been hitherto, and in a few instants a
dead lull in what is now a gale ensues with almost preternatural abruptness. I take advantage of this to sidle down the
second counterscarp, but by the time the ditch is reached the
lull reveals itself to be but the precursor of a storm. It begins
with a heave of the whole atmosphere, like the sigh of a weary
strong man on turning to recommence unusual exertion, just
as I stand here in the second fosse. That which now radiates
from the sky upon the scene is not so much light as vaporous
phosphorescence.

The wind, quickening, abandons the natural direction it has
pursued on the open upland, and takes the course of the
gorge's length rushing along therein helter-skelter, and carrying thick rain upon its back. The rain is followed by
hailstones which fly through the defile in battalions – rolling,
hopping, ricochetting, snapping, clattering down the shelving
banks in an undefinable haze of confusion. The earthen sides
of the fosse seem to quiver under the drenching onset, though
it is practically no more to them than the blows of Thor upon
the giant of Jotun-land. It is impossible to proceed further till
the storm somewhat abates, and I draw up behind a spur of
the inner scarp, where possibly a barricade stood two
thousand years ago; and thus await events.

The roar of the storm can be heard travelling the complete
circuit of the castle – a measured mile – coming round at
intervals like a circumambulating column of infantry. Doubt-

less such a column has passed this way in its time, but the only columns which enter in these latter days are the columns of sheep and oxen that are sometimes seen here now; while the only semblance of heroic voices heard are the utterances of such, and of many winds which make their passage through the ravines.

The expected lightning radiates round and a rumbling as from its subterranean vaults – if there are any – fills the castle. The lightning repeats itself, and, coming after the aforesaid thoughts of martial men, it bears a fanciful resemblance to swords moving in combat. It has the very brassy hue of the ancient weapons that here were used. The so sudden entry upon the scene of this metallic flame is as the entry of a presiding exhibitor who unrolls the maps, uncurtains the pictures, unlocks the cabinets, and effects a transformation by merely exposing the materials of his science, unintelligibly cloaked till then. The corner-stones, plinths, and architraves were carried away to build neighbouring villages even before mediaeval or modern history began. Many a block which once may have helped to form a bastion here rests now in broken and diminished shape as part of the chimney-corner of some shepherd's cottage within the distant horizon, and the corner-stones of this heathen altar may form the base-course of some adjoining village church.

Yet the very bareness of these inner courts and wards, their condition of mere pasturage, protects what remains of them as no defences could do. Nothing is left visible that the hands can seize on or the weather overturn, and a permanence of general outline at least results, which no other condition could ensure.

The position of the castle on this isolated hill bespeaks deliberate and strategic choice exercised by some remote mind capable of prospective reasoning to a far extent. The natural configuration of the surrounding country and its bearing upon such a stronghold were obviously long considered and viewed mentally before its extensive design was carried into execution. Who was the man that said, 'Let it be built here!' – not on that hill yonder, or on that ridge behind, but on this best spot of all? Whether he were some great one of the Belgae, or of the Durotriges, or the travelling engineer of Britain's united tribes, must for ever remain time's secret; his form cannot be realized, nor his countenance, nor the tongue that he spoke, when he set down his foot with a thud and said, 'Let it be here!'

Within the innermost enclosure, though it is so wide that at a superficial glance the beholder has only a sense of standing on a breezy down, the solitude is rendered yet more solitary by the knowledge that between the benighted sojourner herein and all kindred humanity are those three concentric walls of earth which no being would think of scaling on such a night as this, even were he to hear the most pathetic cries issuing hence that could be uttered by a spectre-chased soul. I reach a central mound or platform – the crown and axis of the whole structure. The view from here by day must be of almost limitless extent. On this raised floor, daïs, or rostrum, harps have probably twanged more or less tuneful notes in celebration of daring, strength, or cruelty; of worship, super-stition, love, birth, and death; of simple loving-kindness perhaps never. Many a time must the king or leader have directed his keen eyes hence across the open lands towards the ancient road, the Icening Way, still visible in the distance, on the watch for armed companies approaching either to succour or to attack.

I am startled by a voice pronouncing my name. Past and present have become so confusedly mingled under the associa-tions of the spot that for a time it has escaped my memory that this mound was the place agreed on for the aforesaid appoint-ment. I turn and behold my friend. He stands with a dark lantern in his hand and a spade and light pickaxe over his shoulder. He expresses both delight and surprise that I have come. I tell him I had set out before the bad weather began.

He, to whom neither weather, darkness, nor difficulty seems to have any relation or significance, so entirely is his soul wrapped up in his own deep intentions, asks me to take the lantern and accompany him. I take it and walk by his side. He is a man about sixty, small in figure, with grey old-fashioned whiskers cut to the shape of a pair of crumb-brushes. He is entirely in black broadcloth – or rather, at present, black and brown, for he is bespattered with mud from his heels to the crown of his low hat. He has no consciousness of this – no sense of anything but his purpose, his ardour for which causes his eyes to shine like those of a lynx, and gives his motions all the elasticity of an athlete's.

'Nobody to interrupt us at this time of night!' he chuckles with fierce enjoyment.

We retreat a little way and find a sort of angle, an elevation in the sod, a suggested squareness amid the mass of irregularities around. Here, he tells me, if anywhere, the king's house stood. Three months of measurement and calculation have confirmed him in this conclusion.

He requests me now to open the lantern, which I do, and the light streams out upon the wet sod. At last divining his proceedings I say that I had no idea, in keeping the tryst, that he was going to do more at such an unusual time than meet me for a meditative ramble through the stronghold. I ask him why, having a practicable object, he should have minded interruptions and not have chosen the day? He informs me, quietly pointing to his spade, that it was because his purpose is to dig, then signifying with a grim nod the gaunt notice-post against the sky beyond. I inquire why as a professed and well-known antiquary with capital letters at the tail of his name, he did not obtain the necessary authority, considering the stringent penalties for this sort of thing; and he chuckles fiercely again with suppressed delight, and says, 'because they wouldn't have given it!'

He at once begins cutting up the sod, and, as he takes the pickaxe to follow on with, assures me that, penalty or no penalty, honest men or marauders, he is sure of one thing, that we shall not be disturbed at our work till after dawn.

I remember to have heard of men who, in their enthusiasm for some special science, art, or hobby, have quite lost the moral sense which would restrain them from indulging it illegitimately and I conjecture that here, at last, is an instance of such an one. He probably guesses the way my thoughts travel, for he stands up and solemnly asserts that he has a distinctly justifiable intention in this matter; namely, to uncover, to search, to verify a theory or displace it, and to cover up again. He means to take away nothing – not a grain of sand. In this he says he sees no such monstrous sin. I inquire if this is really a promise to me? He repeats that it is a promise, and resumes digging. My contribution to the labour is that of

directing the light constantly upon the hole. When he has
reached something more than a foot deep he digs more
cautiously, saying that, be it much or little there, it will not lie
far below the surface; such things never are deep. A few
minutes later the point of the pickaxe clicks upon a stony
substance. He draws the implement out as feelingly as if it had
entered a man's body. Taking up the spade he shovels with
care, and a surface, level as an altar, is presently disclosed. His
eyes flash anew; he pulls handfuls of grass and mops the
surface clean, finally rubbing it with his handkerchief. Grasping the lantern from my hand he holds it close to the ground,
when the rays reveal a complete mosaic – a pavement of
minute tesserae of many colours, of intricate pattern, a work
of much art, of much time, and of much industry. He
exclaims in a shout that he knew it always – that it is not a
Celtic stronghold exclusively, but also a Roman; the former
people having probably contributed little more than the
original framework which the latter took and adapted till it
became the present imposing structure.

I ask, What if it is Roman?

A great deal, according to him. That it proves all the world
to be wrong in this great argument, and himself alone to be
right! Can I wait while he digs further?

I agree – reluctantly; but he does not notice my reluctance.
At an adjoining spot he begins flourishing the tools anew with
the skill of a navvy, this venerable scholar with letters after his
name. Sometimes he falls on his knees, burrowing with his
hands in the manner of a hare, and where his old-fashioned
broadcloth touches the sides of the hole it gets plastered with
the damp earth. He continually murmurs to himself how
important, how very important, this discovery is! He draws
out an object; we wash it in the same primitive way by
rubbing it with the wet grass, and it proves to be a semi-
transparent bottle of iridescent beauty, the sight of which
draws groans of luxurious sensibility from the digger. Further
and further search brings out a piece of a weapon. It is strange
indeed that by merely peeling off a wrapper of modern
accumulations we have lowered ourselves into an ancient
world. Finally a skeleton is uncovered, fairly perfect. He lays
it out on the grass, bone to its bone.

My friend says the man must have fallen fighting here, as this is no place of burial. He turns again to the trench, scrapes, feels, till from a corner he draws out a heavy lump – a small image four or five inches high. We clean it as before. It is a statuette, apparently of gold, or, more probably, of bronze gilt – a figure of Mercury, obviously, its head being surmounted with the petasus or winged hat, the usual accessory of that deity. Further inspection reveals the workmanship to be of good finish and detail, and, preserved by the limy earth, to be as fresh in every line as on the day it left the hands of its artificer.

We seem to be standing in the Roman Forum and not on a hill in Wessex. Intent upon this truly valuable relic of the old empire of which even this remote spot was a component part, we do not notice what is going on in the present world till reminded of it by the sudden renewal of the storm. Looking up I perceive that the wide extinguisher of cloud has again settled down upon the fortress-town, as if resting upon the edge of the inner rampart, and shutting out the moon. I turn my back to the tempest, still directing the light across the hole. My companion digs on unconcernedly; he is living two thousand years ago, and despises things of the moment as dreams. But at last he is fairly beaten, and standing up beside me looks round on what he has done. The rays of the lantern pass over the trench to the tall skeleton stretched upon the grass on the other side. The beating rain has washed the bones clean and smooth, and the forehead, cheek-bones, and two and thirty teeth of the skull glisten in the candle-shine as they lie.

This storm, like the first, is of the nature of a squall, and it ends as abruptly as the other. We dig no further. My friend says that it is enough – he has proved his point. He turns to replace the bones in the trench and covers them. But they fall to pieces under his touch: the air has disintegrated them, and he can only sweep in the fragments. The next act of his plan is more than difficult, but is carried out. The treasures are inhumed again in their respective holes: they are not ours. Each deposition seems to cost him a twinge; and at one moment I fancied I saw him slip his hand into his coat pocket.

'We must re-bury them *all*,' say I.

'O yes,' he answers with integrity. 'I was wiping my hand.'

The beauties of the tesselated floor of the governor's house are once again consigned to darkness; the trench is filled up; the sod laid smoothly down; he wipes the perspiration from his forehead with the same handkerchief he had used to mop the skeleton and tesserae clean; and we make for the eastern gate of the fortress.

Dawn bursts upon us suddenly as we reach the opening. It comes by the lifting and thinning of the clouds that way till we are bathed in a pink light. The direction of his homeward journey is not the same as mine, and we part under the outer slope.

Walking along quickly to restore warmth I muse upon my eccentric friend, and cannot help asking myself this question: Did he really replace the gilded image of the god Mercurius with the rest of the treasures? He seemed to do so; and yet I could not testify to the fact. Probably, however, he was as good as his word.

It was thus I spoke to myself, and so the adventure ended. But one thing remains to be told, and that is concerned with seven years after. Among the effects of my friend, at that time just deceased, was found, carefully preserved, a gilt statuette representing Mercury, labelled 'Debased Roman.' No record was attached to explain how it came into his possession. The figure was bequeathed to the Casterbridge Museum.

Detroit Post,
March 1885

WHAT THE SHEPHERD SAW

FIRST NIGHT

The genial Justice of the Peace – now, alas, no more – who made himself responsible for the facts of this story, used to begin in the good old-fashioned way with a bright moonlight night and a mysterious figure, an excellent stroke for an opening, even to this day, if well followed up.

The Christmas moon (he would say) was showing her cold face to the upland, the upland reflecting the radiance in frost-sparkles so minute as only to be discernible by an eye near at hand. This eye, he said, was the eye of a shepherd lad, young for his occupation, who stood within a wheeled hut of the kind commonly in use among sheep-keepers during the early lambing season, and was abstractedly looking through the loophole at the scene without.

The spot was called Lambing Corner, and it was a sheltered portion of that wide expanse of rough pastureland known as the Marlbury Downs, which you directly traverse when following the turnpike-road across Mid-Wessex from London, through Aldbrickham, in the direction of Bath and Bristol. Here, where the hut stood, the land was high and dry, open, except to the north, and commanding an undulating view for miles. On the north side grew a tall belt of coarse furze with enormous stalks, a clump of the same standing detached in front of the general mass. The clump was hollow, and the interior had been ingeniously taken advantage of as a position for the before-mentioned hut, which was thus completely screened from winds, and almost invisible, except through the narrow approach. But the furze twigs had been cut away from the two little windows of the hut, that the occupier might keep his eye on his sheep.

In the rear, the shelter afforded by the belt of furze bushes was artificially improved by an inclosure of upright stakes,

142

interwoven with boughs of the same prickly vegetation, and within the inclosure lay a renowned Marlbury-Down breeding flock of eight hundred ewes.

To the south, in the direction of the young shepherd's idle gaze, there rose one conspicuous object above the uniform moonlit plateau, and only one. It was a Druidical trilithon, consisting of three oblong stones in the form of a doorway, two on end, and one across as a lintel. Each stone had been worn, scratched, washed, nibbled, split, and otherwise attacked by ten thousand different weathers; but now the blocks looked shapely and little the worse for wear, so beautifully were they silvered over by the light of the moon. The ruin was locally called the Devil's Door.

An old shepherd presently entered the hut from the direction of the ewes, and looked around in the gloom. 'Be ye sleepy?' he asked in cross accents of the boy.

The lad replied rather timidly in the negative.

'Then,' said the shepherd, 'I'll get me home along, and rest for a few hours. There's nothing to be done here now as I can see. The ewes can want no more tending till daybreak – 'tis beyond the bounds of reason that they can. But as the order is that one of us must bide, I'll leave 'ee, d'ye hear. You can sleep by day, and I can't. And you can be down to my house in ten minutes if anything should happen. I can't afford 'ee candle; but as 'tis Christmas week, and the time that folks have hollerdays, you can enjoy yerself by falling asleep a bit in the chair instead of biding awake all the time. But mind, no longer at once than while the shade of the Devil's Door moves a couple of spans, for you must keep an eye upon the ewes.'

The boy made no definite reply, and the old man, stirring the fire in the stove with his crook-stem, closed the door upon his companion and vanished.

As this had been more or less the course of events every night since the season's lambing had set in, the boy was not at all surprised at the charge, and amused himself for some time by lighting straws at the stove. He then went out to the ewes and new-born lambs, re-entered, sat down, and finally fell asleep. This was his customary manner of performing his watch, for though special permission for naps had this week been accorded, he had, as a matter of fact, done the same thing on every preceding night, sleeping often till awakened by a smack on the shoulder at three or four in the morning from the crook-stem of the old man.

It might have been about eleven o'clock when he awoke. He was so surprised at awaking without, apparently, being called or struck, that on second thoughts he assumed that somebody must have called him in spite of appearances, and looked out of the hut window towards the sheep. They all lay as quiet as when he had visited them, very little bleating being audible, and no human soul disturbing the scene. He next looked from the opposite window, and here the case was different. The frost-facets glistened under the moon as before; an occasional furze bush showed as a dark spot on the same; and in the foreground stood the ghostly form of the trilithon. But in front of the trilithon stood a man.

That he was not the shepherd or any one of the farm labourers was apparent in a moment's observation his dress being a dark suit, and his figure of slender build and graceful carriage. He walked backwards and forwards in front of the trilithon.

The shepherd lad had hardly done speculating on the strangeness of the unknown's presence here at such an hour, when he saw a second figure crossing the open sward towards the locality of the trilithon and furze clump that screened the hut. This second personage was a woman; and immediately on sight of her the male stranger hastened forward, meeting her just in front of the hut window. Before she seemed to be aware of his intention he clasped her in his arms.

The lady released herself and drew back with some dignity.

'You have come, Harriet – bless you for it!' he exclaimed fervently.

'But not for this,' she answered, in offended accents. And then, more good-naturedly, 'I have come, Fred, because you entreated me so! What can have been the object of your writing such a letter? I feared I might be doing you grievous ill by staying away. How did you come here?'

'I walked all the way from my father's.'

'Well, what is it? How have you lived since we last met?'

'But roughly; you might have known that without asking. I have seen many lands and many faces since I last walked these downs, but I have only thought of you.'

'Is it only to tell me this that you have summoned me so strangely?'

A passing breeze blew away the murmur of the reply and several succeeding sentences, till the man's voice again became audible in the words, 'Harriet – truth between us two! I have heard that the Duke does not treat you too well.'

'He is warm-tempered, but he is a good husband.'

'He speaks roughly to you, and sometimes even threatens to lock you out of doors.'

'Only once, Fred! On my honour, only once. The Duke is a fairly good husband, I repeat. But you deserve punishment for this night's trick of drawing me out. What does it mean?'

'Harriet, dearest, is this fair or honest? Is it not notorious that your life with him is a sad one – that, in spite of the sweetness of your temper, the sourness of his embitters your days. I have come to know if I can help you. You are a Duchess, and I am Fred Ogbourne; but it is not impossible that I may be able to help you. . . . By God! the sweetness of that tongue ought to keep him civil, especially when there is added to it the sweetness of that face!'

'Captain Ogbourne!' she exclaimed, with an emphasis of playful fear. 'How can such a comrade of my youth behave to me as you do? Don't speak so, and start at me so! Is this really all you have to say? I see I ought not to have come. 'Twas thoughtlessly done.'

Another breeze broke the thread of discourse for a time.

'Very well. I perceive you are dead and lost to me,' he could next be heard to say, ' "Captain Ogbourne" proves that. As I once loved you I love you now, Harriet, without one jot of abatement; but you are not the woman you were – you once were honest towards me; and now you conceal your heart in made-up speeches. Let it be: I can never see you again.'

'You need not say that in such a tragedy tone, you silly. You may see me in an ordinary way – why should you not? But, of course, not in such a way as this. I should not have come now, if it had not happened that the Duke is away from home, so that there is nobody to check my erratic impulses.'

'When does he return?'

'The day after tomorrow, or the day after that.'

'Then meet me again tomorrow night.'

'No, Fred, I cannot.'

'If you cannot tomorrow night, you can the night after; one of the two before he comes please bestow on me. Now, your hand upon it! Tomorrow or next night you will see me to bid me farewell!' He seized the Duchess's hand.

'No, but Fred – let go my hand! What do you mean by holding me so? If it be love to forget all respect to a woman's present position in thinking of her past, then yours may be so, Frederick. It is not kind and gentle of you to induce me to come to this place for pity of you, and then to hold me tight here.'

'But see me once more! I have come two thousand miles to ask it.'

'O, I must not! There will be slanders – Heaven knows what! I cannot meet you. For the sake of old times don't ask it.'

'Then own two things to me; that you did love me once, and that your husband is unkind to you often enough now to make you think of the time when you cared for me.'

'Yes – I own them both,' she answered faintly. 'But owning such as that tells against me; and I swear the inference is not true.'

'Don't say that; for you have come – let me think the reason of your coming what I like to think it. It can do you no harm. Come once more!'

He still held her hand and waist. 'Very well, then,' she said. 'Thus far you shall persuade me. I will meet you tomorrow night or the night after. Now, let me go.'

He released her, and they parted. The Duchess ran rapidly down the hill towards the outlying mansion of Shakeforest Towers, and when he had watched her out of sight, he turned and strode off in the opposite direction. All then was silent and empty as before.

Yet it was only for a moment. When they had quite departed, another shape appeared upon the scene. He came from behind the trilithon. He was a man of stouter build than the first, and wore the boots and spurs of a horseman. Two things were at once obvious from this phenomenon: that he had watched the interview between the Captain and the Duchess; and that, though he probably had seen every movement of the couple, including the embrace, he had been too remote to hear the reluctant words of the lady's conversation – or, indeed, any words at all – so that the meeting must have exhibited itself to his eye as the assignation of a pair of well-agreed lovers. But it was necessary that several years should elapse before the shepherd-boy was old enough to reason out this.

The third individual stood still for a moment, as if deep in meditation. He crossed over to where the lady and gentleman had stood, and looked at the ground; then he too turned and went away in a third direction, as widely divergent as possible from those taken by the two interlocutors. His course was towards the highway; and a few minutes afterwards the trot of a horse might have been heard upon its frosty surface, lessening till it died away upon the ear.

The boy remained in the hut, confronting the trilithon as if he expected yet more actors on the scene, but nobody else appeared. How long he stood with his little face against the loophole he hardly knew; but he was rudely awakened from his reverie by a punch in his back, and in the feel of it he familiarly recognized the stem of the old shepherd's crook.

'Blame thy young eyes and limbs, Bill Mills – now you have let the fire out, and you know I want it kept in! I thought something would go wrong with 'ee up here, and I couldn't bide in bed no more than thistledown on the wind, that I could not! Well, what's happened, fie upon 'ee?'

'Nothing.'

'Ewes all as I left 'em?'

'Yes.'

'Any lambs want bringing in?'

'No.'

The shepherd relit the fire, and went out among the sheep with a lantern, for the moon was getting low. Soon he came in again.

'Blame it all – thou'st say that nothing have happened; when one ewe have twinned and is like to go off, and another is dying for want of half an eye of looking to! I told 'ee, Bill

Mills, if anything went wrong to come down and call me; and this is how you have done it.'

'You said I could go to sleep for a hollerday, and I did.'

'Don't you speak to your betters like that, young man, or you'll come to the gallows-tree! You didn't sleep all the time, or you wouldn't have been peeping out of that there hole! Now you can go home, and be up here again by breakfast time. I be an old man, and there's old men that deserve well of the world; but no – I must rest how I can!'

The elder shepherd then lay down inside the hut, and the boy went down the hill to the hamlet where he dwelt.

SECOND NIGHT

When the next night drew on the actions of the boy were almost enough to show that he was thinking of the meeting he had witnessed, and of the promise wrung from the lady that she would come there again. As far as the sheep-tending arrangements were concerned, tonight was but a repetition of the foregoing one. Between ten and eleven o'clock the old shepherd withdrew as usual for what sleep at home he might chance to get without interruption, making up the other necessary hours of rest at some time during the day; the boy was left alone.

The frost was the same as on the night before, except perhaps that it was a little more severe. The moon shone as usual, except that it was three-quarters of an hour later in its course; and the boy's condition was much the same, except that he felt no sleepiness whatever. He felt, too, rather afraid; but upon the whole he preferred witnessing an assignation of strangers to running the risk of being discovered absent by the old shepherd.

It was before the distant clock of Shakeforest Towers had struck eleven that he observed the opening of the second act of this midnight drama. It consisted in the appearance of neither lover nor Duchess, but of the third figure – the stout man, booted and spurred – who came up from the easterly direction in which he had retreated the night before. He walked once round the trilithon, and next advanced towards the clump

concealing the hut, the moonlight shining full upon his face
and revealing him to be the Duke. Fear seized upon the
shepherd-boy: the Duke was Jove himself to the rural population, whom to offend was starvation, homelessness, and
death, and whom to look at was to be mentally scathed and
dumbfounded. He closed the stove, so that not a spark of
light appeared, and hastily buried himself in the straw that lay
in a corner.

The Duke came close to the clump of furze and stood by the
spot where his wife and the Captain had held their dialogue;
he examined the furze as if searching for a hiding-place, and in
doing so discovered the hut. The latter he walked round and
then looked inside; finding it to all seeming empty, he entered,
closing the door behind him and taking his place at the little
circular window against which the boy's face had been pressed
just before.

The Duke had not adopted his measures too rapidly, if his
object were concealment. Almost as soon as he had stationed
himself there eleven o'clock struck, and the slender young
man who had previously graced the scene promptly reap-
peared from the north quarter of the down. The spot of
assignation having, by the accident of his running forward on
the foregoing night, removed itself from the Devil's Door to
the clump of furze, he instinctively came thither, and waited
for the Duchess where he had met her before.

But a fearful surprise was in store for him tonight, as well as
for the trembling juvenile. At his appearance the Duke
breathed more and more quickly, his breathings being distinctly audible to the crouching boy. The young man had hardly
paused when the alert nobleman softly opened the door of the
hut, and, stepping round the furze, came full upon Captain
Fred.

'You have dishonoured her, and you shall die the death you
deserve!' came to the shepherd's ears, in a harsh, hollow
whisper through the boarding of the hut.

The apathetic and taciturn boy was excited enough to run
the risk of rising and looking from the window, but he could
see nothing for the intervening furze boughs, both the men
having gone round to the side. What took place in the few
following moments he never exactly knew. He discerned

portion of a shadow in quick muscular movement; then there was the fall of something on the grass; then there was stillness.

Two or three minutes later the Duke became visible round the corner of the hut, dragging by the collar the now inert body of the second man. The Duke dragged him across the open space towards the trilithon. Behind this ruin was a hollow, irregular spot, overgrown with furze and stunted thorns, and riddled by the old holes of badgers, its former inhabitants, who had now died out or departed. The Duke vanished into this depression with his burden, reappearing after the lapse of a few seconds. When he came forth he dragged nothing behind him.

He returned to the side of the hut, cleansed something on the grass, and again put himself on the watch, though not as before, inside the hut, but without, on the shady side. 'Now for the second!' he said.

It was plain, even to the unsophisticated boy, that he now awaited the other person of the appointment – his wife, the Duchess – for what purpose it was terrible to think. He seemed to be a man of such determined temper that he would scarcely hesitate in carrying out a course of revenge to the bitter end. Moreover – though it was what the shepherd did not perceive – this was all the more probable, in that the moody Duke was labouring under the exaggerated impression which the sight of the meeting in dumb show had conveyed.

The jealous watcher waited long, but he waited in vain. From within the hut the boy could hear his occasional exclamations of surprise, as if he were almost disappointed at the failure of his assumption that his guilty Duchess would surely keep the tryst. Sometimes he stepped from the shade of the furze into the moonlight, and held up his watch to learn the time.

About half-past eleven he seemed to give up expecting her. He then went a second time to the hollow behind the trilithon, remaining there nearly a quarter of an hour. From this place he proceeded quickly over a shoulder of the declivity, a little to the left, presently returning on horseback, which proved that his horse had been tethered in some secret place down there. Crossing anew the down between the hut and the trilithon, and scanning the precincts as if finally to assure himself that she had not come, he rode slowly downwards in the direction of Shakeforest Towers.

The juvenile shepherd thought of what lay in the hollow yonder; and no fear of the crook-stem of his superior officer was potent enough to detain him longer on that hill alone. Any live company, even the most terrible, was better than the company of the dead; so, running with the speed of a hare in the direction pursued by the horseman, he overtook the revengeful Duke at the second descent (where the great western road crossed before you came to the old park entrance on that side – now closed up and the lodge cleared away, though at the time it was wondered why, being considered the most convenient gate of all).

Once within the sound of the horse's footsteps, Bill Mills felt comparatively comfortable; for, though in awe of the Duke because of his position, he had no moral repugnance to his companionship on account of the grisly deed he had committed, considering that powerful nobleman to have a right to do what he chose on his own lands. The Duke rode steadily on beneath his ancestral trees, the hoofs of his horse sending up a smart sound now that he had reached the hard road of the drive, and soon drew near the front door of his house, surmounted by parapets with square-cut battlements that cast a notched shade upon the gravelled terrace. These outlines were quite familiar to little Bill Mills, though nothing within their boundary had ever been seen by him.

When the rider approached the mansion a small turret door was quickly opened and a woman came out. As soon as she saw the horseman's outlines she ran forward into the moonlight to meet him.

'Ah dear – and are you come?' she said. 'I heard Hero's tread just when you rode over the hill, and I knew it in a moment. I would have come further if I had been aware –'

'Glad to see me, eh?'

'How can you ask that?'

'Well; it a lovely night for meetings.'

'Yes, it is a lovely night.'

The Duke dismounted and stood by her side. 'Why should you have been listening at this time of night, and yet not expecting me?' he asked.

'Why, indeed! There is a strange story attached to that, which I must tell you at once. But why did you come a night sooner than you said you would come? I am rather sorry – I really am!' (shaking her head playfully) 'for as a surprise to you I had ordered a bonfire to be built, which was to be lighted on your arrival tomorrow; and now it is wasted. You can see the outline of it just out there.'

The Duke looked across to a spot of rising glade, and saw the faggots in a heap. He then bent his eyes with a bland and puzzled air on the ground, 'what is this strange story you have to tell me that kept you awake?' he murmured.

'It is this – and it is really rather serious. My cousin Fred Ogbourne – Captain Ogbourne as he is now – was in his boyhood a great admirer of mine, as I think I have told you, though I was six years his senior. In strict truth, he was absurdly fond of me.'

'You have never told me of that before.'

'Then it was your sister I told – yes, it was. Well, you know I have not seen him for many years, and naturally I had quite forgotten his admiration of me in old times. But guess my surprise when the day before yesterday, I received a mysterious note bearing no address, and found on opening it that it came from him. The contents frightened me out of my wits. He had returned from Canada to his father's house, and conjured me by all he could think of to meet him at once. But I think I can repeat the exact words, though I will show it to you when we get indoors.

"MY DEAR COUSIN HARRIET," the note said, "After this long absence you will be surprised at my sudden reappearance, and more by what I am going to ask. But if my life and future are of any concern to you at all, I beg that you will grant my request. What I require of you is, dear Harriet, that you meet me about eleven tonight by the Druid stones on Marlbury Downs, about a mile or more from your house. I cannot say more, except to entreat you to come. I will explain all when you are there. The one thing is, I want to see you. Come alone. Believe me, I would not ask this if my happiness did not hang upon it – God knows how entirely! I am too agitated to say more – Yours. FRED"

'That was all of it. Now, of course, I ought not to have gone, as it turned out, but that I did not think of then. I remembered his impetuous temper, and feared that something grievous was impending over his head, while he had not a friend in the world to help him, or any one except myself to whom he would care to make his trouble known. So I wrapped myself up and went to Marlbury Downs at the time he had named. Don't you think I was courageous?'

'Very.'

'Well I got there – but shall we not walk on; it is getting cold?' The Duke, however, did not move. 'When I got there he came, of course, as a full grown man and officer, and not as the lad that I had known him. When I saw him I was sorry I had come. I can hardly tell you how he behaved. What he wanted I don't know even now; it seemed to be no more than the mere meeting with me. He held me by the hand and waist – O so tight – and would not let me go till I had promised to meet him again. His manner was so strange and passionate that I was afraid of him in such a lonely place, and I promised to come. Then I escaped – then I ran home – and that's all. When the time drew on this evening for the appointment – which, of course, I never intended to keep, I felt uneasy, lest when he found I meant to disappoint him he would come on to the house; and that's why I could not sleep. But you are so silent!'

'I have had a long journey.'

'Then let us get into the house. Why did you come alone and unattended like this?'

'It was my humour.'

After a moment's silence, during which they moved on, she said, 'I have thought of something which I hardly like to suggest to you. He said that if I failed to come tonight he would wait again tomorrow night. Now, shall we tomorrow night go to the hill together – just to see if he is there; and if he is, read him a lesson on his foolishness in nourishing this old passion, and sending for me so oddly, instead of coming to the house?'

'Why should we see if he's there?' said her husband moodily.

'Because I think we ought to do something in it. Poor Fred! He would listen to you if you reasoned with him, and set our positons in their true light before him. It would be no more than Christian kindness to a man who unquestionably is very miserable from some cause or other. His head seems quite turned.'

By this time they had reached the door, rung the bell, and waited. All the house seemed to be asleep; but soon a man came to them, the horse was taken away, and the Duke and Duchess went in.

THIRD NIGHT

There was no help for it. Bill Mills was obliged to stay on duty, in the old shepherd's absence, this evening as before, or give up his post and living. He thought as bravely as he could of what lay behind the Devil's Door, but with no great success, and was therefore in a measure relieved, even if awe-stricken, when he saw the forms of the Duke and Duchess strolling across the frosted greensward. The Duchess was a few yards in front of her husband and tripped on lightly.

'I tell you he has not thought it worth while to come again!' the Duke insisted, as he stood still, reluctant to walk further.

'He is more likely to come and wait all night; and it would be harsh treatment to let him do it a second time.'

'He is not here; so turn and come home.'

'He seems not to be here, certainly: I wonder if anything has happened to him. If it has, I shall never forgive myself!'

The Duke, uneasily, 'O, no. He has some other engagement.'

'That is very unlikely.'

'Or perhaps he has found the distance too far.'

'Nor is that probable.'

'Then he may have thought better of it.'

'Yes, he may have thought better of it; if, indeed, he is not here all the time – somewhere in the hollow behind the Devil's Door. Let us go and see; it will serve him right to surpise him.'

'O, he's not there.'

'He may be lying very quiet because of you,' she said archly.

'O, no – not because of me!'

'Come, then. I declare, dearest, you lag like an unwilling schoolboy tonight, and there's no responsiveness in you! You are jealous of that poor lad, and it is quite absurd of you.'

'I'll come! I'll come! Say no more, Harriet!' And they crossed over the green.

Wondering what they would do, the young shepherd left the hut, and doubled behind the belt of furze intending to stand near the trilithon unperceived. But, in crossing the few yards of open ground he was for a moment exposed to view.

'Ah, I see him at last!' said the Duchess.

'See him!' said the Duke. 'Where?'

'By the Devil's Door; don't you notice a figure there? Ah, my poor lover-cousin, won't you catch it now?' And she laughed half-pityingly. 'But what's the matter?' she asked, turning to her husband.

'It is not he!' said the Duke hoarsely. 'It can't be he!'

'No, it is not he. It is too small for him. It is a boy.'

'Ah, I thought so! Boy, come here.'

The youthful shepherd advanced with apprehension.

'What are you doing here?'

'Keeping sheep, your Grace.'

'Ah, you know me! Do you keep sheep here every night?'

'Off and on, my Lord Duke.'

'And what have you seen here tonight or last night?' inquired the Duchess. 'Any person waiting or walking about?'

The boy was silent.

'He has seen nothing,' interrupted her husband, his eyes so forbiddingly fixed on the boy that they seemed to shine like points of fire. 'Come, let us go. The air is too keen to stand in long.'

When they were gone the boy retreated to the hut and sheep, less fearful now than at first – familiarity with the situation having gradually overpowered his thoughts of the buried man. But he was not to be left alone long. When an interval had elapsed of about sufficient length for walking to and from Shakeforest Towers, there appeared from that direction the heavy form of the Duke. He now came alone.

The nobleman, on his part seemed to have eyes no less sharp than the boy's, for he instantly recognized the latter among the ewes, and came straight towards him.

'Are you the shepherd lad I spoke to a short time ago?'

'I be, my Lord Duke.'

'Now listen to me. Her Grace asked you what you had seen this last night or two up here, and you made no reply. I now ask the same thing, and you need not be afraid to answer. Have you seen anything strange these nights you have been watching here?'

'My Lord Duke, I be a poor heedless boy, and what I see I don't bear in mind.'

'I ask you again,' said the Duke, coming nearer, 'have you seen anything strange these nights you have been watching here?'

'O, my Lord Duke! I be but the under-shepherd boy, and my father he was but your humble Grace's hedger, and my mother only the cinder-woman in the backyard! I fall asleep when left alone, and I see nothing at all!'

The Duke grasped the boy by the shoulder, and, directly impending over him, stared down into his face, 'Did you see anything strange done here last night, I say?'

'O, my Lord Duke, have mercy, and don't stab me!' cried the shepherd, falling on his knees. 'I have never seen you walking here, or riding here, or lying-in-wait for a man, or dragging a heavy load!'

'H'm!' said his interrogator, grimly, relaxing his hold. 'It is well to know that you have never seen those things. Now, which would you rather – *see me do those thing now*, or keep a secret all your life?'

'Keep a secret, my Lord Duke!'

'Sure you are able?'

'O, your Grace, try me!'

'Very well. And now, how do you like sheepkeeping?'

'Not at all. 'Tis lonely work for them that think of spirits, and I'm badly used.'

'I believe you. You are too young for it. I must do something to make you more comfortable. You shall change this smock-frock for a real cloth jacket, and your thick boots for polished shoes. And you shall be taught what you have never yet heard of, and be put to school, and have bats and balls for the holidays, and be made a man of. But you must never say you have been a shepherd boy, and watched on the hills at night, for shepherd boys are not liked in good company.'

'Trust me, my Lord Duke.'

'The very moment you forget yourself, and speak of your shepherd days – this year, next year, in school, out of school, or riding in your carriage twenty years hence – at that moment my help will be withdrawn, and smash down you come to shepherding forthwith. You have parents, I think you say?'

'A widowed mother only, my Lord Duke.'

'I'll provide for her, and make a comfortable woman of her, until you speak of – what?'

'Of my shepherd days, and what I saw here.'

'Good. If you do speak of it?'

'Smash down she comes to widowing forthwith!'

'That's well – very well. But it's not enough. Come here.' He took the boy across to the trilithon, and made him kneel down.

'Now, this was once a holy place,' resumed the Duke. 'An altar stood here, erected to a venerable family of gods, who were known and talked of long before the God we know now. So that an oath sworn here is doubly an oath. Say this after me: "May all the host above – angels and archangels, and principalities and powers – punish me; may I be tormented wherever I am – in the house or in the garden, in the fields or in the roads, in church or in chapel, at home or abroad, on land or at sea; may I be afflicted in eating and in drinking, in growing up and in growing old, in living and dying, inwardly and outwardly, and for always, if I ever speak of my life as a shepherd boy, or of what I have seen done on this Marlbury Down. So be it, and so let it be. Amen and amen." Now kiss the stone.'

The trembling boy repeated the words, and kissed the stone, as desired.

The Duke led him off by the hand. That night the junior shepherd slept in Shakeforest Towers, and the next day he was sent away for tuition to a remote village. Thence he went to a preparatory establishment, and in due course to a public school.

FOURTH NIGHT

On a winter evening many years subsequent to the above-mentioned occurrences, the *ci-devant* shepherd sat in a well-furnished office in the north wing of Shakeforest Towers in the guise of an ordinary educated man of business. He appeared at this time as a person of thirty-eight or forty, though actually he was several years younger. A worn and restless glance of the eye now and then, when he lifted his head to search for some letter or paper which had been mislaid, seemed to denote that his was not a mind so thoroughly at ease as his surroundings might have led an observer to expect. His pallor, too, was remarkable for a countryman. He was professedly engaged in writing, but he shaped not a word. He had sat there only a few minutes, when, laying down his pen and pushing back his chair, he rested a hand uneasily on each of the chair-arms and looked on the floor.

Soon he arose and left the room. His course was along a passage which ended in a central octagonal hall; crossing this he knocked at a door. A faint, though deep, voice told him to come in. The room he entered was the library, and it was tenanted by a single person only – his patron the Duke.

During this long interval of years the Duke had lost all his heaviness of build. He was, indeed almost a skeleton; his white hair was thin, and his hands were nearly transparent. 'Oh – Mills?' he murmured. 'Sit down. What is it?'

'Nothing new, your Grace. Nobody to speak of has written, and nobody has called.'

'Ah – what then? You look concerned.'

'Old times have come to life, owing to something waking them.'

'Old times be cursed – which old times are they?'

'That Christmas week twenty-two years ago, when the late Duchess's cousin Frederick implored her to meet him on Marlbury Downs. I saw the meeting – it was just such a night as this – and I, as you know, saw more. She met him once, but not the second time.'

'Mills, shall I recall some words to you – the words of an oath taken on that hill by a shepherd-boy?'

'It is unnecessary. He has strenuously kept that oath and promise. Since that night no sound of his shepherd life has crossed his lips – even to yourself. But do you wish to hear more, or do you not, your Grace?'

'I wish to hear no more,' said the Duke sullenly.

'Very well; let it be so. But a time seems coming – may be quite near at hand -- when, in spite of my lips, that episode will allow itself to go undivulged no longer.'

'I wish to hear no more!' repeated the Duke.

'You need be under no fear of treachery from me,' said the steward, somewhat bitterly. 'I am a man to whom you have been kind – no patron could have been kinder. You have clothed and educated me; have installed me here; and I am not unmindful. But what of it – has your Grace gained much by my staunchness? I think not. There was great excitement about Captain Ogbourne's disappearance, but I spoke not a word. And his body has never been found. For twenty-two years I have wondered what you did with him. Now I know. A circumstance that occurred this afternoon recalled the time to me most forcibly. To make it certain to myself that all was not a dream, I went up there with a spade; I searched, and saw enough to know that something decays there in a closed badger's hole.'

'Mills, do you think the Duchess guessed?'

'She never did, I am sure, to the day of her death.'

'Did you leave all as you found it on the hill?'

'I did.'

'What made you think of going up there this particular afternoon?'

'What your Grace says you don't wish to be told.'

The Duke was silent; and the stillness of the evening was so marked that there reached their ears from the outer air the sound of a tolling bell.

'What is that bell tolling for?' asked the nobleman.

'For what I came to tell you of, your Grace.'

'You torment me – it is your way!' said the Duke querulously. 'Who's dead in the village?'

'The oldest man – the shepherd.'

'Dead at last – how old is he?'

'Ninety-four.'

'And I am only seventy. I have four-and-twenty years to the good!'

'I served under that old man when I kept sheep on Marlbury Downs. And he was on the hill that second night, when I first exchanged words with your Grace. He was on the hill *all the time*; but I did not know he was there – nor did you.'

'Ah!' said the Duke, starting up. 'Go on – I yield the point – you may tell!'

'I heard this afternoon that he was at the point of death. It was that which set me thinking of that past time – and induced me to search on the hill for what I have told you. Coming back I heard that he wished to see the vicar to confess to him a secret he had kept for more than twenty years – "out of respect to my Lord the Duke" – something that he had seen committed on Marlbury Downs when returning to the flock on a December night twenty-two years ago. I have thought it over. He had left me in charge that evening; but he was in the habit of coming back suddenly, lest I should have fallen asleep. That night I saw nothing of him, though he had promised to return. He must have returned, and – found reason to keep in hiding. It is all plain. The next thing is that the Vicar went to him two hours ago. Further than that I have not heard.'

'It is quite enough. I will see the Vicar at daybreak tomorrow.'

'What to do?'

'Stop his tongue for four-and-twenty years – till I am dead at ninety-four, like the shepherd.'

'Your Grace – while you impose silence on me, I will not speak, even though my neck should pay the penalty. I promised to be yours, and I am yours. But is this persistence of any avail?'

'I'll stop his tongue, I say!' cried the Duke with some of his old rugged force. 'Now, you go home to bed, Mills, and leave me to manage him.'

The interview ended, and the steward withdrew. The night, as he had said, was just such as one as the night of twenty-two years before, and the events of the evening destroyed in him all regard for the season as one of cheerfulness and goodwill. He went off to his own house on the further verge of the park, where he led a lonely life, scarcely calling any man friend. At eleven he prepared to retire to bed – but did not retire. He sat down and reflected. Twelve o'clock struck; he looked out at the colourless moon, and, prompted by he knew not what, put on his hat and emerged into the air. Here William Mills strolled on and on, till he reached the top of Marlbury Downs, a spot he had not visited at this hour of the night during the whole score-and-odd years.

He placed himself, as nearly as he could guess, on the spot where the shepherd's hut had stood. No lambing was in progress there now, and the old shepherd who had used him so roughly had ceased from his labours that very day. But the trilithon stood up white as ever; and crossing the intervening sward, the steward fancifully placed his mouth against the stone. Restless and self-reproachful as he was, he could not resist a smile as he thought of the terrifying oath of compact, sealed by a kiss upon the stones of a Pagan temple. But he had kept his word, rather as a promise than as a formal vow, with much worldly advantage to himself, though not much happiness; till increase of years had bred reactionary feelings which led him to receive the news of tonight with emotions akin to relief.

While leaning against the Devil's Door and thinking on these things, he became conscious that he was not the only inhabitant of the down. A figure in white was moving across his front with long, noiseless strides. Mills stood motionless, and when the form drew quite near he perceived it to be that of the Duke himself in his nightshirt – apparently walking in his sleep. Not to alarm the old man, Mills clung close to the shadow of the stone. The Duke went straight on into the hollow. There he knelt down, and began scratching the earth with his hands like a badger. After a few minutes he arose, sighed heavily, and retraced his steps as he had come.

Fearing that he might harm himself, yet unwilling to arouse him, the steward followed noiselessly. The Duke kept on his path unerringly, entered the park, and made for the house, where he let himself in by a window that stood open – the one probably by which he had come out. Mills softly closed the window behind his patron, and then retired homeward to await the revelations of the morning, deeming it unnecessary to alarm the house.

However, he felt uneasy during the remainder of the night,

no less on account of the Duke's personal condition than because of that which was imminent next day. Early in the morning he called at Shakeforest Towers. The blinds were down, and there was something singular upon the porter's face when he opened the door. The steward inquired for the Duke.

The man's voice was subdued as he replied: 'Sir, I am sorry to say his Grace is dead! He left his room some time in the night, and wandered about nobody knows where. On returning to the upper floor he lost his balance and fell downstairs.'

The steward told the tale of the Down before the vicar had spoken. Mills had always intended to do so after the death of the Duke. The consequences to himself he underwent cheerfully; but his life was not prolonged. He died, a farmer at the Cape, when still somewhat under forty-nine years of age.

The splendid Marlbury breeding flock is as renowned as ever, and, to the eye, seems the same in every particular that it was in earlier times; but the animals which composed it on the occasion of the events gathered from the Justice are divided by many ovine generations from its members now. Lambing Corner has long since ceased to be used for lambing purposes, though the name still lingers on as the appellation of the spot. This abandonment of site may be partly owing to the removal of the high furze bushes which lent such convenient shelter at that date. Partly, too, it may be due to another circumstance. For it is said by present shepherds in that district that during the nights of Christmas week flitting shapes are seen in the open space around the trilithon, together with a gleam of a weapon, and the shadow of a man dragging a burden into the hollow. But of these things there is not certain testimony.

Christmas 1881

A COMMITTEE-MAN OF 'THE TERROR'

We had been talking of the Georgian glories of our old-fashioned watering-place, which now, with its substantial russet-red and dun brick buildings in the style of the year eighteen hundred, looks like one side of a Soho or Blooms-bury Street transported to the shore, and draws a smile from the modern tourist who has no eye for solidity of build. The writer, quite a youth, was present merely as a listener. The conversation proceeded from general subjects to particular, until old Mrs. H—, whose memory was as perfect at eighty as it had ever been in her life, interested us all by the obvious fidelity with which she repeated a story many times related to her by her mother when our aged friend was a girl – a domestic drama much affecting the life of an acquaintance of her said parent, one Mademoiselle V—, a teacher of French. The incidents occurred in the town during the heyday of its fortunes, at the time of our brief peace with France in 1802–3.

'I wrote it down in the shape of a story some years ago, just after my mother's death,' said Mrs. H—. 'It is locked up in my desk there now.'

'Read it!' said we.

'No,' said she; 'the light is bad, and I can remember it well enough, word for word, flourishes and all.' We could not be choosers in the circumstances, and she began.

'There are two in it, of course, the man and the woman, and it was on an evening in September that she first got to know him. There had not been such a grand gathering on the Esplanade all the season. His Majesty King George the Third was present, with all the princesses and royal dukes, while upwards of three hundred of the general nobility and other persons of distinction were also in the town at the time. Carriages and other conveyances were arriving every minute from London and elsewhere; and when among the rest a shabby stage-coach came in by a by-route along the coast from Havenpool, and drew up at a second-rate tavern, it attracted comparatively little notice.

'From this dusty vehicle a man alighted, left his small quantity of luggage temporarily at the office, and walked along the street as if to look for lodgings.

'He was about forty-five – possibly fifty – and wore a long coat of faded superfine cloth, with a heavy collar, and a bunched-up neckcloth. He seemed to desire obscurity.

'But the display appeared presently to stike him, and he asked of a rustic he met in the street what was going on; his accent being that of one to whom English pronunciation was difficult.

'The countryman looked at him with a slight surprise, and said, "King Jarge is here and his royal Cwort."

'The stranger inquired if they were going to stay long.

'"Don't know, Sir. Same as they always do, I suppose."

'"How long is that?"

'"Till some time in October. They've come here every zummer since eighty-nine."

'The stranger moved onward down St. Thomas Street, and approached the bridge over the harbour backwater, that then, as now, connected the old town with the more modern portion. The spot was swept with the rays of a low sun, which lit up the harbour lengthwise, and shone under the brim of the man's hat and into his eyes as he looked westward. Against the radiance figures were crossing in the opposite direction to his own; among them this lady of my mother's later acquaintance, Mademoiselle V—. She was the daughter of a good old French family, and at that date a pale woman, twenty-eight or thirty years of age, tall and elegant in figure, but plainly dressed and wearing that evening (she said) a small muslin shawl crossed over the bosom in the fashion of the time, and tied behind.

'At sight of his face, which, as she used to tell us, was unusually distinct in the peering sunlight, she could not help giving a little shriek of horror, for a terrible reason connected with her history, and after walking a few steps further, she sank down against the parapet of the bridge in a fainting fit.

'In his preoccupation the foreign gentleman had hardly noticed her, but her strange collapse immediately attracted his attention. He quickly crossed the carriageway, picked her up, and carried her into the first shop adjoining the bridge, explaining that she was a lady who had been taken ill outside.

'She soon revived; but, clearly much puzzled, her helper perceived that she still had a dread of him which was sufficient to hinder her complete recovery of self-command. She spoke in a quick and nervous way to the shopkeeper, asking him to call a coach.

'This the shopkeeper did, Mademoiselle V— and the stranger remaining in constrained silence while he was gone. The coach came up, and giving the man the address, she entered it and drove away.

'"Who is that lady?" said the newly arrived gentleman.

'"She's of your nation, as I should make bold to suppose," said the shopkeeper. And he told the other that she was Mademoiselle V—, governess at General Newbold's, in the same town.

'"You have many foreigners here?" the stranger inquired.

'"Yes, though mostly Hanoverians. But since the peace they are learning French a good deal in genteel society, and French instructors are rather in demand."

'"Yes, I teach it," said the visitor. "I am looking for a tutorship in an academy."

'The information given by the burgess to the Frenchman seemed to explain to the latter nothing of his countrywoman's conduct – which, indeed, was the case – and he left the shop, taking his course again over the bridge and along the south way to the Old Rooms Inn, where he engaged a bedchamber.

'Thoughts of the woman who had betrayed such agitation at sight of him lingered naturally enough with the newcomer. Though, as I stated, not much less than thirty years of age, Mademoiselle V—, one of his own nation, and of highly refined and delicate appearance, had kindled a singular interest in the middle-aged gentleman's breast, and her large dark eyes, as they had opened and shrunk from him, exhibited a pathetic beauty to which hardly any man could have been insensible.

'The next day, having written some letters, he went out and made known at the office of the town "Guide" and of the newspaper, that a teacher of French and calligraphy had arrived, leaving a card at the bookseller's to the same effect.

He then walked on aimlessly, but at length inquired the way to General Newbold's. At the door, without giving his name, he asked to see Mademoiselle V——, and was shown into a little back parlour, where she came to him with a gaze of surprise.

'"My God! Why do you intrude here, Monsieur?" she gasped in French as soon as she saw his face.

'"You were taken ill yesterday. I helped you. You might have been run over if I had not picked you up. It was an act of simple humanity certainly; but I thought I might come to ask if you had recovered?"

'She had turned aside, and had scarcely heard a word of his speech. "I hate you, infamous man!" she said. "I cannot bear your helping me. Go away!"

'"But you are a stranger to me."

'"I know you too well!"

'"You have the advantage then, Mademoiselle. I am a newcomer here. I never have seen you before to my knowledge; and I certainly do not, could not, hate you."

'"Are you not Monsieur B——?"

'He flinched. "I am – in Paris," he said. "But here I am Monsieur G——."

'"That is trivial. You are the man I say you are."

'"How did you know my real name, Mademoiselle?"

'"I saw you in years gone by, when you did not see me. You were formerly Member of the Committee of Public Safety, under the Convention."

'"I was."

'"You guillotined my father, my brother, my uncle – all my family, nearly, and broke my mother's heart. They had done nothing but keep silence. Their sentiments were only guessed. Their headless corpses were thrown indiscriminately into the ditch of the Mousseaux Cemetry, and destroyed with lime."

'He nodded.

'"You left me without a friend, and here I am now, alone in a foreign land."

'"I am sorry for you," said he. "Sorry for the consequence, not for the intent. What I did was a matter of conscience, and, from a point of view indiscernible by you, I did right. I profited not a farthing. But I shall not argue this. You have the satisfaction of seeing me here an exile also, in poverty, betrayed by comrades, as friendless as yourself."

'"It is no satisfaction to me, Monsieur."

'"Well, things done cannot be altered. Now to the question: are you quite recovered?"

'"Not from dislike and dread of you – otherwise, yes."

'"Good morning, Mademoiselle."

'"Good morning."

'They did not meet again till one evening at the theatre (which my mother's friend was with great difficulty induced to frequent, to perfect herself in English pronunciation, the idea she entertained at that time being to become a teacher of English in her own country later on). She found him sitting next to her, and it made her pale and restless.

'"You are still afraid of me?"

'"I am. O cannot you understand!"

'He signified the affirmative.

'"I follow the play with difficulty," he said, presently.

'"So do I – *now*," said she.

'He regarded her long, and she was conscious of his look; and while she kept her eyes on the stage they filled with tears. Still she would not move, and the tears ran visibly down her cheek, though the play was a merry one, being no other than Mr. Sheridan's comedy of "The Rivals," with Mr. S. Kemble as Captain Absolute. He saw her distress, and that her mind was elsewhere; and abruptly rising from his seat at candle-snuffing time he left the theatre.

'Though he lived in the old town, and she in the new, they frequently saw each other at a distance. One of these occasions was when she was on the north side of the harbour, by the ferry, waiting for the boat to take her across. He was standing by Cove Row, on the quay opposite. Instead of entering the boat when it arrived she stepped back from the quay; but looking to see if he remained she beheld him pointing with his finger to the ferry-boat.

'"Enter!" he said, in a voice loud enough to reach her.

'Mademoiselle V— stood still.

'"Enter!" he said, and, as she did not move, he repeated the word a third time.

'She had really been going to cross, and now approached and stepped down into the boat. Though she did not raise her eyes she knew that he was watching her over. At the landing steps she saw from under the brim of her hat a hand stretched down. The steps were steep and slippery.

'"No, Monsieur," she said. "Unless, indeed, you believe in God, and repent of your evil past!"

'"I am sorry you were made to suffer. But I only believe in the god called Reason, and I do not repent. I was the instrument of a national principle. Your friends were not sacrificed for any ends of mine."

'She thereupon withheld her hand, and clambered up unassisted. He went on, ascending the Look-out Hill, and disappearing over the brow. Her way was in the same direction, her errand being to bring home the two young girls under her charge, who had gone to the cliff for an airing. When she joined them at the top she saw his solitary figure at the further edge, standing motionless against the sea. All the while that she remained with her pupils he stood without turning, as if looking at the frigates in the roadstead, but more probably in meditation, unconscious where he was. In leaving the spot one of the children threw away half a sponge-biscuit that she had been eating. Passing near it he stooped, picked it up carefully, and put it in his pocket.

'Mademoiselle V— came homeward, asking herself, "Can he be starving?"

'From that day he was invisible for so long a time that she thought he had gone away altogether. But one evening a note came to her, and she opened it trembling.

"I am here ill," it said, "and, as you know, alone. There are one or two little things I want done, in case my death should occur, and I should prefer not to ask the people here, if it could be avoided. Have you enough of the gift of charity to come and carry out my wishes before it is too late?"

'Now so it was that, since seeing him possess himself of the broken cake, she had insensibly begun to feel something that was more than curiosity, though perhaps less than anxiety,

about this fellow-countryman of hers; and it was not in her
nervous and sensitive heart to resist his appeal. She found his
lodging (to which he had removed from the Old Rooms inn
for economy) to be a room over a shop, half-way up the steep
and narrow street of the old town, to which the fashionable
visitors seldom penetrated. With some misgiving she entered
the house, and was admitted to the chamber where he lay.

'"You are too good, too good," he murmured. And
presently, "You need not shut the door. You will feel safer,
and they will not understand what we say."

'"Are you in want, Monsieur? Can I give you –"

'"No, no. I merely want you to do a trifling thing or two
that I have not strength enough to do myself. Nobody in the
town but you knows who I really am – unless you have told?"

'"I have not told . . . I thought you *might* have acted from
principle in those sad days, even –"

'"You are kind to concede that much. However, to the
present. I was able to destroy my few papers before I became
so weak. . . . But in the drawer there you will find some
pieces of linen clothing – only two or three – marked with
initials that may be recognized. Will you rip them out with a
penknife?"

'She searched as bidden, found the garments, cut out the
stitches of the lettering, and replaced the linen as before. A
promise to post, in the event of his death, a letter he put in her
hand, completed all that he required of her.

'He thanked her. "I think you seem sorry for me," he
murmured. "And I am surprised. You are sorry?"

'She evaded the question. "Do you repent and believe?" she
asked.

'"No."

'Contrary to her expectations and his own he recovered,
though very slowly; and her manner grew more distant
thenceforward, though his influence upon her was deeper than
she knew. Weeks passed away, and the month of May arrived.
One day at this time she met him walking slowly along the
beach to the northward.

'"You know the news?" he said.

'"You mean of the rupture between France and England
again?"

'"Yes; and the feeling of antagonism is stronger than it was in the last war, owing to Bonaparte's high-handed arrest of the innocent English who were travelling in our country for pleasure. I feel that the war will be long and bitter; and that my wish to live unknown in England will be frustrated. See here."

'He took from his pocket a piece of the single newspaper which circulated in the county in those days, and she read –

"The magistrates acting under the Alien Act have been requested to direct a very scrutinizing eye to the Academies in our towns and other places, in which French tutors are employed, and to all of that nationality who profess to be teachers in this country. Many of them are known to be inveterate Enemies and Traitors to the nation among whose people they have found a livelihood and a home."

'He continued: "I have observed since the declaration of war a marked difference in the conduct of the rougher class of people here towards me. If a great battle were to occur – as it soon will, no doubt – feeling would grow to a pitch that would make it impossible for me, a disguised man of known occupation, to stay here. With you, whose duties and antecedents are known, it may be less difficult, but still unpleasant. Now I propose this. You have probably seen how my deep sympathy with you has quickened to a warm feeling; and what I say is, will you agree to give me a title to protect you by honouring me with your hand? I am older than you, it is true, but as husband and wife we can leave England together, and make the whole world our country. Though I would propose Quebec, in Canada, as the place which offers the best promise of a home."

'"My God! You surprise me!" said she.

'"But you accept my proposal?"

'"No, no!"

'"And yet I think you will, Mademoiselle, some day!"

'"I think not."

'"I won't distress you further now."

'"Much thanks. . . . I am glad to see you looking better, Monsieur; I mean you are looking better."

'"Ah, yes. I am improving. I walk in the sun every day."

'And almost every day she saw him – sometimes nodding stiffly only, sometimes exchanging formal civilities. "You are not gone yet," she said on one of these occasions.

'"No. At present I don't think of going without you."

'"But you find if uncomfortable here?"

'"Somewhat. So when will you have pity on me?"

'She shook her head and went on her way. Yet she was a little moved. "He did it on principle," she would murmur. "He had no animosity towards them, and profited nothing!"

'She wondered how he lived. It was evident that he could not be so poor as she had thought; his pretended poverty might be to escape notice. She could not tell, but she knew that she was dangerously interested in him.

'And he still mended, till his thin, pale face became more full and firm. As he mended she had to meet that request of his, advanced with even stronger insistency.

'The arrival of the King and Court for the season as usual brought matters to a climax for these two lonely exiles and fellow country-people. The King's awkward preference for a part of the coast in such dangerous proximity to France made it necessary that a strict military vigilance should be exercised to guard the royal residents. Half-a-dozen frigates were every night posted in a line across the bay, and two lines of sentinels, one at the water's edge and another behind the Esplanade, occupied the whole sea-front after eight every night. The watering-place was growing an inconvenient residence even for Mademoiselle V— herself, her friendship for this strange French tutor and writing-master who never had any pupils having been observed by many who slightly knew her. The General's wife, whose dependent she was, repeatedly warned her against the acquaintance; while the Hanoverian and other soldiers of the Foreign Legion, who had discovered the nationality of her friend, were more aggressive than the English military gallants who made it their business to notice her.

'In this tense state of affairs her answers became more agitated. "O Heaven, how can I marry you!" She would say.

'"You will; surely you will!" he answered again. "I don't leave without you. and I shall soon be interrogated before the magistrates if I stay here; probably imprisoned. You will come?"

'She felt her defences breaking down. Contrary to all reason and sense of family honour she was, by some abnormal craving, inclining to a tenderness for him that was founded on its opposite. Sometimes her warm sentiments burnt lower than at others, and then the enormity of her conduct showed itself in more staring hues.

'Shortly after this he came with a resigned look on his face. "It is as I expected," he said. "I have received a hint to go. In good sooth, I am no Bonapartist – I am no enemy to England; but the presence of the King made it impossible for a foreigner with no visible occupation, and who may be a spy, to remain at large in the town. The authorities are civil, but firm. They are no more than reasonable. Good. I must go. You must come also."

'She did not speak. But she nodded assent, her eyes drooping.

'On her way back to the house on the Esplanade she said to herself, "I am glad, I am glad! I could not do otherwise. It is rendering good for evil!" But she knew how she mocked herself in this, and that the moral principle had not operated one jot in her acceptance of him. In truth she had not realized till now the full presence of the emotion which had unconsciously grown up in her for this lonely and severe man, who, in her tradition, was vengeance and irreligion personified. He seemed to absorb her whole nature, and, absorbing, to control it.

'A day or two before the one fixed for the wedding there chanced to come to her a letter from the only acquaintance of her own sex and country she possessed in England, one to whom she had sent intelligence of her approaching marriage, without mentioning with whom. This friend's misfortunes had been somewhat similar to her own, which fact had been one cause of their intimacy; her friend's sister, a nun of the Abbey of Montmartre, having perished on the scaffold at the hands of the same Comité de Salut Public which had numbered Mademoiselle V—'s affianced among its members. The writer had felt her position much again of late, since the renewal of the war, she said; and the letter wound up with a fresh denunciation of the authors of their mutual bereavement and subsequent troubles.

'Coming just then, its contents produced upon Mademoiselle V— the effect of a pail of water upon a somnambulist. What had she been doing in betrothing herself to this man! Was she not making herself a parricide after the event? At this crisis in her feelings her lover called. He beheld her trembling, and, in reply to his question, she told him of her scruples with impulsive candour.

'She had not intended to do this, but his attitude of tender command coerced her into frankness. Thereupon he exhibited an agitation never before apparent in him. He said, "But all that is past. You are the symbol of Charity, and we are pledged to let bygones be."

His words soothed her for the moment, but she was sadly silent, and he went away.

'That night she saw (as she firmly believed to the end of her life) a divinely sent vision. A procession of her lost relatives – father, brother, uncle, cousin – seemed to cross her chamber between her bed and the window, and when she endeavoured to trace their features she perceived them to be headless, and that she had recognized them by their familiar clothes only. In the morning she could not shake off the effects of this appearance on her nerves. All that day she saw nothing of her wooer, he being occupied in making arrangements for their departure. It grew towards evening – the marriage eve; but, in spite of his reassuring visit, her sense of family duty waxed stronger now that she was left alone. Yet, she asked herself, how could she, alone and unprotected, go at this eleventh hour and reassert to an affianced husband that she could not and would not marry him while admitting at the same time that she loved him? The situation dismayed her. She had relinquished her post as governess, and was staying temporarily in a room near the coach-office, where she expected him to call in the morning to carry out the business of their union and departure.

'Wisely or foolishly, Mademoiselle V— came to a resolution: that her only safety lay in flight. His contiguity influenced her too sensibly; she could not reason. So packing up her few possessions and placing on the table the small sum she owed, she went out privately, secured a last available seat in the London coach, and, almost before she had fully weighed her action, she was rolling out of the town in the dusk of the September evening.

'Having taken this startling step she began to reflect upon her reasons. He had been one of that tragic Committee the sound of whose name was a horror to the civilized world; yet he had been only *one* of several members, and, it seemed, not the most active. He had marked down names on principle, had felt no personal enmity against his victims, and had enriched himself not a sou out of the office he had held. Nothing could change the past. Meanwhile he loved her, and her heart inclined to as much of him as she could detach from the past. Why not, as he had suggested, bury memories, and inaugurate a new era by this union? In other words, why not indulge her tenderness, since its nullification could do no good.

'Thus she held self-communion in her seat in the coach, passing through Casterbridge and Shottsford, and on to the White Hart at Melchester, at which place the whole fabric of her recent intentions crumbled down. Better be staunch having got so far; let things take their course, and marry boldly the man who had so impressed her. How great he was; how small was she! And she had presumed to judge him! Abandoning her place in the coach with the precipitancy that had characterized her taking it, she waited till the vehicle had driven off, something in the departing shapes of the outside passengers against the starlit sky giving her a start, as she afterwards remembered. Presently the down coach, "The Morning Herald," entered the city, and she hastily obtained a place on the top.

'"I'll be firm – I'll be his – if it cost me my immortal soul!" she said. And with troubled breathings she journeyed back over the road she had just traced.

'She reached our royal watering-place by the time the day broke, and her first aim was to get back to the hired room in which her last few days had been spent. When the landlady appeared at the door in response to Mademoiselle V—'s summons, she explained her sudden departure and return as best she could; and no objection being offered to her re-en-

gagement of the room for one day longer she ascended to the
chamber and sat down panting. She was back once more, and
her wild tergiversations were a secret from him whom alone
they concerned.

'A sealed letter was on the mantlepiece. "Yet, it is directed
to you, Mademoiselle," said the woman who had followed
her. "But we were wondering what to do with it. A town
messenger brought it after you had gone last night."

'When the landlady had left, Mademoiselle V— opened the
letter and read –

"MY DEAR AND HONOURED FRIEND. – You have been
throughout our acquaintance absolutely candid concerning
your misgivings. But I have been reserved concerning
mine. That is the difference between us. You probably have
not guessed that every qualm you have felt on the subject of
our marriage has been paralleled in my heart to the full.
Thus it happened that your involuntary outburst of remorse
yesterday, though mechanically deprecated by me in your
presence, was a last item in my own doubts on the wisdom
of our union, giving them a force that I could no longer
withstand. I came home; and, on reflection, much as I
honour and adore you, I decide to set you free.

"As one whose life has been devoted, and I may say
sacrificed, to the cause of Liberty, I cannot allow your
judgment (probably a permanent one) to be fettered beyond
release by a feeling which may be transient only.

"It would be no less than excruciating to both that I
should announce this decision to you by word of mouth. I
have therefore taken the less painful course of writing.
Before you receive this I shall have left the town by the
evening coach for London, on reaching which city my
movements will be revealed to none.

"Regard me, Mademoiselle, as dead, and accept my
renewed assurances of respect, remembrance, and affection."

'When she had recovered from her shock of surprise and grief,
she remembered that at the starting of the coach out of
Melchester before dawn, the shape of a figure among the

outside passengers against the starlit sky had caused her a
momentary start, from its resemblance to that of her friend.
Knowing nothing of each other's intentions, and screened
from each other by the darkness, they had left the town by the
same conveyance. "He, the greater, persevered; I, the smaller, returned!" she said.

'Recovering from her stupor, Mademoiselle V— bethought
herself again of her employer, Mrs. Newbold, whom recent
events had estranged. To that lady she went with a full heart,
and explained everything. Mrs. Newbold kept to herself her
opinion of the episode, and reinstalled the deserted bride in
her old position as governess to the family.

'A governess she remained to the end of her days. After the
final peace with France she became acquainted with my
mother, to whom by degrees she imparted these experiences
of hers. As her hair grew white, and her features pinched,
Mademoiselle V— would wonder what nook of the world
contained her lover, if he lived, and if by any chance she might
see him again. But when, some time in the 'twenties, death
came to her, at no great age, that outline against the stars of
the morning remained as the last glimpse she ever obtained of
her family's foe and her once affianced husband.'

1895

MASTER JOHN HORSELEIGH, KNIGHT

In the earliest and mustiest volume of the Havenpool marriage registers (said the thin-faced gentleman) this entry may still be read by any one curious enough to decipher the crabbed handwriting of the date. I took a copy of it when I was last there; and it runs thus (he had opened his pocket-book, and now read aloud the extract; afterwards handing round the book to us, wherein we saw transcribed the following) –

> *Mastr John Horseleigh, Knyght, of the p'ysshe of Clyffton was maryd to Edith the wyffe late off John Stocker, m'chawnte of Havenpool the xiiij daie of December be p'vylegge gevyn by our sup'me hedd of the chyrche of Ingelonde Kynge Henry the viiith 1539.*

Now, if you turn to the long and elaborate pedigree of the ancient family of the Horseleighs of Clyfton Horseleigh, you will find no mention whatever of this alliance, notwithstanding the privilege given by the Sovereign and head of the Church; the said Sir John being therein chronicled as marrying, at a date apparently earlier than the above, the daughter and heiress of Richard Phelipson, of Montislope, in Nether Wessex, a lady who outlived him, of which marriage there were issue two daughters and a son, who succeeded him in his estates. How are we to account for these, as it would seem, contemporaneous wives? A strange local tradition only can help us, and this can be briefly told.

One evening in the autumn of the year 1540 or 1541, a young sailor, whose Christian name was Roger, but whose surname is not known, landed at his native place of Havenpool, on the south Wessex coast, after a voyage in the Newfoundland trade, then newly sprung into existence. He returned in the ship *Primrose* with a cargo of 'trayne oyle brought home from the New Founde Lande,' to quote from the town records of the date. During his absence of two summers and a winter, which made up the term of a New-foundland 'spell,' many unlooked-for changes had occurred within the quiet little seaport, some of which closely affected Roger the sailor. At the time of his departure his only sister Edith had become the bride of one Stocker, a respectable townsman, and part owner of the brig in which Roger had sailed; and it was to the house of this couple, his only relatives, that the young man directed his steps. On trying the door in Quay Street he found it locked, and then observed that the windows were boarded up. Inquiring of a bystander, he learnt for the first time of the death of his brother-in-law, though that event had taken place nearly eighteen months before.

'And my sister Edith?' asked Roger.

'She's married again – as they do say, and hath been so these twelve months. I don't vouch for the truth o't, though if she isn't she ought to be.'

Roger's face grew dark, He was a man with a considerable reserve of strong passion, and he asked his informant what he meant by speaking thus.

The man explained that shortly after the young woman's bereavement a stranger had come to the port. He had seen her moping on the quay, had been attracted by her youth and loneliness, and in an extraordinarily brief wooing had com-pletely fascinated her – had carried her off, and, as was reported, had married her. Though he had come by water, he was supposed to live no very great distance off by land. They were last heard of at Oozewood, in Upper Wessex, at the house of one Wall, a timber-merchant, where, he believed, she still had a lodging, though her husband, if he were lawfully that much, was but an occasional visitor to the place.

'The stranger?' asked Roger. 'Did you see him? What manner of man was he?'

'I liked him not,' said the other. 'He seemed of that kind that hath something to conceal, and as he walked with her he ever and anon turned his head and gazed behind him, as if he much feared an unwelcome pursuer. But, faith,' continued he, 'it may have been the man's anxiety only. Yet did I not like him.'

'Was he older than my sister?' Roger asked.

'Ay – much older; from a dozen to a score of years older. A man of some position, maybe, playing an amorous game for the pleasure of the hour. Who knoweth but that he have a wife already? Many have done the thing hereabouts of late.'

Having paid a visit to the graves of his relatives, the sailor next day went along the straight road which, then a lane, now a highway, conducted to the curious little inland town named by the Havenpool man. It is unnecessary to describe Oozewood on the South-Avon. It has a railway at the present day; but thirty years of steam traffic past its precincts have hardly modified its original features. Surrounded by a sort of fresh-water lagoon, dividing it from meadows and coppice, its ancient thatch and timber houses have barely made way even in the front street for the ubiquitous modern brick and slate. It neither increases nor diminishes in size; it is difficult to say what the inhabitants find to do, for, though trades in woodware are still carried on, there cannot be enough of this class of work nowadays to maintain all the householders, the forests around having been so greatly thinned and curtailed. At the time of this tradition the forests were dense, artificers in wood abounded, and the timber trade was brisk. Every house in the town, without exception, was of oak framework, filled in with plaster, and covered with thatch, the chimney being the only brick portion of the structure. Inquiry soon brought Roger the sailor to the door of Wall, the timber-dealer referred to, but it was some time before he was able to gain admission to the lodging of his sister, the people having plainly received directions not to welcome strangers.

She was sitting in an upper room on one of the lathbacked, willow-bottomed 'shepherd's' chairs, made on the spot then as to this day, and as they were probably made there in the days of the Heptarchy. In her lap was an infant, which she had been suckling, though now it had fallen asleep; so had the young mother herself for a few minutes, under the drowsing effects of solitude. Hearing footsteps on the stairs, she awoke, started up with a glad cry, and ran to the door, opening which she met her brother on the threshold.

'O, this is merry; I didn't expect 'ee!' she said. 'Ah Roger – I though it was John.' Her tones fell to disappointment.

The sailor kissed her, looked at her sternly for a few moments, and pointing to the infant, said, 'You mean the father of this?'

'Yes, my husband,' said Edith.

'I hope so,' he answered.

'Why, Roger, I'm married – of a truth am I!' she cried.

'Shame upon 'ee, if true! If not true, worse. Master Stocker was an honest man, and ye should have respected his memory longer. Where is thy husband?'

'He comes often. I though it was he now. Our marriage has to be kept secret for a while – it was done privily for certain reasons; but we was married at church like honest folk – afore God we were, Roger, six months after poor Stocker's death.'

''Twas too soon,' said Roger.

'I was living in a house alone; I had nowhere to go to. You were far over sea in the New Found Land, and John took me and brought me here.'

'How often doth he come?' says Roger again.

'Once or twice weekly,' says she.

'I wish th' 'dst waited till I returned, dear Edy,' he said. 'it mid be you are a wife – I hope so. But, if so, why this mystery? Why this mean and cramped lodging in this lonely copse-circled town? Of what standing is your husband, and of where?'

'He is of gentle breeding – his name is John. I am not free to tell his family-name. He is said to be of London, for safety's sake: but he really lives in the county next adjoining this.'

'Where in the next county?'

'I do not know. He has preferred not to tell me, that I may not have the secret forced from me, to his and my hurt, by bringing the marriage to the ears of his kinsfolk and friends.'

Her brother's face flushed. 'Our people have been honest townsmen, well-reputed for long; why should you readily take such humbling from a sojourner of whom th'st know nothing?'

They remained in constrained converse till her quick ear caught a sound, for which she might have been waiting – a horse's footfall. 'It is John!' said she. 'This is his night – Saturday.'

'Don't be frightened lest he should find me here!' said Roger. 'I am on the point of leaving. I wish not to be a third party. Say nothing at all about my visit, if it will incommode you so to do. I will see thee before I go afloat again.'

Speaking thus he left the room, and descending the staircase let himself out by the front door, thinking he might obtain a glimpse of the approaching horseman. But that traveller had in the meantime gone stealthily round to the back of the homestead, and peering along the pinion-end of the house Roger discerned him unbridling and haltering his horse with his own hands in the shed there.

Roger retired to the neighbouring inn called the Black Lamb, and meditated. This mysterious method of approach determined him, after all, not to leave the place till he had ascertained more definite facts of his sister's position – whether she were the deluded victim of the stranger or the wife she obviously believed herself to be. Having eaten some supper, he left the inn, it being now about eleven o'clock. He first looked into the shed, and, finding the horse still standing there, waited irresolutely near the door of his sister's lodging. Half an hour elapsed, and, while thinking he would climb into a loft hard by for a night's rest, there seemed to be a movement within the shutters of the sitting-room that his sister occupied. Roger hid himself behind a faggot-stack near the back door, rightly divining that his sister's visitor would emerge by the way he had entered. The door opened, and the candle she held in her hand lighted for a moment the stranger's form, showing it to be that of a tall and handsome personage, abourt forty years of age, and apparently of a superior position in life. Edith was assisting him to cloak himself, which being done he took leave of her with a kiss and left the house. From the door she watched him bridle and saddle his horse, and having mounted and waved an adieu to her as she stood candle in hand, he turned out of the yard and rode away.

The horse which bore him was, or seemed to be, a little lame, and Roger fancied from this that the rider's journey was not likely to be a long one. Being light of foot he followed apace, having no great difficulty on such a still night in keeping within earshot some few miles, the horseman pausing more than once. In this pursuit Roger discovered the rider to choose bridletracks and open commons in preference to any high road. The distance soon began to prove a more trying one than he had bargained for; and when out of breath and in some despair of being able to ascertain the man's identity, he perceived an ass standing in the starlight under a hayrick, from which the animal was helping itself to periodic mouthfuls.

The story goes that Roger caught the ass, mounted, and again resumed the trail of the unconscious horseman, which feat may have been possible to a nautical young fellow, though one can hardly understand how a sailor would ride such an animal without bridle or saddle, and strange to his hands, unless the creature were extraordinarily docile. This question, however, is immaterial. Suffice it to say that at dawn the following morning Roger beheld his sister's lover or husband entering the gates of a large and well-timbered park on the south-western verge of the White Hart Forest (as it was then called), now known to everybody as the Vale of Blackmoor. Thereupon the sailor discarded his steed, and finding for himself an obscurer entrance to the same park a little further on, he crossed the grass to reconnoitre.

He presently perceived amid the trees before him a mansion which, new to himself, was one of the best known in the county at that time. Of this fine manorial residence hardly a trace now remains; but a manuscript dated some years later than the events we are regarding describes it in terms from which the imagination may construct a singularly clear and vivid picture. This record presents it as consisting of 'a faire yellow freestone building, partly two and partly three storeys; a faire halle and parlour, both waynscotted, a faire dyning roome and withdrawing roome, and many good lodgings; a kitchen adjoyninge backwarde to one end of the dwelling-house, with a faire passage from it into the halle, parlour, and dyninge roome, and sellars adjoyninge.

'In the front of the house a square greene court, and a curious gatehouse with lodgings in it, standing with the front of the house to the south; in a large outer court three stables, a coach-house, a large barne, and a stable for oxen and kyne, and all houses necessary.

'Without the gatehouse, paled in, a large square greene, in which standeth a faire chappell; of the south-east side of the greene court, towards the river, a large garden.

'Of the south-west side of the greene court is a large bowling green, with fower mounted walks about it, all walled about with a batteled wall, and sett with all sorts of fruit; and out of it into the feildes there are large walks under many tall elmes orderly planted.'

Then follows a description of the orchards and gardens; the servants' offices, brewhouse, bakehouse, dairy, pigeon-houses, and corn-mill; the river and its abundance of fish; the warren, the coppices, the walks; ending thus:—

'And all the country north of the house, open champaign, sandy feildes, very dry and pleasant for all kindes of recreation, huntinge, and hawkinge, and profitable for tillage. . . . The house hath a large prospect east, south, and west, over a very large and pleasant vale . . . is seated from the good markett towns of Sherton Abbas, three miles, and Ivel a mile, that plentifully yield all manner of provision; and within twelve miles of the south sea.'

It was on the grass before this seductive and picturesque structure that the sailor stood at gaze under the elms in the dim dawn of Sunday morning, and saw to his surprise his sister's lover and horse vanish within the court of the building.

Perplexed and weary, Roger slowly retreated, more than ever convinced that something was wrong in his sister's position. He crossed the bowling green to the avenue of elms, and, bent on further research, was about to climb into one of these, when, looking below, he saw a heap of hay apparently for horses or deer. Into this he crept, and, having eaten a crust of bread which he had hastily thrust into his pocket at the inn, he curled up and fell asleep, the hay forming a comfortable bed, and quite covering him over.

He slept soundly and long, and was awakened by the sound of a bell. On peering from the hay he found the time had advanced to full day; the sun was shining brightly. The bell was that of the 'faire chappell' on the green outside the gatehouse, and it was calling to matins. Presently the priest crossed the green to a little side-door in the chancel, and then from the gateway of the mansion emerged the household, the

tall man whom Roger had seen with his sister on the previous
night, on his arm being a portly dame, and, running beside the
pair, two little girls and a boy. These all entered the chapel,
and the bell having ceased and the environs become clear, the
sailor crept from his hiding.

He sauntered towards the chapel, the opening words of the
service being audible within. While standing by the porch he
saw a belated servitor approaching from the kitchen-court to
attend the service also. Roger carelessly accosted him, and
asked, as an idle wanderer, the name of the family he had just
seen cross over from the mansion.

'Od zounds! if ye modden be a stranger here in very truth,
goodman. That wer Sir John and his dame, and his children
Elizabeth, Mary, and John.'

'I be from foreign parts. Sir John what d'ye call'n?'

'Master John Horseleigh, Knight, who had a'most as much
lond by inheritance of his mother as 'a had by his father, and
likewise some by his wife. Why, bain't his arms dree goolden
horses' heads, and idden his lady the daughter of Master
Richard Phelipson, of Montislope, in Nether Wessex, known
to us all?'

'It mid be so, and yet it mid not. However, th' 'lt miss thy
prayers for such an honest knight's welfare, and I have to
traipse seaward many miles.'

He went onward, and as he walked continued saying to
himself, 'Now to that poor wronged fool Edy. The fond
thing! I thought it; 'twas too quick – she was ever amorous.
What's to become of her! God wot! How be I going to face
her with the news, and how be I to hold it from her? To bring
this disgrace on my father's honoured name, a double-
tongued knave!' He turned and shook his fist at the chapel and
all in it, and resumed his way.

Perhaps it was owing to the perplexity of his mind that,
instead of returning by the direct road towards his sister's
obscure lodging in the next county, he followed the highway
to Casterbridge, some fifteen miles off, where he remained
drinking hard all that afternoon and evening, and where he lay
that and two or three succeeding nights, wandering thence
along the Anglebury road to some village that way, and lying
the Friday night after at his native place of Havenpool. The

sight of the familiar objects there seems to have stirred him anew to action, and the next morning he was observed pursuing the way to Oozewood that he had followed on the Saturday previous, reckoning, no doubt, that Saturday night would, as before, be a time for finding Sir John with his sister again.

He delayed to reach the place till just before sunset. His sister was walking in the meadows at the foot of the garden, with a nursemaid who carried the baby, and she looked up pensively when he approached. Anxiety as to her position had already told upon her once rosy cheeks and lucid eyes. But concern for herself and child was displaced for the moment by her regard of Roger's worn and haggard face.

'Why – you are sick, Roger – you are tired! Where have you been these many days? Why not keep me company a bit – my husband is much away? And we have hardly spoke at all of dear father and of your voyage to the New Land. Why did you go away so suddenly? There is a spare chamber at my lodging.'

'Come indoors,' he said. 'We'll talk now – talk a good deal. As for him [nodding to the child], better heave him into the river; better for him and you!'

She forced a laugh, as if she tried to see a good joke in the remark, and they went silently indoors.

'A miserable hole!' said Roger, looking round the room.

'Nay, but 'tis very pretty!'

'Not after what I've seen. Did he marry 'ee at church in orderly fashion?'

'He did sure – at our church at Havenpool.'

'But in a privy way?'

'Ay – because of his friends – it was at night-time.'

'Ede, ye fond one – for all that he's not thy husband! Th' 'rt not his wife; and the child is a bastard. He hath a wife and children of his own rank, and bearing his name; and that's Sir John Horseleigh, of Clyfton Horseleigh, and not plain Jack, as you think him, and your lawful husband. The sacrament of marriage is no safeguard nowadays. The King's new-made headship of the Church hath led men to practise these tricks lightly.'

She had turned white. 'That's not true, Roger!' she said.

'You are in liquor, my brother, and you know not what you say! Your seafaring years have taught 'ee bad things!'

'Edith – I've seen them; wife and family – all. How canst —'

They were sitting in the gathered darkness, and at that moment steps were heard without. 'Go out this way,' she said. 'It is my husband. He must not see thee in this mood. Get away till tomorrow, Roger, as you care for me.'

She pushed her brother through a door leading to the back stairs, and almost as soon as it was closed her visitor entered. Roger, however, did not retreat down the stairs; he stood and looked through the bobbinhole. If the visitor turned out to be Sir John, he had determined to confront him.

It was the knight. She had struck a light on his entry, and he kissed the child, and took Edith tenderly, by the shoulders, looking into her face.

'Something's gone awry wi' my dear!' he said. 'What is it? What's the matter?'

'O, Jack!' she cried. 'I have heard such a fearsome rumour – what doth it mean? He who told me is my best friend. He must be deceived! But who deceived him, and why? Jack, I was just told that you had a wife living when you married me, and have her still!'

'A wife? – H'm.'

'Yes, and children. Say no, say no!'

'By God! I have no lawful wife but you; and as for children, many or few, they are all bastards, save this one alone!'

'And that you be Sir John Horseleigh of Clyfton?'

'I mid be. I have never said so to 'ee.

'But Sir John is known to have a lady, and issue of her!'

The knight looked down. 'How did thy mind get filled with such as this?' he asked.

'One of my kindred came.'

'A traitor! why should he mar our life? Ah! you said you had a brother at sea – where is he now?'

'*Here!*' came from close behind him. And flinging open the door, Roger faced the intruder. 'Liar!' he said, 'to call thyself her husband!'

Sir John fired up, and made a rush at the sailor, who seized him by the collar, and in the wrestle they both fell, Roger under. But in a few seconds he contrived to extricate his right

arm, and drawing from his belt a knife which he wore
attached to a cord round his neck he opened it with his teeth,
and struck it into the breast of Sir John stretched above him.
Edith had during these moments run into the next room to
place the child in safety, and when she came back the knight
was relaxing his hold of Roger's throat. He rolled over upon
his back and groaned.

The only witness of the scene save the three concerned was
the nursemaid, who had brought in the child on its father's
arrival. She stated afterwards that nobody suspected Sir John
had received his death wound; yet it was so, though he did not
die for a long while, meaning thereby an hour or two; that
Mistress Edith continually endeavoured to staunch the blood,
calling her brother Roger a wretch, and ordering him to get
himself gone; on which order he acted, after a gloomy pause,
by opening the window, and letting himself down by the sill
to the ground.

It was then that Sir John, in difficult accents, made his dying
declaration to the nurse and Edith, and, later, the apothecary;
which was to this purport, that the Dame Horseleigh who
passed as his wife at Clyfton, and who had borne him three
children, was in truth and deed, though unconsciously, the
wife of another man. Sir John had married her several years
before, in the face of the whole county, as the widow of one
Decimus Strong, who had disappeared shortly after her union
with him, having adventured to the North to join the revolt of
the Nobles, and on that revolt being quelled retreated across
the sea. Two years ago, having discovered this man to be still
living in France, and not wishing to distrub the mind and
happiness of her who believed herself his wife, yet wishing for
legitimate issue, Sir John had informed the King of the facts,
who had encouraged him to wed honestly, though secretly,
the young merchant's widow at Havenpool; she being, therefore, his lawful wife, and she only. That to avoid all scandal
and hubbub he had purposed to let things remain as they were
till fair opportunity should arise of making the true case
known with least pain to all parties concerned, but that,
having been thus suspected and attacked by his own brother-
in-law, his zest for such schemes and for all things had died
out in him, and he only wished to commend his soul to God.

That night, while the owls were hooting from the forest that encircled the sleeping townlet, and the South-Avon was gurgling through the wooden piles of the bridge, Sir John died there in the arms of his wife. She concealed nothing of the cause of her husband's death save the subject of the quarrel, which she felt it would be premature to announce just then, until proof of her status should be forthcoming. But before a month had passed, it happened, to her inexpressible sorrow, that the child of this clandestine union fell sick and died. From that hour all interest in the name and fame of the Horseleighs forsook the younger of the twain who called themselves wives of Sir John, and, being careless about her own fame, she took no steps to assert her claims, her legal position having, indeed, grown hateful to her in her horror at the tragedy. And Sir William Byrt, the curate who had married her to her husband, being an old man and feeble, was not disinclined to leave the embers unstirred of such a fiery matter as this, and to assist her in letting established things stand. Therefore, Edith retired with the nurse, her only companion and friend, to her native town, where she lived in absolute obscurity till her death in middle age. Her brother was never seen again in England.

A strangely corroborative sequel to the story remains to be told. Shortly after the death of Sir John Horseleigh, a soldier of fortune returned from the continent, called on Dame Horseleigh the fictitious, living in widowed state at Clyfton Horseleigh, and, after a singularly brief courtship, married her. The tradition at Havenpool and elsewhere has ever been that this man was already her husband, Decimus Strong, who remarried her for appearance' sake only.

The illegitmate son of this lady by Sir John succeeded to the estates and honours, and his son after him, there being nobody on the alert to investigate their pretensions. Little difference would it have made to the present generation, however, had there been such a one, for the family in all its branches, lawful and unlawful, has been extinct these many score years, the last representative but one being killed at the siege of Sherton Castle, while attacking in the service of the Parliament, and the other being outlawed later in the same century for a debt of ten pounds, and dying in the county jail.

The mansion house and its appurtenances were, as I have previously stated, destroyed, excepting one small wing, which now forms part of a farmhouse, and is visible as you pass along the railway from Casterbridge to Ivel. The outline of the old bowling-green is also distinctly to be seen.

This, then is the reason why the only lawful marriage of Sir John, as recorded in the obscure register at Havenpool, does not appear in the pedigree of the house of Horseleigh.

Spring 1893

THE DUKE'S REAPPEARANCE

A FAMILY TRADITION

According to the kinsman who told me the story, Christopher Swetman's house, on the outskirts of King's-Hintock village, was in those days larger and better kept than when, many years later, it was sold to the lord of the manor adjoining; after having been in the Swetman family, as one may say, since the Conquest.

Some people would have it to be that the thing happened at the house opposite, belonging to one Childs, with whose family the Swetmans afterwards intermarried. But that it was at the original homestead of the Swetmans can be shown in various ways; chiefly by the unbroken traditions of the family, and indirectly by the evidence of the walls themselves, which are the only ones thereabout with windows mullioned in the Elizabethan manner, and plainly of a date anterior to the event; while those of the other house might well have been erected fifty or eighty years later, and probably were; since the choice of Swetman's house by the fugitive was doubtless dictated by no other circumstance than its then suitable loneliness.

It was a cloudy July morning just before dawn, the hour of two having been struck by Swetman's one-handed clock on the stairs, that is still preserved in the family. Christopher heard the strokes from his chamber, immediately at the top of the staircase, and overlooking the front of the house. He did not wonder that he was sleepless. The rumours and excitements which had latterly stirred the neighbourhood, to the effect that the rightful King of England had landed from Holland, at a port only eighteen miles to the south-west of Swetman's house, were enough to make wakeful and anxious even a contented yeoman like him. Some of the villagers, intoxicated by the news, had thrown down their scythes, and rushed to the ranks of the invader. Christopher Swetman had weighed both sides of the question, and had remained at home.

Now as he lay thinking of these and other things he fancied that he could hear the footfall of a man on the road leading up to his house – a byway, which led scarce anywhere else; and therefore, a tread was at any time more apt to startle the inmates of the homestead than if it had stood in a thorough-fare. The footfall came opposite the gate, and stopped there. One minute, two minutes passed, and the pedestrian did not proceed. Christopher Swetman got out of bed, and opened the casement. 'Hoi! who's there?' cries he.

'A friend,' came from the darkness.

'And what mid ye want at this time o' night?' says Swetman.

'Shelter. I've lost my way.'

'What's thy name?'

There came no answer.

'Be ye one of King Monmouth's men?'

'He that asks no questions will hear no lies from me. I am a stranger; and I am spent, and hungered. Can you let me lie with you tonight?'

Swetman was generous to people in trouble, and his house was roomy. 'Wait a bit,' he said, 'and I'll come down and have a look at thee, anyhow.'

He struck a light, put on his clothes, and descended, taking his horn-lantern from a nail in the passage, and lighting it before opening the door. The rays fell on the form of a tall, dark man in cavalry accoutrements and wearing a sword. He was pale with fatigue and covered with mud, though the weather was dry.

'Prithee take no heed of my appearance,' said the stranger. 'But let me in.'

That his visitor was in sore distress admitted of no doubt, and the yeoman's natural humanity assisted the other's sad importunity and gentle voice. Swetman took him in, not without a suspicion that this man represented in some way Monmouth's cause, to which he was not unfriendly in his secret heart. At his earnest request the newcomer was given a suit of the yeoman's old clothes in exchange for his own, which, with his sword, were hidden in a closet in Swetman's chamber; food was then put before him and a lodging provided for him in a room at the back.

Here he slept till quite late in the morning, which was Sunday, the sixth of July, and when he came down in the garments that he had borrowed he met the household with a melancholy smile. Besides Swetman himself, there were only his two daughters, Grace and Leonard (the latter was, oddly enough, a woman's name here), and both had been enjoined to secrecy. They asked no question and received no information; though the stranger regarded their fair countenances with an interest almost too deep. Having partaken of their usual breakfast of ham and cider he professed weariness and retired to the chamber whence he had come.

In a couple of hours or thereabout he came down again, the two young women having now gone off to morning service. Seeing Christopher bustling about the house without assistance, he asked if he could do anything to aid his host.

As he seemed anxious to hide all differences and appear as one of themselves, Swetman set him to get vegetables from the garden and fetch water from Buttock's Spring in the dip near the house (though the spring was not called by that name till years after, by the way).

'And what can I do next?' says the stranger when these services had been performed.

His meekness and docility struck Christopher much, and won upon him. 'Since you be minded to,' says the latter, 'you can take down the dishes and spread the table for dinner. Take a pewter plate for thyself, but the trenchers will do for we.'

But the other would not, and took a trencher likewise, in doing which he spoke of the two girls and remarked how comely they were.

This quietude was put an end to by the stir out of doors, which was sufficient to draw Swetman's attention to it, and he went out. Farm hands who had gone off and joined the Duke on his arrival had begun to come in with news that a midnight battle had been fought on the moors to the north, the Duke's men, who had attacked, being entirely worsted; the Duke himself, with one or two lords and other friends, had fled, no one knew whither.

'There has been a battle,' says Swetman, on coming indoors after these tidings, and looking earnestly at the stranger.

'May the victory be to the rightful in the end, whatever the issue now,' says the other, with a sorrowful sigh.

'Dost really know nothing about it? said Christopher. 'I could have sworn you was one from that very battle!'

'I was here before three o' the clock this morning; and these men have only arrived now.'

'True,' said the yeoman. 'But still, I think –'

'Do not press your question,' the stranger urged. 'I am in a strait, and can refuse a helper nothing; such inquiry is, therefore, unfair.'

'True again,' said Swetman, and held his tongue.

The daughters of the house returned from church where the service had been hurried by reason of the excitement. To their father's questioning if they had spoken of him who sojourned there they replied that they had said never a word; which, indeed, was true, as events proved.

He bade them serve the dinner; and, as the visitor had withdrawn since the news of the battle, prepared to take a platter to him upstairs. But he preferred to come down and dine with the family.

During the afternoon more fugitives passed through the village, but Christopher Swetman, his visitor, and his family kept indoors. In the evening, however, Swetman came out from his gate, and, harkening in silence to these tidings and more, wondered what might be in store for him for his last night's work.

He returned homeward by a path across the mead that skirted his own orchard. Passing here, he heard the voice of his daughter Leonard expostulating inside the hedge, her words being:

'Don't ye, sir; don't! I prithee let me go!'

'Why, sweetheart?'

'Because I've a-promised another!'

Peeping through, as he could not help doing, he saw the girl struggling in the arms of the stranger, who was attempting to kiss her; but finding her resistance to be genuine, and her distress unfeigned, he reluctantly let her go.

Swetman's face grew dark, for his girls were more to him than himself. He hastened on, meditating moodily all the way. He entered the gate, and made straight for the orchard. When he reached it his daughter had disappeared, but the stranger was still standing there.

'Sir!' said the yeoman, his anger having in no wise abated, 'I've seen what has happened! I have taken 'ee into my house, at some jeopardy to myself; and, whoever you be, the least I expected of 'ee was to treat the maidens with a seemly respect. You have not done it, and I no longer trust you. I am the more watchful over them in that they are motherless; and I must ask 'ee to go after dark this night!'

The stranger seemed dazed at discovering what his impulse had brought down upon his head, and his pale face grew paler. He did not reply for a time. When he did speak his soft voice was thick with feeling.

'Sir,' says he, 'I own that I am in the wrong, if you take the matter gravely. We do not what we would but what we must. Though I have not injured your daughter as a woman, I have been treacherous to her as a hostess and friend in need. I'll go, as you say; I can do no less. I shall doubtless find a refuge elsewhere.'

They walked towards the house in silence, where Swetman insisted that his guest should have supper before departing. By the time this was eaten it was dusk and the stranger announced that he was ready.

They went upstairs to where the garments and sword lay hidden, till the departing one said that on further thought he would ask another favour: that he should be allowed to retain the clothes he wore, and that his host would keep the others and the sword till he, the speaker, should come or send for them.

'As you will,' said Swetman. 'The gain is on my side; for those clouts were but kept to dress a scarecrow next fall.'

'They suit my case,' said the stranger sadly. 'However much they may misfit me, they do not misfit my sorry fortune now!'

'Nay, then,' said Christopher relenting, 'I was too hasty. Sh'lt bide!'

But the other would not, saying that it was better that things should take their course. Notwithstanding that Swetman importuned him, he only added, 'If I never come again, do with my belongings as you list. In the pocket you will find a gold snuff-box, and in the snuff-box fifty gold pieces.'

'But keep 'em for thy use, man!' said the yeoman.

'No,' says the parting guest; 'they are foreign pieces and would harm me if I were taken. Do as I bid thee. Put away these things again and take especial charge of the sword. It belonged to my father's father and I value it much. But something more common becomes me now.'

Saying which, he took, as he went downstairs, one of the ash sticks used by Swetman himself for walking with. The yeoman lighted him out to the garden hatch, where he disappeared through Clammers Gate by the road that crosses King's-Hintock Park to Evershead.

Christopher returned to the upstairs chamber, and sat down on his bed reflecting. Then he examined the things left behind, and surely enough in one of the pockets the gold snuff-box was revealed, containing the fifty gold pieces as stated by the fugitive. The yeoman next looked at the sword which its owner had stated to have belonged to his grandfather. It was two-edged, sò that he almost feared to handle it. On the blade was inscribed the words 'ANDREA FERARA', and among the many fine chasings were a rose and crown, the plume of the Prince of Wales, and two portraits; portraits of a man and a woman, the man's having the face of the first King Charles, and the woman's apparently, that of his Queen.

Swetman, much awed and surprised, returned the articles to the closet, and went downstairs pondering. Of his surmise he said nothing to his daughters, merely declaring to them that the gentleman was gone; and never revealing that he had been an eye-witness of the unpleasant scene in the orchard that was the immediate cause of the departure.

Nothing occured in Hintock during the week that followed, beyond the fitful arrival of more decided tidings concerning the utter defeat of the Duke's army and his own disappearance at an early stage of the battle. Then it was told that Monmouth was taken, not in his own clothes but in the disguise of a countryman. He had been sent to London, and was confined in the Tower.

The possibility that his guest had been no other than the Duke made Swetman unspeakably sorry now; his heart smote him at the thought that, acting so harshly for such a small breach of good faith, he might have been the means of forwarding the unhappy fugitive's capture. On the girls coming up to him he said, 'Get away with ye, wenches: I fear you have been the ruin of an unfortunate man!'

On the Tuesday night following, when the yeoman was sleeping as usual in his chamber, he was, he said, conscious of the entry of some one. Opening his eyes, he beheld by the light of the moon, which shone upon the front of his house, the figure of a man who seemed to be the stranger moving from the door towards the closet. He was dressed somewhat differently now, but the face was quite that of his late guest in its tragical pensiveness, as was also the tallness of his figure. He neared the closet; and, feeling his visitor to be within his rights, Christopher refrained from stirring. The personage turned his large haggard eyes upon the bed where Swetman lay, and then withdrew from their hiding the articles that belonged to him, again giving a hard gaze at Christopher as he went noiselessly out of the chamber with his properties on his arm. His retreat down the stairs was just audible, and also his departure by the side door, through which entrance or exit was easy to those who knew the place.

Nothing further happened, and towards morning Swetman slept. To avoid all risk he said not a word to the girls of the visit of the night, and certainly not to any one outside the house; for it was dangerous at that time to avow anything.

Among the killed in opposing the recent rising had been a younger brother of the lord of the manor, who lived at King's-Hintock Court hard by. Seeing the latter ride past in mourning clothes next day, Swetman ventured to condole with him.

'He'd no business there!' answered the other. His words and manner showed the bitterness that was mingled with his regret. 'But say no more of him. You know what has happened since, I suppose?'

'I know they say Momouth is taken, Sir Thomas, but I can't think it true,' answered Swetman.

'O zounds! 'tis true enough,' cried the knight, 'and that's not all. The Duke was executed on Tower Hill two days ago.'

'D'ye say it verily?' says Swetman.

'And a very hard death he had, worse luck for 'n,' said Sir Thomas. 'Well, 'tis over for him and over for my brother. But not for the rest. There'll be searchings and siftings down here anon; and happy is the man who has had nothing to do with this matter!'

Now Swetman had hardly heard the latter words, so much was he confounded by the strangeness of the tidings that the Duke had come to his death on the previous Tuesday. For it had been only the night before this present day of Friday that he had seen his former guest, whom he had ceased to doubt could be other than the Duke, come into his chamber and fetch away his accoutrements as he had promised.

'It couldn't have been a vision,' said Christopher to himself when the knight had ridden on. 'But I'll go straight and see if the things be in the closet still; and thus I shall surely learn if t'were a vision or no.'

To the closet he went, which he had not looked into since the stranger's departure. And searching behind the articles placed to conceal the things hidden, he found that, as he had never doubted, they were gone.

When the rumour spread abroad in the West that the man beheaded in the Tower was not indeed the Duke, but one of his officers taken after the battle and that the Duke had been assisted to escape out of the country, Swetman found in it an explanation of what so deeply mystified him. That his visitor might have been a friend of the Duke's whom the Duke had asked to fetch the things in a last request, Swetman would never admit. His belief in the rumour that Monmouth lived, like that of thousands of others, continued to the end of his days.

Such, briefly, concluded my kinsman, is the tradition which has been handed down in Christopher Swetman's family for the last two hundred years.

Christmas 1896

A MERE INTERLUDE

I

The traveller in school-books, who vouched in dryest tones for the fidelity to fact of the following narrative, used to add a ring of truth to it by opening with a nicety of criticism on the heroine's personality. People were wrong, he declared, when they surmised that Baptista Trewthen was a young woman with scarcely emotions or character. There was nothing in her to love, and nothing to hate – so ran the general opinion. That she showed few positive qualities was true. The colours and tones which changing events paint on the faces of active womankind were looked for in vain upon hers. But still waters run deep; and no crisis had come in the years of her early maidenhood to demonstrate what lay hidden within her, like metal in a mine.

She was the daughter of a small farmer in St. Maria's one of the Isles of Lyonesse beyond Off-Wessex, who had spent a large sum, as there understood, on her education, by sending her to the mainland for two years. At nineteen she was entered at the Training College for Teachers, and at twenty-one nominated to a school in the country, near Tor-upon-Sea, whither she proceeded after the Christmas examination and holidays.

The months passed by from winter to spring and summer, and Baptista applied herself to her new duties as best she could, till an uneventful year had elapsed. Then an air of abstraction pervaded her bearing as she walked to and fro, twice a day, and she showed the traits of a person who had something on her mind. A widow, by name Mrs. Wace, in whose house Baptista Trewthen had been provided with a sitting-room and bedroom till the school-house should be built, noticed this change in her youthful tenant's manner, and at last ventured to press her with a few questions.

'It has nothing to do with the place, nor with you,' said Miss Trewthen.

'Then it is the salary?'

'No, nor the salary.'

'Then it is something you have heard from home, my dear.'

Baptista was silent for a few moments. 'It is Mr. Heddegan,' she murmured. 'Him they used to call David Heddegan before he got his money.'

'And who is the Mr. Heddegan they used to call David?'

'An old bachelor at Giant's Town, St. Maria's, with no relations whatever, who lives about a stone's throw from father's. When I was a child he used to take me on his knee and say he'd marry me some day. Now I am a woman the jest has turned earnest, and he is anxious to do it. And father and mother says I can't do better than have him.'

'He's well off?'

'Yes – he's the richest man we know – as a friend and neighbour.'

'How much older did you say he was than yourself?'

'I didn't say. Twenty years at least.'

'And an unpleasant man in the bargain perhaps?'

'No – he's not unpleasant.'

'Well, child, all I can say is that I'd resist any such engagement if it's not palatable to 'ee. You are comfortable here, in my little house, I hope. All the parish like 'ee: and I've never been so cheerful, since my poor husband left me to wear his wings, as I've been with 'ee as my lodger.'

The schoolmistress assured her landlady that she could return the sentiment. 'But here comes my perplexity.' she said. 'I don't like keeping school. Ah, you are surprised – you didn't suspect it. That's because I've concealed my feeling. Well, I simply hate school. I don't care for children – they are unpleasant, troublesome little things, whom nothing would delight so much as to hear that you had fallen down dead. Yet I would even put up with them if it was not for the inspector. For three months before his visit I didn't sleep soundly. And the Committee of Council are always changing the Code, so that you don't know what to teach, and what to leave untaught. I think father and mother are right. They say I shall never excel as a schoolmistress if I dislike the work so, and

that therefore I ought to get settled by marrying Mr. Heddegan. Between us two, I like him better than school; but I don't
like him quite so much as to wish to marry him.'

These conversations, once begun, were continued from day
to day; till at length, the young girl's elderly friend and
landlady threw in her opinion on the side of Miss Trewthen's
parents. All things considered, she declared, the uncertainty of
the school, the labour, Baptista's natural dislike for teaching,
it would be as well to take what fate offered, and make the
best of matters by wedding her father's old neighbour and
prosperous friend.

The Easter holidays came round, and Baptista went to
spend them as usual in her native isle, going by train into
Off-Wessex and crossing by packet from Penzephyr. When
she returned in the middle of April her face wore a more
settled aspect.

'Well?' said the expectant Mrs. Wace.

'I have agreed to have him as my husband,' said Baptista, in
an off-hand way. 'Heaven knows if it will be for the best or
not. But I have agreed to do it, and so the matter is settled.'

Mrs. Wace commended her; but Baptista did not care to
dwell on the subject; so that allusion to it was very infrequent
between them. Nevertheless, among other things, she repeated to the window from time to time in monosyllabic
remarks that the wedding was really impending; that it was
arranged for the summer, and that she had given notice of
leaving the school at the August holidays. Later on she
announced more specifically that her marriage was to take
place immediately after her return home at the beginning of
the month aforesaid.

She now corresponded regularly with Mr. Heddegan. Her
letters from him were seen, at least on the outside, and in part
within, by Mrs. Wace, Had she read more of their interiors
than the occasional sentences shown her by Baptista she
would have perceived that the scratchy, rusty handwriting of
Miss Trewthen's betrothed conveyed little more matter than
details of their future housekeeping, and his preparations for
the same, with innumerable 'my dears' sprinkled in discon-
nectedly, to show the depth of his affection without the
inconveniences of syntax.

II

It was the end of July – dry, too dry, even for the season, the delicate green herbs and vegetables that grew in this favoured end of the kingdom tasting rather of the watering-pot than of the pure fresh moisture from the skies. Baptista's boxes were packed, and one Saturday morning she departed by a waggonette to the station, and thence by train to Pen-zephyr, from which port she was, as usual, to cross the water immediately to her home, and become Mr. Heddegan's wife on the Wednesday of the week following.

She might have returned a week sooner. But though the wedding day had loomed so near, and the banns were out, she delayed her departure till this last moment, saying it was not necessary for her to be at home long beforehand. As Mr. Heddegan was older than herself, she said, she was to be married in her ordinary summer bonnet and grey silk frock, and there were no preparations to make that had not been amply made by her parents and intended husband.

In due time, after a hot and tedious journey, she reached Pen-zephyr. She here obtained some refreshment, and then went toward the pier, where she learnt to her surprise that the little steamboat plying between the town and the islands had left at eleven o'clock; the usual hour of departure in the afternoon having been forestalled in consequence of the fogs which had for a few days prevailed towards evening, making twilight navigation dangerous.

This being Saturday, there was now no other boat till Tuesday, and it became obvious that here she would have to remain for the three days, unless her friends should think fit to rig out one of the island sailing-boats and come to fetch her – a not very likely contingency, the sea distance being nearly forty miles.

Baptista, however, had been detained in Pen-zephyr on more than one occasion before, either on account of bad weather or some such reason as the present, and she was therefore not in any personal alarm. But, as she was to be married on the following Wednesday, the delay was certainly inconvenient to a more than ordinary degree, since it would leave less than a day's interval between her arrival and the wedding ceremony.

Apart from this awkwardness she did not much mind the accident. It was indeed curious to see how little she minded. Perhaps it would not be too much to say that, although she was going to do the critical deed of her life quite willingly, she experienced an indefinable relief at the postponement of her meeting with Heddegan. But her manner after making discovery of the hindrance was quiet and subdued, even to passivity itself; as was instanced by her having, at the moment of receiving information that the steamer had sailed, replied 'Oh,' so coolly to the porter with her luggage, that he was almost disappointed at her lack of disappointment.

The question now was, should she return again to Mrs. Wace, in the village of Lower Wessex, or wait in the town at which she had arrived. She would have preferred to go back, but the distance was too great; moreover, having left the place for good, and somewhat dramatically, to become a bride, a return, even for so short a space, would have been a trifle humiliating.

Leaving, then, her boxes at the station, her next anxiety was to secure a respectable, or rather genteel, lodging in the popular seaside resort confronting her. To this end she looked about the town, in which, though she had passed through it half-a-dozen times, she was practically a stranger.

Baptista found a room to suit her over a fruiterer's shop; where she made herself at home, and set herself in order after her journey. An early cup of tea having revived her spirits she walked out to reconnoitre.

Being a schoolmistress she avoided looking at the schools, and having a sort of trade connection with books, she avoided looking at the booksellers; but wearying of the other shops she inspected the churches; not that for her own part she cared much about ecclesiastical edifices; but tourists looked at them, and so would she – a proceeding for which no one would have credited her with any great originality, such, for instance, as that she subsequently showed herself to possess. The churches soon oppressed her. She tried the Museum, but came out because it seemed lonely and tedious.

Yet the town and the walks in this land of strawberries, these headquarters of early English flowers and fruit, were then, as always, attractive. From the more picturesque streets she went to the town gardens, and the Pier, and the Harbour, and looked at the men at work there, loading and unloading as in the time of the Phoenicians.

'Not Baptista? Yes, Baptista it is!'

The words were uttered behind her. Turning round she gave a start, and became confused, even agitated, for a moment. Then she said in her usual undemonstrative manner, 'O – is it really you, Charles?'

Without speaking again at once, and with a half-smile, the newcomer glanced her over. There was much criticism, and some resentment – even temper – in his eye.

'I am going home,' continued she. 'But I have missed the boat.'

He scarcely seemed to take in the meaning of this explanation, in the intensity of his critical survey. 'Teaching still? What a fine schoolmistress you make, Baptista, I warrant!' he said with a slight flavour of sarcasm, which was not lost upon her.

'I know I am nothing to brag of,' she replied. 'That's why I have given up.'

'O – given up? You astonish me.'

'I hate the profession.'

'Perhaps that's because I am in it.'

'O no, it isn't. But I am going to enter on another life altogether. I am going to be married next week to Mr. David Heddegan.'

The young man – fortified as he was by a natural cynical pride and passionateness – winced at this unexpected reply, notwithstanding.

'Who is Mr. David Heddegan?' he asked, as indifferently as lay in his power.

She informed him the bearer of the name was a general merchant of Giant's Town, St. Maria's Island – her father's nearest neighbour and oldest friend.

'Then we shan't see anything more of you on the mainland?' inquired the schoolmaster.

'O, I don't know about that,' said Miss Trewthen.

'Here endeth the career of the belle of the boarding-school your father was foolish enough to send you to. A "general merchant's" wife in the Lyonesse Isles. Will you sell pounds of soap and pennyworths of tin tacks, or whole bars of saponaceous matter, and great tenpenny nails?'

'He's not in such a small way as that!' she almost pleaded. 'He owns ships, though they are rather little ones!'

'O, well, it is much the same. Come, let us walk on; it is tedious to stand still. I thought you would be a failure in education,' he continued, when she obeyed him and strolled ahead. 'You never showed power that way. You remind me much of some of those women who think they are sure to be great actresses if they go on the stage, because they have a pretty face, and forget that what we require is acting. But you found your mistake, didn't you?'

'Don't taunt me, Charles.' It was noticeable that the young schoolmaster's tone caused her no anger or retaliatory passion; far otherwise: there was a tear in her eye. 'How is it you are at Pen-zephyr?' she inquired.

'I don't taunt you. I speak the truth, purely in a friendly way, as I should to any one I wished well. Though for that matter I might have some excuse even for taunting you. Such a terrible hurry as you've been in. I hate a woman who is in such a hurry.'

'How do you mean that?'

'Why, to be somebody's wife or other – anything's wife rather than nobody's. You couldn't wait for me. O, no. Well, thank God, I'm cured of all that!'

'How merciless you are!' she said bitterly. 'Wait for you? What does that mean, Charley? You never showed – anything to wait for – anything special towards me.'

'O come, Baptista dear; come!'

'What I mean is, nothing definite,' she expostulated. 'I suppose you liked me a little; but it seemed to me to be only a pastime on your part, and that you never meant to make an honourable engagement of it.'

'There, that's just it! You girls expect a man to mean businss at the first look. No man when he first becomes interested in a woman has any definite scheme of engagement to marry her in his mind, unless he is meaning a vulgar mercenary marriage. However, I *did* at least mean an honourable engagement, as you call it, come to that.'

'But you never said so, and an indefinite courtship soon injures a woman's position and credit, sooner than you think.'

'Baptista, I solemnly declare that in six months I should have asked you to marry me.'

She walked along in silence, looking on the ground, and appearing very uncomfortable. Presently he said, 'Would you have waited for me if you had known?' To this she whispered in a sorrowful whisper, 'Yes!'

They went still farther in silence – passing along one of the beautiful walks on the outskirts of the town, yet not observant of scene or situation. Her shoulder and his were close together, and he clasped his fingers round the small of her arm – quite lightly, and without any attempt at impetus; yet the act seemed to say, 'Now I hold you, and my will must be yours.'

Recurring to a previous question of hers he said, 'I have merely run down here for a day or two from school near Trufal, before going off to the north for the rest of my holiday. I have seen my relations at Redrutin quite lately, so I am not going there this time. How little I thought of meeting you! How very different the circumstances would have been if, instead of parting again as we must in half-an-hour or so, possibly for ever, you had been now just going off with me, as my wife, on our honeymon trip. Ha – ha – well – so humorous is life!'

She stopped suddenly. 'I must go back now – this is altogether too painful, Charley! It is not at all a kind mood you are in today.'

'I don't want to pain you – you know I do not,' he said more gently. 'Only it just exasperates me – this you are going to do. I wish you would not.'

'What?'

'Marry him. There, now I have showed you my true sentiments.'

'I must do it now,' said she.

'Why?' he asked, dropping the off-hand masterful tone he had hitherto spoken in, and becoming earnest; still holding her arm, however, as if she were his chattel to be taken up or put down at will. 'It is never too late to break off a marriage that's distasteful to you. Now I'll say one thing; and it is truth: I wish you would marry me instead of him, even now, at the last moment, though you have served me so badly.'

'O, it is not possible to think of that!' she answered hastily, shaking her head. 'When I get home all will be prepared – it is ready even now – the things for the party, the furniture, Mr. Heddegan's new suit, and everything. I should require the courage of a tropical lion to go home there and say I wouldn't carry out my promise!'

'Then go, in Heaven's name! But there would be no necessity for you to go home and face them in that way. If we were to marry, it would have to be at once, instantly; or not at all. I should think your affection not worth the having unless you agreed to come back with me to Trufal this evening, where we could be married by licence on Monday morning. And then no Mr. David Heddegan or anybody else could get you away from me.'

'I must go home by the Tuesday boat,' she faltered. 'What would they think if I did not come?'

'You could go home by that boat just the same. All the difference would be that I should go with you. You could leave me on the quay, where I'd have a smoke, while you went and saw your father and mother privately; you could then tell them what you had done, and that I was waiting not far off; that I was a schoolmaster in a fairly good position, and a young man you had known when you were at the Training College. Then I would come boldly forward; and they would see that it could not be altered, and so you wouldn't suffer a lifelong misery by being the wife of a wretched old gaffer you don't like at all. Now, honestly; you do like me best, don't you, Baptista?'

'Yes.'

'Then we will do as I say.'

She did not pronounce a clear affirmative. But that she consented to the novel propositon at some moment or other of that walk was apparent by what occurred a little later.

III

An enterprise of such pith required, indeed, less talking than consideration. The first thing they did in carrying it out was to return to the railway station, where Baptista took from her luggage a small trunk of immediate necessaries which she would in any case have required after missing the boat. That same afternoon they travelled up the line to Trufal.

Charles Stow (as his name was), despite his disdainful indifference to things, was very careful of appearances, and made the journey independently of her though in the same train. He told her where she could get board and lodgings in the city; and with merely a distant nod to her of a provisional kind, went off to his own quarters, and to see about the licence.

On Sunday she saw him in the morning across the nave of the pro-cathedral. In the afternoon they walked together in the fields, where he told her that the licence would be ready the next day, and would be available the day after, when the ceremony could be performed as early after eight o'clock as they should choose.

His courtship, thus renewed after an interval of two years, was as impetuous, violent even, as it was short. The next day came and passed, and the final arrangements were made. Their agreement was to get the ceremony over as soon as they possibly could the next morning, so as to go on to Pen-zephyr at once, and reach that place in time for the boat's departure the same day. It was in obedience to Baptista's earnest request that Stow consented thus to make the whole journey to Lyonesse by land and water at one heat, and not break it at Pen-zephyr; she seemed to be oppressed with a dread of lingering anywhere, this great first act of disobedience to her parents once accomplished, with the weight on her mind that her home had to be convulsed by the disclosure of it. To face her difficulties over the water immediately she had created them was, however, a course more desired by Baptista than by her lover; though for once he gave way.

The next morning was bright and warm as those which had preceded it. By six o'clock it seemed nearly noon, as is often the case in that part of England in the summer season. By nine they were husband and wife. They packed up and departed by the earliest train after the service; and on the way discussed at length what she should say on meeting her parents, Charley dictating the turn of each phrase. In her anxiety they had travelled so early that when they reached Pen-zephyr they found there were nearly two hours on their hands before the steamer's time of sailing.

Baptista was extremely reluctant to be seen promenading the streets of the watering-place with her husband till, as above stated, the household at Giant's Town should know the unexpected course of events from her own lips; and it was just possible, if not likely, that some Lyonessian might be prowling about there, or even have come across the sea to look for her. To meet any one to whom she was known, and to have to reply to awkward questions about the strange young man at her side before her well-framed announcement had been delivered at proper time and place, was a thing she could not contemplate with equanimity. So, instead of looking at the shops and harbour, they went along the coast a little way.

The heat of the morning was by this time intense. They clambered up on some cliffs, and while sitting there, looking around at St. Michael's Mount and other objects, Charles said to her that he thought he would run down to the beach at their feet, and take just one plunge into the sea.

Baptista did not much like the idea of being left alone; it was gloomy, she said. But he assured her he would not be gone more than a quarter of an hour at the outside, and she passively assented.

Down he went, disappeared, appeared again, and looked back. Then he again proceeded, and vanished, till, as a small waxen object, she saw him emerge from the nook that had screened him, cross the white fringe of foam, and walk into the undulating mass of blue. Once in the water he seemed less inclined to hurry than before; he remained a long time; and, unable either to appreciate his skill or criticize his want of it at that distance, she withdrew her eyes from the spot, and gazed at the still outline of St. Michael's – now beautifully toned in grey.

Her anxiety for the hour of departure, and to cope at once with the approaching incidents that she would have to manipulate as best she could, sent her into a reverie. It was now Tuesday; she would reach home in the evening – a very late time they would say; but, as the delay was a pure accident, they would deem her marriage to Mr. Heddegan tomorrow

still practicable. Then Charles would have to be produced
from the background. It was a terrible undertaking to think
of, and she almost regretted her temerity in wedding so hastily
that morning. The rage of her father would be so crushing;
the reproaches of her mother so bitter; and perhaps Charles
would answer hotly, and perhaps cause estrangement till
death. There had obviously been no alarm about her at St.
Maria's, or somebody would have sailed across to inquire for
her. She had, in a letter written at the beginning of the week,
spoken of the hour at which she intended to leave her country
schoolhouse; and from this her friends had probably perceived
that by such timing she would run a risk of losing the
Saturday boat. She had missed it, and as a consequence sat here
on the shore as Mrs. Charles Stow.

This brought her to the present, and she turned from the
outline of St. Michael's Mount to look about for her husband's form. He was, as far as she could discover, no longer in
the sea. Then he was dressing. By moving a few steps she
could see where his clothes lay. But Charles was not beside
them.

Baptista looked back again at the water in bewilderment, as
if her senses were the victim of some sleight of hand. Not a
speck or spot resembling a man's head or face showed
anywhere. By this time she was alarmed, and her alarm
intensified when she perceived a little beyond the scene of her
husband's bathing a small area of water, the quality of whose
surface differed from that of the surrounding expanse as the
coarse vegetation of some foul patch in a mead differs from
the fine green of the remainder. Elsewhere it looked flexuous,
here it looked vermiculated and lumpy, and her marine
experiences suggested to her in a moment that two currents
met and caused a turmoil at this place.

She descended as hastily as her trembling limbs would allow.
The way down was terribly long, and before reaching the heap
of clothes it occurred to her that, after all, it would be best to
run first for help. Hastening along in a lateral direction she
proceeded inland till she met a man, and soon afterwards two
others. To them she exclaimed, 'I think a gentleman who was
bathing is in some danger. I cannot see him as I could. Will you
please run and help him, at once, if you will be so kind?'

She did not think of turning to show them the exact spot, indicating it vaguely by the direction of her hand, and still going on her way with the idea of gaining more assistance. When she deemed, in her faintness, that she had carried the alarm far enough, she faced about and dragged herself back again. Before reaching the now dreaded spot she met one of the men.

'We can see nothing at all, Miss,' he declared.

Having gained the beach, she found the tide in, and no sign of Charley's clothes. The other men whom she had besought to come had disappeared, it must have been in some other direction, for she had not met them going away. They, finding nothing, had probably thought her alarm a mere conjecture, and given up the quest.

Baptista sank down upon the stones near at hand. Where Charley had undressed was now sea. There could not be the least doubt that he was drowned, and his body sucked under the current; while his clothes, lying within high-water mark, had probably been carried away by the rising tide.

She remained in a stupor for some minutes, till a strange sensation succeeded the aforesaid perceptions, mystifying her intelligence, and leaving her physically almost inert. With his personal disappearance, the last three days of her life with him seemed to be swallowed up, also his image, in her mind's eye, waned curiously, receded far away, grew stranger and stranger, less and less real. Their meeting and marriage had been so sudden, unpremeditated, adventurous, that she could hardly believe that she had played her part in such a reckless drama. Of all the few hours of her life with Charles, the portion that most insisted in coming back to memory was their fortuitous encounter on the previous Saturday, and those bitter reprimands with which he had begun the attack, as it might be called, which had piqued her to an unexpected consummation.

A sort of cruelty, an imperiousness, even in his warmth, had characterized Charles Stow. As a lover he had ever been a bit of a tyrant: and it might pretty truly have been said that he had stung her into marriage with him at last. Still more alien from her life did these reflections operate to make him; and then they would be chased away by an interval of passionate weeping and mad regret. Finally, there returned upon the confused mind of the young wife the recollection that she was on her way homeward, and that the packet would sail in three-quarters of an hour.

Except the parasol in her hand, all she possessed was at the station awaiting her onward journey.

She looked in that direction; and, entering one of those undemonstrative phases so common with her, walked quietly on.

At first she made straight for the railway; but suddenly turning she went to a shop and wrote an anonymous line announcing his death by drowning to the only person she had ever heard Charles mention as a relative. Posting this stealthily, and with a fearful look around her, she seemed to acquire a terror of the late events, pursuing her way to the station as if followed by a spectre.

When she got to the office she asked for the luggage that she had left there on the Saturday as well as the trunk left on the morning just lapsed. All were put in the boat, and she herself followed. Quickly as these things had been done, the whole proceeding, nevertheless, had been almost automatic on Baptista's part, ere she had come to any definite conclusion on her course.

Just before the bell rang she heard a conversation on the pier, which removed the last shade of doubt from her mind, if any had existed, that she was Charles Stow's widow. The sentences were but fragmentary, but she could easily piece them out.

'A man drowned – swam out too far – was a stranger to the place – people in boat – saw him go down – couldn't get there in time.'

The news was little more definite than this as yet; though it may as well be stated once and for all that the statement was true. Charley, with the over-confidence of his nature, had ventured out too far for his strength, and succumbed in the absence of assistance, his lifeless body being at that moment suspended in the transparent mid-depths of the bay. His clothes, however, had merely been gently lifted by the rising tide, and floated into a nook hard by, where they lay out of sight of the passers-by till a day or two after.

IV

In ten minutes they were steaming out of the harbour for their voyage of four or five hours, at whose ending she would have to tell her strange story.

As Pen-zephyr and all its environing scenes disappeared behind Mousehole and St. Clement's Isle, Baptista's ephemeral, meteor-like husband impressed her yet more as a fantasy. She was still in such a trance-like state that she had been an hour on the little packet-boat before she became aware of the agitating fact that Mr. Heddegan was on board with her. Involuntarily she slipped from her left hand the symbol of her wifehood.

'Hee-hee! Well, the truth is, I wouldn't interrupt 'ee. "I reckon she don't see me, or won't see me," I said, "and what's the hurry? She'll see enough o' me soon!" I hope ye be well, mee deer?'

He was a hale, well-conditioned man of about five and fifty, of the complexion common to those whose lives are passed on the bluffs and beaches of an ocean isle. He extended the four quarters of his face in a genial smile, and his hand for a grasp of the same magnitude. She gave her own in surprised docility, and he continued.

'I couldn't help coming across to meet 'ee. What an unfortunate thing you missing the boat and not coming Saturday! They meant to have warned 'ee that the time was changed, but forgot it at the last moment. The truth is that I should have informed 'ee myself, but I was that busy finishing up a job last week, so as to have this week free, that I trusted to your father for attending to these little things. However, so plain and quiet as it is all to be, it really do not matter so much as it might otherwise have done, and I hope ye haven't been greatly put out. Now, if you'd sooner that I should not be seen talking to 'ee – if 'ee feel shy at all before strangers – just say. I'll leave 'ee to yourself till we get home.'

'Thank you much. I am indeed a little tired, Mr. Heddegan.'

He nodded urbane acquiescence, strolled away immediately, and minutely inspected the surface of the funnel, till some female passengers of Giant's Town tittered at what they must have thought a rebuff – for the approaching wedding was known to many on St. Maria's Island, though to nobody elsewhere. Baptista coloured at their satire, and called him back, and forced herself to commune with him in at least a mechanically friendly manner.

The opening event had been thus different from her expectation, and she had adumbrated no act to meet it. Taken aback she passively allowed circumstances to pilot her along; and so the voyage was made.

It was near dusk when they touched the pier of Giant's Town, where several friends and neighbours stood awaiting them. Her father had a lantern in his hand. Her mother, too, was there, reproachfully glad that the delay had at last ended so simply. Mrs. Trewthen and her daughter went together along the Giant's Walk, or promenade, to the house, rather in advance of her husband and Mr. Heddegan, who talked in loud tones which reached the women over their shoulders.

Some would have called Mrs. Trewthen a good mother; but though well meaning she was maladroit, and her intentions missed their mark. This might have been partly attributable to the slight deafness from which she suffered. Now, as usual, the chief utterances came from her lips.

'Ah, yes, I'm so glad, my child, that you've got over safe. It is all ready, and everything so well arranged, that nothing but misfortune could hinder you settling as, with God's grace, becomes 'ee. Close to your mother's door a'most, 'twill be a great blessing, I'm sure; and I was very glad to find from your letters that you'd held your word sacred. That's right – make your word your bond always. Mrs. Wace seems to be a sensible woman. I hope the Lord will do for her as he's doing for you no long time hence. And how did 'ee get over the terrible journey from Tor-upon-Sea to Pen-Zephyr? Once you'd done with the railway, of course, you seemed quite at home. Well, Baptista, conduct yourself seemly, and all will be well.'

Thus admonished, Baptista entered the house, her father and Mr. Heddegan immediately at her back. Her mother had been so didactic that she had felt herself absolutely unable to broach the subjects in the centre of her mind.

The familiar room, with the dark ceiling, the well-spread table, the old chairs, had never before spoken so eloquently of the times ere she knew or had heard of Charley Stow. She went upstairs to take off her things, her mother remaining below to complete the disposition of the supper, and attend to the preparation of tomorrow's meal, altogether composing such an array of pies, from pies of fish to pies of turnips, as was never heard of outside the Western Duchy. Baptista, once alone, sat down and did nothing; and was called before she had taken off her bonnet.

'I'm coming,' she cried, jumping up, and speedily disapparelling herself, brushed her hair with a few touches and went down.

Two or three of Mr. Heddegan's and her father's friends had dropped in, and expressed their sympathy for the delay she had been subjected to. The meal was a most merry one except to Baptista. She had desired privacy, and there was none; and to break the news was already a greater difficulty than it had been at first. Everything around her, animate and inanimate, great and small, insisted that she had come home to be married; and she could not get a chance to say nay.

One or two people sang songs, as overtures to the melody of the morrow, till at length bedtime came, and they all withdrew, her mother having retired a little earlier. When Baptista found herself again alone in her bedroom the case stood as before: she had come home with much to say, and she had said nothing.

It was now growing clear even to herself that Charles being dead, she had not determination sufficient within her to break tidings which, had he been alive, would have imperatively announced themselves. And thus with the stroke of midnight came the turning of the scale; her story should remain untold. It was not that upon the whole she thought it best not to attempt to tell it; but that she could not undertake so explosive a matter. To stop the wedding now would cause a convulsion in Giant's Town little short of volcanic. Weakened, tired, and terrified as she had been by the day's adventures, she could not make herself the author of such a catastrophe. But how refuse Heddegan without telling? It really seemed to her as if her marriage with Mr.

Heddegan were about to take place as if nothing had inter-
vened.

Morning came. The events of the previous days were cut
off from her present existence by scene and sentiment more
completely than ever. Charles Stow had grown to be a special
being of whom, owing to his character, she entertained rather
fearful than loving memory. Baptista could hear when she
awoke that her parents were already moving about downstairs. But she did not rise till her mother's rather rough voice
resounded up the staircase as it had done on the preceding
evening.

'Baptista! Come, time to be stirring! The man will be here,
by Heaven's blessing, in three-quarters of an hour. He has
looked in already for a minute or two – and says he's going to
the church to see if things be well forward.'

Baptista arose, looked out of the window, and took the
easy course. When she emerged from the regions above she
was arrayed in her new silk frock and best stockings, wearing
a linen jacket over the former for breakfasting, and her
common slippers over the latter, not to spoil the new ones on
the rough precincts of the dwelling.

It is unnecessary to dwell at any great length on this part of
the morning's proceedings. She revealed nothing; and married
Heddegan, as she had given her word to do, on that appointed
August day.

V

Mr. Heddegan forgave the coldness of his bride's manner
during and after the wedding ceremony, full well aware that
there had been considerable reluctance on her part to acquiesce
in this neighbourly arrangement, and, as a philosopher of long
standing, holding that whatever Baptista's attitude now, the
conditions would probably be much the same six months
hence as those which ruled among other married couples.

An absolutely unexpected shock was given to Baptista's
listless mind about an hour after the wedding service. They
had nearly finished the midday dinner when the now husband
said to her father, 'We think of starting about two. And the

breeze being so fair we shall bring up inside Pen-zephyr new pier about six at least.'

'What – are we going to Pen-zephyr?' said Baptista. 'I don't know anything of it.'

'Didn't you tell her?' asked her father of Heddegan.

It transpired that, owing to the delay in her arrival, this proposal too, among other things, had in the hurry not been mentioned to her, except some time ago as a general suggestion that they would go somewhere. Heddegan had imagined that any trip would be pleasant, and one to the mainland the pleasantest of all.

She looked so distressed at the announcement that her husband willingly offered to give it up, though he had not had a holiday off the island for a whole year. Then she pondered on the inconvenience of staying at Giant's Town, where all the inhabitants were bonded, by the circumstances of their situation, into a sort of family party, which permitted and encouraged on such occasions as these oral criticism that was apt to disturb the equanimity of newly married girls, and would especially worry Baptista in her strange situation. Hence, unexpectedly, she agreed not to disorganize her husband's plans for the wedding jaunt, and it was settled that, as originally intended, they should proceed in a neighbour's sailing boat to the metropolis of the district.

In this way they arrived at Pen-zephyr without difficulty or mishap. Bidding adieu to Jenkin and his man, who had sailed them over, they strolled arm in arm off the pier, Baptista silent, cold, and obedient. Heddegan had arranged to take her as far as Plymouth before their return, but to go no further than where they had landed that day. Their first business was to find an inn; and in this they had unexpected difficulty, since for some reason or other – possibly the fine weather – many of the nearest at hand were full of tourists and commercial travellers. He led her on till he reached a tavern which, though comparatively unpretending, stood in as attractive spot as any in the town; and this, somewhat to their surprise after their previous experience, they found apparently empty. The considerate old man, thinking that Baptista was educated to artistic notions, though he himself was deficient in them had decided that it was most desir-

able to have, on such an occasion as the present, an apartment with 'a good view' (the expression being one he had
often heard in use among tourists); and he therefore asked
for a favourite room on the first floor, from which a
bow-window protruded, for the express purpose of affording such an outlook.

The landlady, after some hesitation, said she was sorry that
particular apartment was engaged; the next one, however, or
any other in the house, was unoccupied.

'The gentlemen who has the best one will give it up
tomorrow, and then you can change into it,' she added, as
Mr. Heddegan hesitated about taking the adjoining and less
commanding one.

'We shall be gone tomorrow, and shan't want it,' he said.

Wishing not to lose customers, the landlady earnestly
continued that since he was bent on having the best room,
perhaps the other gentleman would not object to move at
once into the one they despised, since, though nothing could
be seen from the window, the room was equally large.

'Well, if he doesn't care for a view,' said Mr. Heddegan,
with the air of a highly artistic man who did.

'O no – I am sure he doesn't,' she said. 'I can promise that
you shall have the room you want. If you would not object to
go for a walk for half an hour, I could have it ready, and your
things in it, and a nice tea laid in the bow-window by the time
you come back?'

This proposal was deemed satisfactory by the fussy old
tradesman, and they went out. Baptista nervously conducted
him in an opposite direction to her walk of the former day in
other company, showing on her wan face, had he observed it,
how much she was beginning to regret her sacrificial step for
mending matters that morning.

She took advantage of a moment when her husband's back
was turned to inquire casually in a shop if anything had been
heard of the gentleman who was sucked down in the eddy
while bathing.

The shopman said, 'Yes, his body has been washed ashore'
and had just handed Baptista a newspaper on which she
discerned the heading, 'A Schoolmaster drowned while bathing,' when her husband turned to join her. She might have

pursued the subject without raising suspicion; but it was more than flesh and blood could do, and completing a small purchase almost ran out of the shop.

'What is your terrible hurry, mee dear?' said Heddegan, hastening after.

'I don't know – I don't want to stay in shops,' she gasped.

'And we won't.' he said. 'They are suffocating this weather. Let's go back and have some tay!'

They found the much desired apartment awaiting their entry. It was a sort of combination bed and sitting-room, and the table was prettily spread with high tea in the bow-window, a bunch of flowers in the midst, and a best-parlour chair on each side. Here they shared the meal by the ruddy light of the vanishing sun. But though the view had been engaged, regardless of expense, exclusively for Baptista's pleasure, she did not direct any keen attention out of the window. Her gaze as often fell on the floor and walls of the room as elsewhere, and on the table as much as on either, beholding nothing at all.

But there was a change. Opposite her seat was the door, upon which her eyes presently became riveted like those of a little bird upon a snake. For, on a peg at the back of the door, there hung a hat; such a hat – surely, from its peculiar make, the actual hat – that had been worn by Charles. Conviction grew to certainty when she saw a railway ticket sticking up from the band. Charles had put the ticket there – she had noticed the act.

Her teeth almost chattered; she murmured something incoherent. Her husband jumped up and said, 'You are not well! What is it? What shall I get 'ee?'

'Smelling salts!' she said, quickly and desperately; 'at the chemist's shop you were in just now.'

He jumped up like the anxious old man that he was, caught up his own hat from a back table, and without observing the other hastened out and downstairs.

Left alone she gazed and gazed at the back of the door, then spasmodically rang the bell. An honest looking country maid-servant appeared in response.

'A hat!' murmured Baptista, pointing with her finger. 'It does not belong to us.'

'O yes, I'll take it away,' said the young woman with some hurry. 'It belongs to the other gentleman.'

She spoke with a certain awkwardness, and took the hat out of the room. Baptista had recovered her outward composure. 'The other gentleman?' she said. 'Where is the other gentleman?'

'He's in the next room, ma'am. He removed out of this to oblige 'ee.'

'How can you say so? I should hear him if he were there,' said Baptista, sufficiently recovered to argue down an apparent untruth.

'He's there,' said the girl, hardily.

'Then it is strange that he makes no noise,' said Mrs. Heddegan, convicting the girl of falsity by a look.

'He makes no noise; but it is not strange,' said the servant.

All at once a dread took possession of the bride's heart, like a cold hand laid thereon; for it flashed upon her that there was a possibility of reconciling the girl's statement with her own knowledge of facts.

'Why does he make no noise?' she weakly said.

The waiting-maid was silent, and looked at her questioner. 'If I tell you, ma'am you won't tell missis?' she whispered.

Baptista promised.

'Because he's a-lying dead!' said the girl. 'He's the schoolmaster that was drownded yesterday.'

'O!' said the bride, covering her eyes. 'Then he was in this room till just now?'

'Yes,' said the maid, thinking the young lady's agitation natural enough. 'And I told missis that I thought she oughtn't to have done it, because I don't hold it right to keep visitors so much in the dark where death's concerned; but she said the gentleman didn't die of anything infectious; she was a poor, honest, innkeeper's wife, she says, who had to get her living by making hay while the sun sheened. And owing to the drownded gentleman being brought here, she said, it kept so many people away that we were empty, though all the other houses were full. So when your good man set his mind upon the room, and she would have lost good paying folk if he'd not had it, it wasn't to be supposed, she said, that she'd let anything stand in the way. Ye won't say that I've told ye, please, m'm? All the linen has been changed, and as the inquest won't be till tomorrow, after you are gone, she thought you wouldn't know a word of it, being strangers here.'

The returning footsteps of her husband broke off further narration. Baptista waved her hand, for she could not speak. The waiting-maid quickly withdrew, and Mr. Heddegan entered with the smelling salts and other nostrums.

'Any better?' he questioned.

'I don't like the hotel,' she exclaimed, almost simultaneously. 'I can't bear it – it doesn't suit me!'

'Is that all that's the matter?' he returned pettishly (this being the first time of his showing such a mood). 'Upon my heart and life such trifling is trying to any man's temper, Baptista! Sending me about from here to yond, and then when I come back saying 'ee don't like the place that I have sunk so much money and words to get for 'ee. 'Od dang it all, 'tis enough to – But I won't say any more at present, mee deer, though it is just too much to expect to turn out of the house now. We shan't get another quiet place at this time of the evening – every other inn in the town is bustling with rackety folk of one sort and t'other, while here 'tis as quiet as the grave – the country, I would say. So bide still, d'ye hear, and tomorrow we shall be out of the town altogether – as early as you like.'

The obstinacy of age had, in short, overmastered its complaisance, and the young woman said no more. The simple course of telling him that in the adjoining room lay a corpse which had lately occupied their own might, it would have seemed, have been an effectual one without further disclosure, but to allude to *that* subject, however it was disguised, was more than Heddegan's young wife had strength for. Horror broke her down. In the contingency one thing only presented itself to her paralyzed regard – that here she was doomed to abide, in a hideous contiguity to the dead husband and the living, and her conjecture did, in fact, bear itself out. That night she lay between the two men she had married – Heddegan on the one hand, and on the other through the partition against which the bed stood, Charles Stow.

VI

Kindly time had withdrawn the foregoing event three days from the present of Baptista Heddegan. It was ten o'clock in the morning; she had been ill, not in an ordinary or definite sense, but in a state of cold stupefaction, from which it was difficult to arouse her so much as to say a few sentences. When questioned she had replied that she was pretty well.

Their trip, as such, had been something of a failure. They had gone as far as Falmouth, but here he had given way to her entreaties to return home. This they could not very well do without repassing through Pen-zephyr, at which place they had now again arrived.

In the train she had seen a weekly local paper, and read there a paragraph detailing the inquest on Charles. It was added that the funeral was to take place at his native town of Redrutin on Friday.

After reading this she had shown no reluctance to enter the fatal neighbourhood of the tragedy, only stipulating that they should take their rest at a different lodging from the first; and now comparatively braced up and calm – indeed a cooler creature altogether than when last in the town, she said to David that she wanted to walk out for a while, as they had plenty of time on their hands.

'To a shop as usual, I suppose, mee deer?'

'Partly for shopping,' she said. 'And it will be best for you, dear, to stay in after trotting about so much, and have a good rest while I am gone.'

He assented; and Baptista sallied forth. As she had stated, her first visit was made to a shop, a draper's. Without the exercise of much choice she purchased a black bonnet and veil, also a black stuff gown; a black mantle she already wore. These articles were made up into a parcel which, in spite of the saleswoman's offers, her customer said she would take with her. Bearing it on her arm she turned to the railway, and at the station got a ticket for Redrutin.

Thus it appeared that, on her recovery from the paralyzed mood of the former day, while she had resolved not to blast utterly the happiness of her present husband by revealing the history of the departed one, she had also determined to indulge a certain odd, inconsequent, feminine sentiment of decency, to the small extent to which it could do no harm to any person. At Redrutin she emerged from the railway carriage in the black attire purchased at the shop, having during the transit made the change in the empty compartment she had chosen. The other clothes were now in the bandbox and parcel. Leaving these at the cloak-room she proceeded onward, and after a wary survey reached the side of a hill whence a view of the burial ground could be obtained.

It was now a little before two o'clock. While Baptista waited a funeral procession ascended the road. Baptista hastened across, and by the time the procession entered the cemetry gates she had unobtrusively joined it.

In addition to the schoolmaster's own relatives (not a few), the paragraph in the newspapers of his death by drowning had drawn together many neighbours, acquaintances, and onlookers. Among them she passed unnoticed, and with a quiet step pursued the winding path to the chapel, and afterwards thence to the grave. When all was over, and the relatives and idlers had withdrawn, she stepped to the edge of the chasm. From beneath her mantle she drew a little bunch of forget-me-nots, and dropped them in upon the coffin. In a few minutes she also turned and went away from the cemetry. By five o'clock she was again in Pen-zephyr.

'You have been a mortal long time!' said her husband, crossly. 'I allowed you an hour at most, mee deer.'

'It occupied me longer,' said she.

'Well – I reckon it is wasting words to complain. Hang it, ye look so tired and wisht that I can't find heart to say what I would!'

'I am – weary and wisht, David; I am. We can get home tomorrow for certain, I hope?'

'We can. And please God we will!' said Mr. Heddegan heartily, as if he too were weary of his brief honeymoon. 'I must be into business again on Monday morning at latest.'

They left by the next morning steamer, and in the afternoon took up their residence in their own house at Giant's Town.

The hour that she reached the island it was as if a material weight had been removed from Baptista's shoulders. Her husband attributed the change to the influence of local breezes after the hot-house atmosphere of the mainland. However that might be, settled here, a few doors from her mother's dwelling, she recovered in no very long time much of her customary bearing, which was never very demonstrative. She accepted her position calmly, and faintly smiled when her neighbours learned to call her Mrs. Heddegan, and said she seemed likely to become the leader of fashion in Giant's Town.

Her husband was a man who had made considerably more money by trade than her father had done: and perhaps the greater profusion of surroundings at her command than she had heretofore been mistress of, was not without an effect upon her. One week, two weeks, three weeks passed; and, being pre-eminently a young woman who allowed things to drift, she did nothing whatever either to disclose or conceal traces of her first marriage; or to learn if there existed possibilities – which there undoubtedly did – by which that hasty contract might become revealed to those about her at any unexpected moment.

While yet within the first month of her marriage, and on an evening just before sunset, Baptista was standing within her garden adjoining the house, when she saw passing along the road a personage clad in a greasy black coat and battered tall hat, which common enough in the slums of a city, had an odd appearance in St. Maria's. The tramp, as he seemed to be, marked her at once – bonnetless and unwrapped as she was her features were plainly recognizable – and with an air of friendly surprise came and leant over the wall.

'What! don't you know me?' said he.

She had some dim recollection of his face, but said that she was not acquainted with him.

'Why, your witness to be sure, ma'am. Don't you mind the man that was mending the church-window when you and your husband walked up to be made one; and the clerk called me down from the ladder, and I came and did my part by writing my name and occupation?'

Baptista glanced quickly around; her husband was out of earshot. That would have been of less importance but for the fact that the wedding witnessed by this personage had not been the wedding with Mr. Heddegan, but the one of the day previous.

'I've had a misfortune since then, that's pulled me under,' continued her friend. 'But don't let me damp yer wedded joy by naming the particulars. Yes, I've seen changes since; though 'tis but a short time ago – let me see, only a month next week, I think; for 'twere the first or second day in August.'

'Yes – that's when it was,' said another man, a sailor, who had come up with a pipe in his mouth, and felt it necessary to join in (Baptista having receded to escape further speech). 'For that was the first time I set foot in Giant's Town; and her husband took her to him the same day.'

A dialogue then proceeded between the two men outside the wall, which Baptista could not help hearing.

'Ay, I signed the book that made her one flesh,' repeated the decayed glazier. 'Where's her goodman?'

'About the premises somewhere; but you don't see 'em together much,' replied the sailor in an undertone. 'You see, he's older than she.'

'Older? I should never have thought it from my own observation,' said the glazier. 'He was a remarkably handsome man.'

'Handsome? Well, there he is – we can see for ourselves.'

David Heddegan had, indeed, just shown himself at the upper end of the garden; and the glazier, looking in bewilderment from the husband to the wife, saw the latter turn pale.

Now that decayed glazier was a far-seeing and cunning man – too far-seeing and cunning to allow himself to thrive by simple and straightforward means – and he held his peace, till he could read more plainly the meaning of this riddle, merely adding carelessly, 'Well – marriage do alter a man, 'tis true. I should never ha' knowed him!'

He then stared oddly at the disconcerted Baptista, and moving on to where he could again address her, asked her to do him a good turn, since he once had done the same for her. Understanding that he meant money, she handed him some, at which he thanked her, and instantly went away.

VII

She had escaped exposure on this occasion; but the incident had been an awkward one, and should have suggested to Baptista that sooner or later the secret must leak out. As it was, she suspected that at any rate she had not heard the last of the glazier.

In a day or two, when her husband had gone to the old town on the other side of the island, there came a gentle tap at the door, and the worthy witness of her first marriage made his appearance a second time.

'It took me hours to get to the bottom of the mystery – hours!' he said with a gaze of deep confederacy which offended her pride very deeply. 'But thanks to a good intellect I've done it. Now, ma'am I'm not a man to tell tales, even when a tale would be so good as this. But I'm going back to the mainland again, and a little assistance would be as rain on thirsty ground.'

'I helped you two days ago,' began Baptista.

'Yes – but what was that, my good lady? Not enough to pay my passage to Pen-zephyr. I came over on your account, for I thought there was a mystery somewhere. Now I must go back on my own. Mind this – 'twould be very awkward for you if your old man were to know. He's a queer temper, though he may be fond.'

She knew as well as her visitor how awkward it would be; and the hush-money she paid was heavy that day. She had, however, the satisfaction of watching the man to the steamer, and seeing him diminish out of sight. But Baptista perceived that the system into which she had been led of purchasing silence thus was one fatal to her peace of mind, particularly if it had to be continued.

Hearing no more from the glazier she hoped the difficulty was past. But another week only had gone by, when, as she was pacing the Giant's Walk (the name given to the promenade), she met the same personage in the company of a fat woman carrying a bundle.

'This is the lady, my dear,' he said to his companion. 'This ma'am, is my wife. We've come to settle in the town for a time, if so be we can find room.'

'That you won't do, said she. 'Nobody can live here who is not privileged.'

'I am privileged,' said the glazier, 'by my trade.'

Baptista went on, but in the afternoon she received a visit from the man's wife. This honest woman began to depict, in forcible colours, the necessity for keeping up the concealment.

'I will intercede with my husband, ma'am' she said. 'He's a true man if rightly managed; and I'll beg him to consider your position. 'Tis a very nice house you've got here,' she added, glancing round, 'and well worth a little sacrifice to keep it.'

The unlucky Baptista staved off the danger on this third occasion as she had done on the previous two. But she formed a resolve that, if the attack were once more to be repeated she would face a revelation – worse though that must now be than before she had attempted to purchase silence by bribes. Her tormentors, never believing her capable of acting upon such an intention, came again; but she shut the door in their faces. They retreated, muttering something; but she went to the back of the house, where David Heddegan was.

She looked at him, unconscious of all. The case was serious; she knew that well; and all the more serious in that she liked him better now than she had done at first. Yet, as she herself began to see, the secret was one that was sure to disclose itself. Her name and Charles's stood indelibly written in the registers; and though a month only had passed as yet it was a wonder that his clandestine union with her had not already been discovered by his friends. Thus spurring herself to the inevitable, she spoke to Heddegan.

'David, come indoors. I have something to tell you.'

He hardly regarded her at first. She had discerned that during the last week or two he had seemed preoccupied, as if some private business harassed him. She repeated her request. He replied with a sigh, 'Yes, certainly, mee deer.'

When they had reached the sitting-room and shut the door she repeated, faintly, 'David, I have something to tell you – a sort of tragedy I have concealed. You will hate me for having so far deceived you; but perhaps my telling you

voluntarily will make you think a little better of me than you
would do otherwise.'

'Tragedy?' he said, awakening to interest. 'Much you can
know about tragedies, mee deer, that have been in the world
so short a time!'

She saw that he suspected nothing, and it made her task
the harder. But on she went steadily. 'It is about something
that happened before we were married,' she said.

'Indeed!'

'Not a very long time before – a short time. And it is
about a lover,' she faltered.

'I don't much mind that,' he said mildly. 'In truth, I was in
hopes 'twas more.'

'In hopes!'

'Well, yes.'

This screwed her up to the necessary effort. 'I met my old
sweetheart. He scorned me, chid me, dared me, and I went
and married him. We were coming straight here to tell you
all what we had done; but he was drowned; and I thought I
would say nothing about him: and I married you, David, for
the sake of peace and quietness. I've tried to keep it from
you, but have found I cannot. There – that's the substance of
it, and you can never, never forgive me, I am sure!'

She spoke desperately. But the old man, instead of turning
black or blue, or slaying her in his indignation, jumped up
from his chair, and began to caper around the room in quite
an ecstatic emotion.

'O, happy thing! How well it falls out!' he exclaimed,
snapping his fingers over his head. 'Ha-ha – the knot is cut –
I see a way out of my trouble – ha-ha!'

She looked at him without uttering a sound, till as he still
continued smiling joyfully, she said, 'O – what do you
mean! Is it done to torment me?'

'No – no! O, mee deer, your story helps me out of the
most heart-aching quandary a poor man ever found himself
in! You see, it is this – *I've* got a tragedy, too; and unless you
had had one to tell, I could never have seen my way to tell
mine!'

'What is your – what is it?' she asked, with altogether a
new view of things.

'Well – it is a bouncer; mine is a bouncer!' said he, looking
on the ground and wiping his eyes.

'Not worse than mine?'

'Well – that depends upon how you look at it. Yours had to
do with the past alone; and I don't mind it. You see, we've
been married a month, and it don't jar upon me as it would if
we'd only been married a day or two. Now mine refers to
past, present, and future; so that –'

'Past, present, and future!' she murmured. 'It never occurred to me that *you* had a tragedy, too.'

'But I have!' he said, shaking his head. 'In fact, four.'

'Then tell 'em!' cried the young woman.

'I will – I will. But be considerate, I beg 'ee, mee deer. Well
– I wasn't a bachelor when I married 'ee, any more than you
were a spinster. Just as you was a widow-woman, I was a
widow-man.'

'Ah!' said she, with some surprise. 'But is that all? – then we
are nicely balanced,' she added, relieved.

'No – it is not all. There's the point. I am not only a
widower.'

'O, David!'

'I am a widower with four tragedies – that is to say, four
strapping girls – the eldest taller than you. Don't 'ee look so
struck – dumb-like! It fell out in this way. I knew the poor
woman, their mother, in Pen-zephyr for some years; and – to
cut a long story short – I privately married her at last, just
before she died. I kept the matter secret, but it is getting
known among the people here by degrees. I've long felt for
the children – that it is my duty to have them here, and do
something for them. I have not had courage to break it to 'ee,
but I've seen lately that it would soon come to your ears, and
that hev worried me.'

'Are they educated?' said the ex-schoolmistress.

'No. I am sorry to say they have been much neglected; in
truth, they can hardly read. And so I thought that by
marrying a young schoolmistress I should get some one in the
house who could teach 'em, and bring 'em into genteel
condition, all for nothing. You see, they are growed up too
tall to be sent to school.'

'O, mercy!' she almost moaned. 'Four great girls to teach

the rudiments to, and have always in the house with me
spelling over their books; and I hate teaching, it kills me. I am
bitterly punished – I am, I am!'

'You'll get used to 'em, mee deer, and the balance of secrets
– mine against yours – will comfort your heart with a sense of
justice. I could send for 'em this week very well – and I will! In
faith, I could send this very day. Baptista, you have relieved
me of all my difficulty.'

Thus the interview ended, so far as this matter was concerned. Baptista was too stupefied to say more, and when she
went away to her room she wept from very mortification at
Mr. Heddegan's duplicity. Education, the one thing she
abhorred; the shame of it to delude a young wife so!

The next meal came round. As they sat, Baptista would not
suffer her eyes to turn towards him. He did not attempt to
intrude upon her reserve, but every now and then looked
under the table and chuckled with satisfaction at the aspect of
affairs. 'How very well matched we be!' he said, comfortably.

Next day, when the steamer came in, Baptista saw her
husband rush down to meet it; and soon after there appeared
at her door four tall, hipless, shoulderless girls, dwindling in
height and size from the eldest to the youngest, like a row of
Pan pipes; at the head of them standing Heddegan. He smiled
pleasantly through the grey fringe of his whiskers and beard,
and turning to the girls said, 'Now come forrard, and shake
hands properly with your stepmother.'

Thus she made their acquaintance, and he went out, leaving
them together. On examination the poor girls turned out to be
not only plain-looking, which she could have forgiven, but to
have such a lamentably meagre intellectual equipment as to be
hopelessly inadequate as companions. Even the eldest, almost
her own age, could only read with difficulty words of two
syllables; and taste in dress was beyond their comprehension. In
the long vista of future years she saw nothing but dreary
drudgery at her detested old trade without prospect of reward.

She went about quite despairing during the next few days –
an unpromising, unfortunate mood for a woman who had not
been married six weeks. From her parents she concealed
everything. They had been amongst the few acquaintances of
Heddegan who knew nothing of his secret, and were indig-

nant enough when they saw such a ready-made household foisted upon their only child. But she would not support them in their remonstrances.

'No, you don't yet know all,' she said.

Thus Baptista had sense enough to see the retributive fairness of this issue. For some time, whenever conversation arose between her and Heddegan, which was not often, she always said, 'I am miserable, and you know it. Yet I don't wish things to be otherwise.'

But one day when he asked, 'How do you like 'em now? her answer was unexpected. 'Much better than I did,' she said, quietly. 'I may like them very much some day.'

This was the beginning of a serener season for the chastened spirit of Baptista Heddegan. She had, in truth, discovered, underneath the crust of uncouthness and meagre articulation which was due to their Troglodytean existence, that her unwelcomed daughters had natures that were unselfish almost to sublimity. The harsh discipline accorded to their young lives before their mother's wrong had been righted, had operated less to crush them than to lift them above all personal ambition. They considered the world and its contents in a purely objective way, and their own lot seemed only to affect them as that of certain human beings among the rest, whose troubles they knew rather than suffered.

This was such an entirely new way of regarding life to a woman of Baptista's nature, that her attention, from being first arrested by it, became deeply interested. By imperceptible pulses her heart expanded in sympathy with theirs. The sentences of her tragi-comedy, her life, confused till now, became clearer daily. That in humanity, as exemplified by these girls, there was nothing to dislike, but infinitely much to pity, she learnt with the lapse of each week in their company. She grew to like the girls of unpromising exterior, and from liking she got to love them; till they formed an unexpected point of junction between her own and her husband's interests, generating a sterling friendship at least, between a pair in whose existence there had threatened to be neither friendship nor love.

October, 1885

THE ROMANTIC ADVENTURES OF A MILKMAID

I

It was half-past four o'clock (by the testimony of the land-surveyor, my authority for the particulars of this story, a gentleman with the faintest curve of humour on his lips); it was half-past four o'clock on a May morning in the eighteen forties. A dense white fog hung over the Valley of the Exe, ending against the hills on either side.

But though nothing in the vale could be seen from higher ground, notes of differing kinds gave pretty clear indications that bustling life was going on there. This audible presence and visual absence of an active scene had a peculiar effect above the fog level. Nature had laid a white hand over the creatures ensconced within the vale, as a hand might be laid over a nest of chirping birds.

The noises that ascended through the pallid coverlid were perturbed lowings, mingled with human voices in sharps and flats, and the bark of a dog. These, followed by the slamming of a gate, explained as well as eyesight could have done, to any inhabitant of the district, that Dairyman Tucker's under-milker was driving the cows from the meads into the stalls. When a rougher accent joined in the vociferations of man and beast, it would have been realized that the dairy-farmer himself had come out to meet the cows, pail in hand, and white pinafore on; and when, moreover, some women's voices joined in the chorus, that the cows were stalled and proceedings about to commence.

A hush followed, the atmosphere being so stagnant that the milk could be heard buzzing into the pails, together with occasional words of the milkmaids and men.

'Don't ye bide about long upon the road, Margery. You can be back again by skimming-time.'

The rough voice of Dairyman Tucker was the vehicle of

this remark. The barton-gate slammed again, and in two or three minutes a something became visible, rising out of the fog in that quarter.

The shape revealed itself as that of a woman having a young and agile gait. The colours and other details of her dress were then disclosed – a bright pink cotton frock (because winter was over); a small woollen shawl of shepherd's plaid (because summer was not come); a white handkerchief tied over her head-gear, because it was so foggy, so damp, and so early; and a straw bonnet and ribbons peeping from under the handker-chief, because it was likely to be a sunny May day.

Her face was of the hereditary type among families down in these parts: sweet in expression, perfect in hue, and somewhat irregular in feature. Her eyes were of a liquid brown. On her arm she carried a withy basket, in which lay several butter-rolls in a nest of wet cabbage-leaves. She was the 'Margery' who had been told not to 'bide about long upon the road.'

She went on her way across the fields, sometimes above the fog, sometimes below it, not much perplexed by its presence except when the track was so indefinite that it ceased to be a guide to the next stile. The dampness was such that innumer-able earthworms lay in couples across the path till, startled even by her light tread, they withdrew suddenly into their holes. She kept clear of all trees. Why was that? There was no danger of lightning on such a morning as this. But though the roads were dry the fog had gathered in the boughs, causing them to set up such a dripping as would go clean through the protecting handkerchief like bullets, and spoil the ribbons beneath. The beech and ash were particularly shunned, for they dripped more maliciously than any. It was an instance of woman's keen appreciativeness of nature's moods and pecu-liarities: a man crossing those fields might hardly have per-ceived that the trees dripped at all.

In less than an hour she had traversed a distance of four miles, and arrived at a latticed cottage in a secluded spot. An elderly woman, scarce awake, answered her knocking. Margery delivered up the butter, and said, 'How is granny this morning? I can't stay to go up to her, but tell her I have returned what we owed her.'

Her grandmother was no worse than usual: and receiving

back the empty basket the girl proceeded to carry out some intention which had not been included in her orders. Instead of returning to the light labours of skimming-time, she hastened on, her direction being towards a little neighbouring town. Before, however, Margery had proceeded far, she met the postman, laden to the neck with letter-bags, of which he had not yet deposited one.

'Are the shops open yet, Samuel?' she said.

'O no,' replied that stooping pedestrian, not waiting to stand upright. 'They won't be open yet this hour, except the saddler and ironmonger and little tacker-haired machine-man for the farm folk. They downs their shutters at half-past six, then the baker's at half-past seven, then the draper's at eight.'

'O, the draper's at eight.' It was plain that Margery had wanted the draper's.

The postman turned up a side-path, and the young girl, as though deciding within herself that if she could not go shopping at once she might as well get back for the skimming, retraced her steps.

The public road home from this point was easy but devious. By far the nearest way was by getting over a fence, and crossing the private grounds of a picturesque old country-house, whose chimneys were just visible through the trees. As the house had been shut up for many months, the girl decided to take the straight cut. She pushed her way through the laurel bushes, sheltering her bonnet with the shawl as an additional safeguard, scrambled over an inner boundary, went along through more shrubberies, and stood ready to emerge upon the open lawn. Before doing so she looked around in the wary manner of a poacher. It was not the first time that she had broken fence in her life; but somehow, and all of a sudden, she had felt herself too near womanhood to indulge in such practices with freedom. However, she moved forth, and the house-front stared her in the face, at this higher level unobscured by fog.

It was a building of the medium size, and unpretending, the façade being of stone; and of the Italian elevation made familiar by Inigo Jones and his school. There was a doorway to the lawn, standing at the head of a flight of steps. The shutters of the house were closed, and the blinds of the bedrooms drawn down. Her perception of the fact that no crusty caretaker could see her from the windows led her at once to slacken her pace, and stroll through the flower-beds coolly. A house unblinded is a possible spy, and must be treated accordingly; a house with the shutters together is an insensate heap of stone and mortar, to be faced with indifference.

On the other side of the house the greensward rose to an eminence, whereon stood one of those curious summer shelters sometimes erected on exposed points of view, called an all-the-year-round. In the present case it consisted of four walls radiating from a centre like the arms of a turnstile, with seats in each angle, so that whencesoever the wind came, it was always possible to find a screened corner from which to observe the landscape.

The milkmaid's trackless course led her up the hill and past this erection. At ease as to being watched and scolded as an intruder, her mind flew to other matters; till, at the moment when she was not a yard from the shelter, she heard a foot or feet scraping on the gravel behind it. Some one was in the all-the-year-round, apparently occupying the seat on the other side; as was proved when, on turning, she saw an elbow, a man's elbow, projecting over the edge.

Now the young woman did not much like the idea of going down the hill under the eyes of this person, which she would have to do if she went on, for as an intruder she was liable to be called back and questioned upon her businss there. Accordingly she crept softly up and sat in the seat behind, intending to remain there until her companion should leave.

This he by no means seemed in a hurry to do. What could possibly have brought him there, what could detain him there, at six o'clock on a morning of mist when there was nothing to be seen or enjoyed of the vale beneath, puzzled her not a little. But he remained quite still, and Margery grew impatient. She discerned the track of his feet in the dewy grass, forming a line from the house steps, which announced that he was an inhabitant and not a chance passer-by. At last she peeped round.

II

A fine-framed dark-mustachioed gentleman, in dressing-gown and slippers, was sitting there in the damp without a hat on. With one hand he was tightly grasping his forehead, the other hung over his knee. The attitude bespoke with sufficient clearness a mental condition of anguish. He was quite a different being from any of the men to whom her eyes were accustomed. She had never seen mustachios before, for they were not worn by civilians in Lower Wessex at this date. His hands and his face were white – to her view deadly white – and he heeded nothing outside his own existence. There he remained as motionless as the bushes around him; indeed, he scarcely seemed to breathe.

Having imprudently advanced thus far, Margery's wish was to get back again in the same unseen manner; but in moving her foot for the purpose it grated on the gravel. He started up with an air of bewilderment, and slipped something into the pocket of his dressing-gown. She was almost certain that it was a pistol. The pair stood looking blankly at each other.

'My Gott, who are you?' he asked sternly, and with not altogether an English articulation. 'What do you do here?'

Margery had already begun to be frightened at her boldness in invading the lawn and pleasure-seat. The house had a master, and she had not known of it. 'My name is Margaret Tucker, sir,' she said meekly. 'My father is Dairyman Tucker. We live at Silverthorn Dairy-house.'

'What were you doing here at this hour of the morning?'

She told him, even to the fact that she had climbed over the fence.

'And what made you peep round at me?'

'I saw your elbow, sir; and I wondered what you were doing?'

'And what was I doing?'

'Nothing. You had one hand on your forehead and the other on your knee. I do hope you are not ill, sir, or in deep trouble?' Margery had sufficient tact to say nothing about the pistol.

'What difference would it make to you if I were ill or in trouble? You don't know me.'

She returned no answer, feeling that she might have taken a liberty in expressing sympathy. But, looking furtively up at him, she discerned to her surprise that he seemed affected by her humane wish, simply as it had been expressed. She had scarcely conceived that such a tall dark man could know what gentle feelings were.

'Well, I am much obliged to you for caring how I am,' said he with a faint smile and an affected lightness of manner which, even to her, only rendered more apparent the gloom beneath. 'I have not slept this past night. I suffer from sleeplessness. Probably you do not.'

Margery laughed a little, and he glanced with interest at the comely picture she presented; her fresh face, brown hair, candid eyes, unpractised manner, country dress, pink hands, empty wicker-basket, and the handkerchief over her bonnet.

'Well,' he said, after his scrutiny, 'I need hardly have asked such a question of one who is Nature's own image. . . . Ah, but my good little friend,' he added, recurring to his bitter tone and sitting wearily down, 'you don't know what great clouds can hang over some people's lives, and what cowards some men are in face of them. To escape themselves they travel, take picturesque houses, and engage in country sports. But here it is so dreary, and the fog was horrible this morning!'

'Why, this is only the pride of the morning!' said Margery. 'By-and-by it will be a beautiful day.'

She was going on her way forthwith; but he detained her – detained her with words, talking on every innocent little subject he could think of. He had an object in keeping her there more serious than his words would imply. It was as if he feared to be left alone.

While they still stood, the misty figure of the postman, whom Margery had left a quarter of an hour earlier to follow his sinuous course, crossed the grounds below them on his way to the house. Signifying to Margery by a wave of his hand that she was to step back out of sight, in the hinder angle of the shelter, the gentleman beckoned to the postman to bring the bag to where he stood. The man did so, and again resumed his journey.

The stranger unlocked the bag and threw it on the seat, having taken one letter from within. This he read attentively, and his countenance changed.

The change was almost phantasmagorial, as if the sun had burst through the fog upon that face: it became clear, bright, almost radiant. Yet it was but a change that may take place in the commonest human being, provided his countenance be not too wooden, or his artifice have not grown to second nature. He turned to Margery, who was again edging off, and, seizing her hand, appeared as though he were about to embrace her. Checking his impulse, he said, 'My guardian child – my good friend – you have saved me!'

'What from?' she ventured to ask.

'That you may never know.'

She thought of the weapon, and guessed that the letter he had just received had effected this change in his mood, but made no observation till he went on to say, 'What did you tell me was your name, dear girl?'

She repeated her name.

'Margaret Tucker.' He stooped, and pressed her hand. 'Sit down for a moment – one moment,' he said, pointing to the end of the seat, and taking the extremest further end for himself, not to discompose her. She sat down.

'It is to ask a question,' he went on, 'and there must be confidence between us. You have saved me from an act of madness! What can I do for you?'

'Nothing, sir.'

'Nothing?'

'Father is very well off, and we don't want anything.'

'But there must be some service I can render, some kindness, some votive offering which I could make, and so imprint on your memory as long as you live that I am not an ungrateful man?'

'Why should you be grateful to me, sir?'

He shook his head. 'Some things are best left unspoken. Now think. What would you like to have best in the world?'

Margery made a pretence of reflecting – then fell to reflecting seriously; but the negative was ultimately as undisturbed as ever: she could not decide on anything she would like best in the world; it was too difficult, too sudden.

'Very well – don't hurry yourself. Think it over all day. I ride this afternoon. You live – where?'

'Silverthorn Dairy-house.'

'I will ride that way homeward this evening. Do you consider by eight o'clock what little article, what little treat you would most like of any.'

'I will, sir,' said Margery, now warming up to the idea. 'Where shall I meet you? Or will you call at the house, sir?'

'Ah – no. I should not wish the circumstances known out of which our acquaintance rose. It would be more proper – but no.'

Margery, too, seemed rather anxious that he should not call. 'I could come out, sir,' she said. 'My father is odd-tempered, and perhaps –'

It was agreed that she should look over a stile at the top of her father's garden, and that he should ride along a bridle-path outside, to receive her answer. 'Margery,' said the gentleman in conclusion, 'now that you have discovered me under ghastly conditions, are you going to reveal them, and make me an object for the gossip of the curious?'

'No, no, sir!' she replied earnestly. 'Why should I do that?'

'You will never tell?'

'Never, never will I tell what has happened here this morning.'

'Neither to your father, nor to your friends, nor to any one?'

'To no one at all', she said.

'It is sufficient,' he answered. 'You mean what you say, my dear maiden. Now you want to leave me. Good-bye!'

She descended the hill, walking with some awkwardness; for she felt the stranger's eyes were upon her till the fog had enveloped her from his gaze. She took no notice now of the dripping from the trees; she was lost in thought on other things. Had she saved this handsome, melancholy, sleepless, foreign gentleman who had had a trouble on his mind till the letter came? What had he been going to do? Margery could guess that he had meditated death at his own hand. Strange as the incident had been in itself, to her it had seemed stranger even than it was. Contrasting colours heighten each other by being juxtaposed; it is the same with contrasting lives.

Reaching the opposite side of the park there appeared before her for the third time that little old man, the foot-post. As the turnpike-road ran, the postman's beat was twelve miles a day;

six miles out from the town, and six miles back at night. But what with zigzags, devious ways, offsets to country seats, curves to farms, looped courses, and triangles to outlying hamlets, the ground actually covered by him was nearer one-and-twenty miles. Hence it was that Margery, who had come straight, was still abreast of him, despite her long pause.

The weighty sense that she was mixed up in a tragical secret with an unknown and handsome stranger prevented her joining very readily in chat with the postman for some time. But a keen interest in her adventure caused her to respond at once when the bowed man of mails said, 'You hit athwart the grounds of Mount Lodge, Miss Margery, or you wouldn't ha' met me here. Well, somebody hev took the old place at last.'

In acknowledging her route Margery brought herself to ask who the new gentleman might be.

'Guide the girl's heart! What! don't she know? And yet how should ye – he's only just a-come. – Well, nominal, he's a fishing gentleman, come for the summer only. But, more to the subject, he's a foreign noble that's lived in England so long as to be without any true country: some of his letters call him Baron, some Squire, so that 'a must be born to something that can't be earned by elbow-grease and Christian conduct. He was out this morning a-watching the fog. "Postman," 'a said, "good-morning: give me the bag." O, yes, 'a's a civil genteel nobleman enough.'

'Took the house for fishing, did he?'

'That's what they say, and as it can be for nothing else I suppose it's true. But, in final, his health's not good, 'a b'lieve; he's been living too rithe. The London smoke got into his wyndpipe, till 'a couldn't eat. However, I shouldn't mind having the run of his kitchen.'

'And what is his name?'

'Ah – there you have me! 'Tis a name no man's tongue can tell, or even woman's except by pen-and-ink and good scholarship. It begins with X, and who, without the machinery of a clock in's inside, can speak that? But here 'tis – from his letters.' The postman with his walking-stick wrote upon the ground,

'BARON VON XANTEN'

III

The day, as she had prognosticated, turned out fine; for weather-wisdom was imbibed with their milk-sops by the children of the Exe Vale. The impending meeting excited Margery, and she performed her duties in her father's house with mechanical unconsciousness.

Milking, skimming, cheesemaking were done. Her father was asleep in the settle, the milkmen and maids were gone home to their cottages, and the clock showed a quarter to eight. She dressed herself with care, went to the top of the garden, and looked over the stile. The view was eastward, and a great moon hung before her in a sky which had not a cloud. Nothing was moving except on the minutest scale, and she remained leaning over, the night-hawk sounding his croud from the bough of an isolated tree on the open hill side.

Here Margery waited till the appointed time had passed by three-quarters of an hour; but no Baron came. She had been full of an idea, and her heart sank with disappointment. Then at last the pacing of a horse became audible on the soft path without, leading up from the water-meads, simultaneously with which she beheld the form of the stranger, riding home, as he had said.

The moonlight so flooded her face as to make her very conspicuous in the garden-gap. 'Ah my maiden – what is your name – Margery!' he said. 'How came you here? But of course I remember – we were to meet. And it was to be eight – *proh pudor!* – I have kept you waiting!'

'It doesn't matter, sir. I've thought of something.'

'Thought of something?'

'Yes, sir. You said this morning that I was to think what I would like best in the world, and I have made up my mind.'

'I did say so – to be sure I did,' he replied, collecting his thoughts. 'I remember to have had good reason for gratitude to you.' He placed his hand to his brow, and in a minute alighted, and came up to her with the bridle in his hand. 'I was to give you a treat or present, and you could not think of one. Now you have done so. Let me hear what it is, and I'll be as good as my word.'

'To go to the Yeomanry Ball that's to be given this month.'

'The Yeomanry Ball – Yeomanry Ball?' he murmured, as if, of all requests in the world, this was what he had least expected. 'Where is what you call the Yeomanry Ball?'

'At Exonbury.'

'Have you ever been to it before?'

'No, sir.'

'Or to any ball?'

'No.'

'But did I not say a gift – a present?'

'Or a treat?'

'Ah, yes, or a treat,' he echoed, with the air of one who finds himself in a slight fix. 'But with whom would you propose to go?'

'I don't know. I have not thought of that yet.'

'You have no friend who could take you, even if I got you an invitation?'

Margery looked at the moon. 'No one who can dance,' she said; adding, with hesitation, 'I was thinking that perhaps –'

'But, my dear Margery,' he said, stopping her, as if he half-divined what her simple dream of a cavalier had been; 'it is very odd that you can think of nothing else than going to a Yeomanry Ball. Think again. You are sure there is nothing else?'

'Quite sure, sir,' she decisively answered. At first nobody would have noticed in that pretty young face any sign of decision; yet it was discoverable. The mouth, though soft, was firm in line; the eyebrows were distinct, and extended near to each other. 'I have thought of it all day,' she continued, sadly. 'Still, sir, if you are sorry you offered me anything, I can let you off.'

'Sorry? – Certainly not, Margery,' he said, rather nettled. 'I'll show you that whatever hopes I have raised in your breast I am honourable enough to gratify. If it lies in my power,' he added with sudden firmness, 'you *shall* go to the Yeomanry Ball. In what building is it to be held?'

'In the Assembly Rooms.'

'And would you be likely to be recognized there? Do you know many people?'

'Not many, sir. None, I may say. I know nobody who goes to balls.'

'Ah, well; you must go, since you wish it; and if there is no other way of getting over the difficulty of having nobody to take you, I'll take you myself. Would you like me to do so? I can dance.'

'O, yes, sir; I know that, and I thought you might offer to do it. But would you bring me back again?'

'Of course I'll bring you back. But, by-the-bye, can *you* dance?'

'Yes.'

'What?'

'Reels, and jigs, and country-dances like the New-Rigged-Ship, and Follow-my-Lover, and Haste-to-the-Wedding, and the College Hornpipe, and the Favourite Quickstep, and Captain White's dance.'

'A very good list – a very good! but unluckily I fear they don't dance any of those now. But if you have the instinct we may soon cure your ignorance. Let me see you dance a moment.'

She stood out into the garden-path, the stile being still between them, and seizing a side of her skirt with each hand, performed the movements which are even yet far from uncommon in the dances of the villagers of merry England. But her motions, though graceful, were not precisely those which appear in the figures of a modern ball-room.

'Well, my good friend, it is a very pretty sight,' he said, warming up to the proceedings. 'But you dance too well – you dance all over your person – and that's too thorough a way for the present day. I should say it was exactly how they danced in the time of your poet Chaucer; but as people don't dance like it now, we must consider. First I must inquire more about this ball, and then I must see you again.'

'If it is a great trouble to you, sir, I –'

'O no, no. I will think it over. So far so good.'

The Baron mentioned an evening and an hour when he would be passing that way again; then mounted his horse and rode away.

On the next occasion, which was just when the sun was changing places with the moon as an illuminator of Silverthorn Dairy, she found him at the spot before her, and unencumbered by a horse. The melancholy that had so weighed him down at their first interview, and had been perceptible at their second, had quite disappeared. He pressed her right hand between both his own across the stile.

'My good maiden, Gott bless you!' said he warmly. 'I cannot help thinking of that morning! I was too much over-shadowed at first to take in the whole force of it. You do not know all; but your presence was a miraculous intervention. Now to more cheerful matters. I have a great deal to tell – that is, if your wish about the ball be still the same?'

'O yes, sir – if you don't object.'

'Never think of my objecting. What I have found out is something which simplifies matters amazingly. In addition to your Yeomanry Ball at Exonbury, there is also to be one in the next county about the same time. This ball is not to be held at the Town Hall of the county-town as usual, but at Lord Toneborough's, who is colonel of the regiment, and who, I suppose, wishes to please the yeomen because his brother is going to stand for the county. Now I find I could take you there very well, and the great advantage of that ball over the Yeomanry Ball in this county is, that there you would be absolutley unknown, and I also. But do you prefer your own neighbourhood?'

'O no, sir. It is a ball I long to see – I don't know what it is like; it does not matter where.'

'Good. Then I shall be able to make much more of you there, where there is no possibility of recognition. That being settled, the next thing is the dancing. Now reels and such things do not do. For think of this – there is a new dance at Almack's and everywhere else, over which the world has gone crazy.'

'How dreadful!'

'Ah – but that is a mere expression – gone mad. It is really an ancient Scythian dance; but, such is the power of fashion, that, having once been adopted by society, this dance has made the tour of the Continent in one season.'

'What is its name, sir?'

'The polka. Young people, who always dance, are ecstatic about it, and old people, who have not danced for years, have begun to dance again on its account. All share the excitement. It arrived in London only some few months ago – it is now all over the country. Now this is your opportunity, my good Margery. To learn this one dance will be enough. They will dance scarce anything else at that ball. While, to crown all, it is the easiest dance in the world, and as I know it quite well I can practise you in the step. Suppose we try?'

Margery showed some hesitation before crossing the stile: it was a Rubicon in more ways than one. But the curious reverence which was stealing over her for all that this stranger said and did was too much for prudence. She crossed the stile.

Withdrawing with her to a nook where two high hedges met, and where the grass was elastic and dry, he lightly rested his arm on her waist, and practised with her the new step of fascination. Instead of music he whispered numbers, and she, as may be supposed, showed no slight aptness in following his instructions. Thus they moved round together, the moon-shadows from the twigs racing over their forms as they turned.

The interview lasted about half an hour. Then he somewhat abruptly handed her over the stile and stood looking at her from the other side.

'Well,' he murmured, 'what has come to pass is strange! My whole business after this will be to recover my right mind!'

Margery always declared that there seemed to be some power in the stranger that was more than human, something magical and compulsory, when he seized her and gently trotted her round. But lingering emotions may have led her memory to play pranks with the scene, and her vivid imagination at that youthful age must be taken into account in believing her. However, there is no doubt that the stranger, whoever he might be and whatever his powers, taught her the elements of modern dancing at a certain interview by moonlight at the top of her father's garden, as was proved by her possession of knowledge on the subject that could have been acquired in no other way.

His was of the first rank of commanding figures, she was one of the most agile of milkmaids, and to casual view it would have seemed all of a piece with nature's doings that things should go on thus. But there was another side to the case; and whether the strange gentleman were a wild olive tree, or not, it was questionable if the acquaintance would lead to happiness. 'A fleeting romance and a possible calamity;' thus it might have been summed up by the practical.

Margery was in Paradise; and yet she was not at this date distinctly in love with the stranger. What she felt was something more mysterious, more of the nature of veneration. As he looked at her across the stile she spoke timidly, on a subject which had apparently occupied her long.

'I ought to have a ball-dress, ought I not, sir?'

'Certainly. And you shall have a ball-dress.'

'Really?'

'No doubt of it. I won't do things by halves for my best friend. I have thought of the ball-dress, and of other things also.'

'And is my dancing good enough?'

'Quite – quite.' He paused, lapsed into thought, and looked at her. 'Margery,' he said, 'do you trust yourself unreservedly to me?'

'O yes, sir,' she replied brightly; 'if I am not too much trouble: if I am good enough to be seen in your society.'

The Baron laughed in a peculiar way. 'Really, I think you may assume as much as that. – However, to business. The ball is on the twenty-fifth, that is next Thursday week; and the only difficulty about the dress is the size. Suppose you lend me this?' And he touched her on the shoulder to signify a tight little jacket she wore.

Margery was all obedience. She took it off and handed it to him. The Baron rolled and compressed it with all his force till it was about as large as an apple-dumpling, and put it into his pocket.

'The next thing,' he said, 'is about getting the consent of your friends to your going. Have you thought of this?'

'There is only my father. I can tell him I am invited to a party, and I don't think he'll mind. Though I would rather not tell him.'

'But it strikes me that you must inform him something of what you intend. I would strongly advise you to do so.' He spoke as if rather perplexed as to the probable custom of the English peasantry in such matters, and added, 'However, it is for you to decide. I know nothing of the circumstances. As to getting to the ball, the plan I have arranged is this. The direction to Lord Toneborough's being the other way from my house, you must meet me at Three-Walks-End in Chillington Wood, two miles or more from here. You know the place? Good. By meeting there we shall save five or six miles of journey – a consideration, as it is a long way. Now, for the last time: are you still firm in your wish for this particular treat and no other? It is not too late to give it up. Cannot you think of something else – something better – some useful household articles you require?'

Margery's countenance, which before had been beaming with expectation, lost its brightness: her lips became close, and her voice broken. 'You have offered to take me, and now –'

'No, no, no,' he said, patting her cheek, 'We will not think of anything else. You shall go.'

IV

But whether the Baron, in naming such a distant spot for the rendezvous, was in hope she might fail him, and so relieve him after all of his undertaking, cannot be said; though it might have been strongly suspected from his manner that he had no great zest for the responsibility of escorting her.

But he little knew the firmness of the young woman he had to deal with. She was one of those soft natures whose power of adhesiveness to an acquired idea seems to be one of the special attributes of that softness. To go to a ball with this mysterious personage of romance was her ardent desire and aim; and none the less in that she trembled with fear and excitement at her position in so aiming. She felt the deepest awe, tenderness, and humility towards the Baron of the strange name; and yet she was prepared to stick to her point.

Thus it was that the afternoon of the eventful day found Margery trudging her way up the slopes from the vale to the place of appointment. She walked to the music of innumerable birds, which increased as she drew away from the open meads towards the groves. She had overcome all difficulties. After thinking out the question of telling or not telling her father, she had decided that to tell him was to be forbidden to go. Her contrivance therefore was this: to leave home this evening on a visit to her invalid grandmother, who lived not far from the Baron's house; but not to arrive at her grandmother's till breakfast-time next morning. Who would suspect an intercalated experience of twelve hours with the Baron at a ball? That this piece of deception was indefensible she afterwards owned readily enough; but she did not stop to think of it then.

It was sunset within Chillington Wood by the time she reached Three-Walks-End – the converging point of radiating track-ways, now floored with a carpet of matted grass, which had never known other scythes than the teeth of rabbits and hares. The twitter overhead had ceased, except from a few braver and larger birds, including the cuckoo, who did not fear night at this pleasant time of year. Nobody seemed to be on the spot when she first drew near; but no sooner did Margery stand at the intersection of the roads than a slight crashing became audible, and her patron appeared. He was so transfigured in dress that she scarcely knew him. Under a light great-coat, which was flung open, instead of his ordinary clothes he wore a suit of thin black cloth, an open waistcoat with a frill all down his shirt-front, a white tie, shining boots, no thicker than a glove, a coat that made him look like a bird, and a hat that seemed as if it would open and shut like an accordion.

'I am dressed for the ball – nothing worse,' he said, drily smiling. 'So will you be soon.'

'Why did you choose this place for our meeting, sir?' she asked, looking around and acquiring confidence.

'Why did I choose it? Well, because in riding past one day I observed a large hollow tree close by here, and it occurred to me when I was last with you that this would be useful for our purpose. Have you told your father?'

'I have not yet told him, sir.'

'That's very bad of you, Margery. How have you arranged it, then?'

She briefly related her plan, on which he made no comment, but, taking her by the hand as if she were a little child, he led her through the undergrowth to a spot where the trees were older, and standing at wider distances. Among them was the tree he had spoken of – an elm; huge, hollow, distorted, and headless, with a rift in its side.

'Now go inside,' he said, 'before it gets any darker. You will find there everything you want. At any rate, if you do not you must do without it. I'll keep watch; and don't be longer than you can help to be.'

'What am I to do, sir?' asked the puzzled maiden.

'Go inside, and you will see. When you are ready wave your handkerchief at that hole.'

She stooped into the opening. The cavity within the tree formed a lofty circular apartment, four or five feet in diameter, to which daylight entered at the top, and also through a round hole about six feet from the ground, marking the spot at which a limb had been amputated in the tree's prime. The decayed wood of cinnamon-brown, forming the inner surface of the tree, and the warm evening glow, reflected in at the top, suffused the cavity with a faint mellow radiance.

But Margery had hardly given herself time to heed these things. Her eye had been caught by objects of quite another quality. A large white oblong paper box lay against the inside of the tree; over it, on a splinter, hung a small oval looking-glass.

Margery seized the idea in a moment. She pressed through the rift into the tree, lifted the cover of the box, and, behold, there was disclosed within a lovely white apparition in a somewhat flattened state. It was the ball-dress.

This marvel of art was, briefly a sort of heavenly cobweb. It was a gossamer texture of precious manufacture, artistically festooned in a dozen flounces or more.

Margery lifted it, and could hardly refrain from kissing it. Had any one told her before this moment that such a dress could exist, she would have said, 'No; it's impossible!' She drew back, went forward, flushed, laughed, raised her hands. To say that the maker of that dress had been an individual of talent was simply understatement: he was a genius, and she sunned herself in the rays of his creation.

She then remembered that her friend without had told her to make haste, and she spasmodically proceeded to array herself. In removing the dress she found satin slippers, gloves, a handkerchief nearly all lace, a fan, and even flowers for the

hair. 'O, how could he think of it!' she said, clasping her
hands and almost crying with agitation. 'And the glass – how
good of him!'

Everything was so well prepared, that to clothe herself in
these garments was a matter of ease. In a quarter of an hour
she was ready, even to shoes and gloves. But what led her
more than anything else into admiration of the Baron's
foresight was the discovery that there were half-a-dozen pairs
each of shoes and gloves, of varying sizes, out of which she
selected a fit.

Margery glanced at herself in the mirror, or at as much as
she could see of herself: the image presented was superb.
Then she hastily rolled up her old dress, put it in the box,
and thrust the latter on a ledge as high as she could reach.
Standing on tiptoe, she waved the handkerchief through the
upper aperture, and bent to the rift to go out.

But what a trouble stared her in the face. The dress was so
airy, so fantastical, and so extensive, that to get out in her
new clothes by the rift which had admitted her in her old
ones was an impossibility. She heard the baron's steps crack-
ling over the dead sticks and leaves.

'O sir!' she began in despair.

'What – can't you dress yourself?' he inquired from the
back of the trunk.

'Yes; but I can't get out of this dreadful tree!'

He came round to the opening, stooped, and looked in. 'It
is obvious that you cannot,' he said, taking in her compass at
a glance; and adding to himself, 'Charming! who would have
thought that clothes could do so much! – Wait a minute, my
little maid: I have it!' he said more loudly.

With all his might he kicked at the sides of the rift, and by
that means broke away several pieces of the rotten touch-
wood. But, being thinly armed about the feet, he abandoned
that process, and went for a fallen branch which lay near. By
using the large end as a lever, he tore away pieces of the
wooden shell which enshrouded Margery and all her loveli-
ness, till the aperture was large enough for her to pass
without tearing her dress. She breathed her relief: the silly
girl had begun to fear that she would not get to the ball after
all.

He carefully wrapped round her a cloak he had brought with him: it was hooded, and of a length which covered her to the heels.

'The carriage is waiting down the other path,' he said, and gave her his arm. A short trudge over the soft dry leaves brought them to the place indicated. There stood the brougham, the horses, the coachman, all as still as if they were growing on the spot, like the trees. Margery's eyes rose with some timidity to the coachman's figure.

'You need not mind him,' said the Baron. 'He is a foreigner, and heeds nothing.'.

In the space of a short minute she was handed inside; the Baron buttoned up his overcoat, and surprised her by mounting with the coachman. The carriage moved off silently over the long grass of the vista, the shadows deepening to black as they proceeded. Darker and darker grew the night as they rolled on; the neighbourhood familiar to Margery was soon left behind, and she had not the remotest idea of the direction they were taking. The stars blinked out, the coachman lit his lamps, and they bowled on again.

In the course of an hour and a half they arrived at a small town, where they pulled up at the chief inn, and changed horses: all being done so readily that their advent had plainly been expected. The journey was resumed immediately. Her companion never descended to speak to her; whenever she looked out there he sat upright on his perch, with the mien of a person who had a difficult duty to perform, and who meant to perform it properly at all costs. But Margery could not help feeling a certain dread at her situation – almost, indeed, a wish that she had not come. Once or twice she thought, 'Suppose he is a wicked man, who is taking me off to a foreign country, and will never bring me home again.'

But her characteristic persistence in an original idea sustained her against these misgivings except at odd moments. One incident in particular had given her confidence in her escort: she had seen a tear in his eye when she expressed her sorrow for his troubles. He may have divined that her thoughts would take an uneasy turn, for when they stopped for a moment in ascending a hill he came to the window. 'Are you tired, Margery?' he asked kindly.

'No, sir.'

'Are you afraid?'

'N – no, sir. But it is a long way.'

'We are almost there,' he answered. 'And now, Margery,' he said in a lower tone, 'I must tell you a secret. I have obtained this invitation in a peculiar way. I thought it best for your sake not to come in my own name, and this is how I have managed. A man in this county, for whom I have lately done a service, one whom I can trust, and who is personally as unknown here as you and I, has (privately) transferred his card of invitation to me. So that we go under his name. I explain this that you may not say anything imprudent by accident. Keep your ears open and be cautious.' Having said this the Baron retreated again to his place.

'Then he is a wicked man after all!' she said to herself; 'for he is going under a false name.' But she soon had the temerity not to mind it: wickedness of that sort was the one ingredient required just now to finish him off as a hero in her eyes.

They descended a hill, passed a lodge, then up an avenue; and presently there beamed upon them the light from other carriages, drawn up in a file, which moved on by degrees; and at last they halted before a large arched doorway, round which a group of people stood.

'We are among the latest arrivals, on account of the distance,' said the Baron, reappearing. 'But never mind; there are three hours at least for your enjoyment.'

The steps were promptly flung down, and they alighted. The steam from the flanks of their swarthy steeds, as they seemed to her, ascended to the parapet of the porch, and from their nostrils the hot breath jetted forth like smoke out of volcanoes, attracting the attention of all.

V

The bewildered Margery was led by the Baron up the steps to the interior of the house, whence the sounds of music and dancing were already proceeding. The tones were strange. At every fourth beat a deep and mighty note throbbed through the air, reaching Margery's soul with all the force of a blow.

'What is that powerful tune, sir – I have never heard anything like it?' she said.

'The Drum Polka,' answered the Baron. 'The strange dance I spoke of and that we practised – introduced from my country and other parts of the continent.'

Her surprise was not lessened when, at the entrance to the ballroom, she heard the names of her conductor and herself announced as 'Mr. and Miss Brown.'

However, nobody seemed to take any notice of the announcement, the room beyond being in a perfect turmoil of gaiety, and Margery's consternation at sailing under false colours subsided. At the same moment she observed awaiting them a handsome, dark-haired, rather *petite* lady in cream-coloured satin. 'Who is she?' asked Margery of the Baron.

'She is the lady of the mansion,' he whispered. 'She is the wife of a peer of the realm, the daughter of a marquis, has five Christian names; and hardly ever speaks to commoners, except for political purposes.'

'How divine – what joy to be here!' murmured Margery, as she contemplated the diamonds that flashed from the head of her ladyship, who was just inside the ball-room door, in front of a little gilded chair, upon which she sat in the intervals between one arrival and another. She had come down from London at great inconvenience to herself, openly to promote this entertainment.

As Mr. and Miss Brown expressed absolutely no meaning to Lady Toneborough (for there were three Browns already present in this rather mixed assembly), and as there was possibly a slight awkwardness in poor Margery's manner, Lady Toneborough touched their hands lightly with the tips of her long gloves, said, 'How d'ye do,' and turned round for more comers.

'Ah, if she only knew we were a rich Baron and his friend, and not Mr. and Miss Brown at all, she wouldn't receive us like that, would she?' whispered Margery confidentially.

'Indeed, she wouldn't!' drily said the Baron. 'Now let us drop into the dance at once; some of the people here, you see, dance much worse than you.'

Almost before she was aware she had obeyed his myste-rious influence, by giving him one hand, placing the other upon his shoulder, and swinging with him round the room to the steps she had learnt on the sward.

At the first gaze the apartment had seemed to her to be floored with black ice; the figures of the dancers appearing upon it upside down. At last she realized that it was highly-polished oak, but she was none the less afraid to move.

'I am afraid of falling down,' she said.

'Lean on me; you will soon get used to it,' he replied. 'You have no nails in your shoes now, dear.'

His words, like all his words to her, were quite true. She found it amazingly easy in a brief space of time. The floor, far from hindering her, was a positive assistance to one of her natural agility and litheness. Moreover, her marvellous dress of twelve flounces inspired her as nothing else could have done. Externally a new creature, she was prompted to new deeds. To feel as well-dressed as the other women around her is to set any woman at her ease, whencesoever she may have come: to feel much better dressed is to add radiance to that ease.

Her prophet's statement on the popularity of the polka at this juncture was amply borne out. It was among the first seasons of its general adoption in country houses; the enthusiasm it excited tonight was beyond description, and scarcely credible to the youth of the present day. A new motive power had been introduced into the world of poesy – the polka, as a counter-poise to the new motive power that had been introduced into the world of prose – steam.

Twenty finished musicians sat in the music gallery at the end, with romantic mop-heads of raven hair, under which their faces and eyes shone like fire under coals.

The nature and object of the ball had led to its being very inclusive. Every rank was there, from the peer to the smallest yeoman, and Margery got on exceedingly well, particularly when the recuperative powers of supper had banished the fatigue of her long drive.

Sometimes she heard people saying, 'Who are they? – brother and sister – father and daughter? And never dancing except with each other – how odd?' But of this she took no notice.

When not dancing the watchful Baron took her through the drawing-rooms and picture-galleries adjoining, which tonight were thrown open like the rest of the house; and there, ensconcing her in some curtained nook, he drew her attention to scrap-books, prints, and albums, and left her to amuse herself with turning them over till the dance in which she was practised should again be called. Margery would much have preferred to roam about during these intervals; but the words of the Baron were law, and as he commanded so she acted. In such alternations the evening winged away; till at last came the gloomy words, 'Margery, our time is up.'

'One more – only one!' she coaxed, for the longer they stayed the more freely and gaily moved the dance. This entreaty he granted; but on her asking for yet another, he was inexorable. 'No,' he said. 'We have a long way to go.'

Then she bade adieu to the wondrous scene, looking over her shoulder as they withdrew from the hall; and in a few minutes she was cloaked and in the carriage. The Baron mounted to his seat on the box, where she saw him light a cigar; they plunged under the trees, and she leant back, and gave herself up to contemplate the images that filled her brain. The natural result followed: she fell asleep.

She did not awake till they stopped to change horses; when she saw against the stars the Baron sitting as erect as ever. 'He watches like the Angel Gabriel, when all the world is asleep!' she thought.

With the resumption of motion she slept again, and knew no more till he touched her hand and said, 'Our journey is done – we are in Chillington Wood.'

It was almost daylight. Margery scarcely knew herself to be awake till she was out of the carriage and standing beside the Baron, who, having told the coachman to drive on to a certain point indicated, turned to her.

'Now,' he said, smiling, 'run across to the hollow tree; you know where it is. I'll wait as before, while you perform the reverse operation to that you did last night.' She took no heed of the path now, nor regarded whether her pretty slippers became scratched by the brambles or no. A walk of a few steps brought her to the particular tree which she had left about nine hours earlier. It was still gloomy at this spot, the morning not being clear.

She entered the trunk, dislodged the box containing her old clothing, pulled off the satin shoes, and gloves, and dress, and in ten minutes emerged in the cotton gown and shawl of shepherd's plaid.

The Baron was not far off. 'Now you look the milkmaid again,' he said, coming towards her. 'Where is the finery?'

'Packed in the box, sir, as I found it.' She spoke with more humility now. The difference between them was greater than it had been at the ball.

'Good,' he said. 'I must just dispose of it; and then away we go.'

He went back to the tree, Margery following at a little distance. Bringing forth the box, he pulled out the dress as carelessly as if it had been rags. But this was not all. He gathered a few dry sticks, crushed the lovely garment into a loose billowy heap, the gloves, fan, and shoes on the top, then struck a light and ruthlessly set fire to the whole.

Margery was agonized. She ran forward; she implored and entreated. 'Please, sir – do spare it – do! My lovely dress – my dear, dear slippers – my fan – it is cruel! Don't burn them, please!'

'Nonsense. We shall have no further use for them if we live a hundred years.'

'But spare a bit of it – one little piece, sir – a scrap of the lace – one bow of the ribbon – the lovely fan – just something!'

But he was as immoveable as Rhadamanthus. 'No,' he said, with a stern gaze of his aristocratic eye. 'It is of no use for you to speak like that. The things are my property. I undertook to gratify you in what you might desire because you had saved my life. To go to a ball, you said. You might much more wisely have said anything else, but no; you said, to go to a ball. Very well – I have taken you to a ball. I have brought you back. The clothes were only the means, and I dispose of them my own way. Have I not a right to?'

'Yes, sir,' she said meekly.

He gave the fire a stir, and lace and ribbons, and the twelve flounces, and the embroidery, and all the rest crackled and disappeared. He then put in her hands the butter basket she had brought to take on to her grandmother's, and accompanied her to the edge of the wood, where it merged in the undulating open country in which her granddame dwelt.

'Now, Margery,' he said, 'here we part. I have performed my contract – at some awkwardness, if I was recognized. But never mind that. How do you feel – sleepy?'

'Not at all, sir,' she said.

'That long nap refreshed you, eh? Now you must make me a promise. That if I require your presence at any time, you will come to me. . . . I am a man of more than one mood,' he went on with sudden solemnity; 'and I may have desperate need of you again, to deliver me from that darkness as of Death which sometimes encompasses me. Promise it, Margery – promise it; that no matter what stands in the way, you will come to me if I require you.'

'I would have if you had not burnt my pretty clothes!' she pouted.

'Ah – ungrateful!'

'Indeed, then, I will promise, sir,' she said from her heart. 'Wherever I am, if I have bodily strength I will come to you.'

He pressed her hand. 'It is a solemn promise,' he replied. 'Now I must go, for you know your way.'

'I shall hardly believe that it has not been all a dream!' she said, with a childish instinct to cry at his withdrawal. 'There will be nothing left of last night – nothing of my dress, nothing of my pleasure, nothing of the place!'

'You shall remember it in this way,' he said. 'We'll cut our initials on this tree as a memorial, so that whenever you walk this path you will see them.'

Then with a knife he inscribed on the smooth bark of a beech tree the letters M.T., and underneath a large X.

'What, have you no Christian name, sir?'

'Yes, but I don't use it. Now, good-bye, my little friend. – What will you do with yourself today, when you are gone from me?' he lingered to ask.

'Oh – I shall go to my granny's,' she replied with some gloom; 'and have breakfast, and dinner, and tea with her, I suppose; and in the evening I shall go home to Silverthorn Dairy, and perhaps Jim will come to meet me, and all will be the same as usual.'

'Who is Jim?'

'O, he's nobody – only the young man I've got to marry some day.'

'What! – you engaged to be married? – Why didn't you tell me this before?'

'I don't know, sir.'

'What is the young man's name?'

'James Hayward.'

'What is he?'

'A master lime-burner.'

'Engaged to a master lime-burner, and not a word of this to me! Margery, Margery! when shall a straightforward one of your sex be found! Subtle even in your simplicity! What mischief have you caused me to do, through not telling me this? I wouldn't have so endangered anybody's happiness for a thousand pounds. Wicked girl that you were; why didn't you tell me?'

'I thought I'd better not!' said Margery, beginning to be frightened.

'But don't you see and understand that if you are already the property of a young man, and he were to find out this night's excursion, he may be angry with you and part from you for ever? With him already in the field I had no right to take you at all; he undoubtedly ought to have taken you; which really might have been arranged, if you had not deceived me by saying you had nobody.'

Margery's face wore that aspect of woe which comes from the repentant consciousness of having been guilty of an enormity. 'But he wasn't good enough to take me, sir!' she said, almost crying; 'and he isn't absolutely my master until I have married him, is he?'

'That's a subject I cannot go into. However, we must alter our tactics. Instead of advising you, as I did at first to tell of this experience to your friends, I must now impress on you that it will be best to keep a silent tongue on the matter – perhaps for ever and ever. It may come right some day, and you may be able to say "All's well that ends well." Now, good morning, my friend. Think of Jim, and forget me.'

'Ah, perhaps I can't do that,' she said, with a tear in her eye, and a full throat.

'Well – do your best. I can say no more.'

He turned and retreated into the wood, and Margery, sighing, went on her way.

VI

Between six and seven o'clock in the evening of the same day a young man descended the hills into the valley of the Exe, at a point about midway between Silverthorn and the residence of Margery's grandmother, four miles to the east.

He was a thoroughbred son of the country, as far removed from what is known as the provincial, as the latter is from the out-and-out gentleman of culture. His trousers and waistcoat were of fustian, almost white, but he wore a jacket of old-fashioned blue West-of-England cloth, so well preserved that evidently the article was relegated to a box whenever its owner engaged in such active occupations as he usually pursued. His complexion was fair, almost florid, and he had scarcely any beard.

A novel attraction about this young man, which a glancing stranger would know nothing of, was a rare and curious freshness of atmosphere that appertained to him, to his clothes, to all his belongings, even to the room in which he had been sitting. It might almost have been said that by adding him and his implements to an over-crowded apartment you made it healthful. This resulted from his trade. He was a lime-burner; he handled lime daily; and in return the lime rendered him an incarnation of salubrity. His hair was dry, fair, and frizzled, the latter possibly by the operation of the same caustic agent. He carried as a walking-stick a green sapling, whose growth had been contorted to a corkscrew pattern by a twining honeysuckle.

As he descended to the level ground of the water-meadows he cast his glance westward, with a frequency that revealed him to be in search of some object in the distance. It was rather difficult to do this, the low sunlight dazzling his eyes by glancing from the river away there, and from the 'carriers' (as they were called) in his path – narrow artificial brooks for conducting the water over the grass. His course was something of a zigzag from the necessity of finding points in these carriers convenient for jumping. Thus peering and leaping and winding, he drew near the Exe, the central river of the miles-long mead.

A moving spot became visible to him in the direction of his scrutiny, mixed up with the rays of the same river. The spot got nearer, and revealed itself to be a slight thing of pink cotton and shepherd's plaid, which pursued a path on the brink of the stream. The young man so shaped his trackless course as to impinge on the path a little ahead of this coloured form, and when he drew near her he smiled and reddened. The girl smiled back to him; but her smile had not the life in it that the young man's had shown.

'My dear Margery – here I am!' he said gladly in an undertone, as with a last leap he crossed the last intervening carrier, and stood at her side.

'You've come all the way from the kiln, on purpose to meet me, and you shouldn't have done it,' she reproachfully returned.

'We finished there at four, so it was no trouble; and if it had been – why, I should ha' come.'

A small sigh was the response.

'What, you are not even so glad to see me as you would be to see your dog or cat!' he continued. 'Come, Mis'ess Margery, this is rather hard. But, by George, how tired you dew look! Why, if you'd been up all night your eyes couldn't be more like tea-saucers. You've walked tew far, that's what it is. The weather is getting warm now, and the air of these low-lying meads is not strengthening in summer. I wish you lived up on higher ground with me, beside the kiln. You'd get as strong as a hoss! Well, there; all that will come in time.'

Instead of saying yes, the fair maid repressed another sigh.

'What, won't it, then?' he said.

'I suppose so,' she answered. 'If it is to be, it is.'

'Well said – very well said, my dear.'

'And if it isn't to be it isn't.'

'What? Who's been putting that into your head? Your grumpy granny, I suppose. However, how is she? Margery, I have been thinking today – in fact, I was thinking it yesterday and all the week – that really we might settle our little business this summer.'

'This summer?' she repeated, with some dismay. 'But the partnership? Remember it was not to be till after that was completed.'

'There I have you!' said he, taking the liberty to pat her shoulder, and the further liberty of advancing his hand behind it to the other. 'The partnership is settled. 'Tis "Vine and Hayward, lime-burners," now, and "Richard Vine" no longer. Yes, Cousin Richard has settled it so, for a time at least, and 'tis to be painted on the carts this week – blue letters – yaller ground. I'll hoss one of 'em, and drive en round to your door as soon as the paint is dry, to show 'ee how it looks?'

'Oh, I am sure you needn't take that trouble, Jim; I can see it quite well enough in my mind,' replied the young girl – not without a flitting accent of superiority.

'Hullo,' said Jim, taking her by the shoulders, and looking at her hard. 'What dew that bit of incivility mean? Now, Margery, let's sit down here, and have this cleared.' He rapped with his stick upon the rail of a little bridge they were crossing, and seated himself firmly, leaving a place for her.

'But I want to get home-along, dear Jim,' she coaxed.

'Fidgets. Sit down, there's a dear. I want a straightforward answer, if you please. In what month, and on what day of the month, will you marry me?'

'O, Jim,' she said, sitting gingerly on the edge, 'that's too plain-spoken for you yet. Before I look at it in that business light I should have to – to –'

'But your father has settled it long ago, and you said it should be as soon as I became a partner. So, dear, you must not mind a plain man wanting a plain answer. Come, name your time.'

She did not reply at once. What thoughts were passing through her brain during the interval? Not images raised by his words, but whirling figures of men and women in red and white and blue, reflected from a glassy floor, in movements timed by the thrilling beats of the Drum Polka. At last she said slowly, 'Jim, you don't know the world, and what a woman's wants can be.'

'But I can make you comfortable. I am in lodgings as yet, but I can have a house for the asking; and as to furniture, you shall choose of the best for yourself – the very best.'

'The best! Far are you from knowing what that is!' said the little woman. 'There be ornaments such as you never dream of; work tables that would set you in amaze; silver candlesticks, tea and coffee pots that would dazzle your eyes; teacups, and saucers, gilded all over with guinea-gold; heavy velvet curtains, gold clocks, pictures, and looking-glasses beyond your very dreams. So don't say I shall have the best.'

'H'm!' said Jim gloomily; and fell into reflection. 'Where did you get those high notions from, Margery?' he presently inquired. 'I'll swear you hadn't got 'em a week ago?' She did not answer, and he added, '*Yew* don't expect to have such things, I hope; deserve them as you may?'

'I was not exactly speaking of what I wanted,' she said severely. 'I said, things a woman *could* want. And since you wish to know what I *can* want to quite satisfy me, I assure you I can want those!'

'You are a pink-and-white conundrum, Margery,' he said; 'and I give you up for tonight. Anybody would think the devil had showed you all the kingdoms of the world since I saw you last!'

She reddened. 'Perhaps he has!' she murmured; then arose, he following her; and they soon reached Margery's home, approaching it from the lower or meadow side – the opposite to that of the garden top, where she had met the Baron.

'You'll come in, won't you, Jim?' she said, with more ceremony than heartiness.

'No – I think not tonight,' he answered. 'I'll consider what you've said.'

'You are very good, Jim,' she returned lightly. 'Goodbye.'

VII

Jim thoughtfully retraced his steps. He was a village character, and he had a villager's simplicity: that is, the simplicity which comes from the lack of a complicated experience. But simple by nature he certainly was not. Among the rank and file of rustics he was quite a Talleyrand, or rather had been one, till he lost a good deal of his self-command by falling in love.

Now, however, that the charming object of his distraction was out of sight he could deliberate, and measure, and weigh things with some approach to keenness. The substance of his queries was, What change had come over Margery – whence these new notions?

Ponder as he would he could evolve no answer save one, which, eminently unsatisfactory as it was, he felt it would be unreasonable not to accept: that she was simply skittish and ambitious by nature, and would not be hunted into matrimony till he had provided a well-adorned home.

Jim retrod the miles to the kiln, and looked to the fires. The kiln stood in a peculiar, interesting, even impressive spot. It was at the end of a short ravine in a limestone formation, and all around was an open hilly down. The nearest house was that of Jim's cousin and partner, which stood on the outskirts of the down beside the turnpike-road. From this house a little lane wound between the steep escarpments of the ravine till it reached the kiln, which faced down the miniature valley, commanding it as a fort might command a defile.

The idea of a fort in this association owed little to imagination. For on the nibbled green steep above the kiln stood a bye-gone, worn-out specimen of such an erection, huge, impressive and difficult to scale even now in its decay. It was a British castle or entrenchment, with triple rings of defence, rising roll behind roll, their outlines cutting sharply against the sky, and Jim's kiln nearly undermining their base. When the lime-kiln flared up in the night, which it often did, its fires lit up the front of these ramparts to a great majesty. They were old friends of his, and while keeping up the heat through the long darkness, as it was sometimes his duty to do, he would imagine the dancing lights and shades about the stupendous earthwork to be the forms of those giants who (he supposed) had heaped it up. Often he clambered upon it, and walked about the summit, thinking out the problems connected with his business, his partner, his future, his Margery.

It was what he did this evening, continuing the meditation on the young girl's manner that he had begun upon the road, and still, as then, finding no clue to the change.

While thus engaged he observed a man coming up the ravine to the kiln. Business messages were almost invariably left at the house below, and Jim watched the man with the interest excited by a belief that he had come on a personal matter. On nearer approach Jim recognized him as the gardener at Mount Lodge some miles away. If this meant business, the Baron (of whose arrival Jim had vaguely heard) was a new and unexpected customer.

It meant nothing else, apparently. The man's errand was simply to inform Jim that the Baron required a load of lime for the garden.

'You might have saved yourself trouble by leaving word at Mr. Vine's,' said Jim.

'I was to see you personally,' said the gardener, 'and to say that the Baron would like to inquire of you about the different qualities of lime proper for such purposes.'

'Couldn't you tell him yourself?' said Jim.

'He said I was to tell you that,' replied the gardener; 'and it wasn't for me to interfere.'

No motive other than the ostensible one could possibly be conjectured by Jim Hayward at this time; and the next morning he started with great pleasure, in his best business suit of clothes. By eleven o'clock he and his horse and cart had arrived on the Baron's premises, and the lime was deposited where directed; an exceptional spot, just within view of the windows of the south front.

Baron von Xanten, pale and melancholy, was sauntering in the sun on the slope between the house and the all-the-year-round. He looked across to where Jim and the gardener were standing and the identity of Hayward being established by what he brought, the Baron came down, and the gardener withdrew.

The Baron's first inquiries were, as Jim had been led to suppose they would be, on the exterminating effects of lime upon slugs and snails in its different conditions of slaked and unslaked, ground and in the lump. He appeared to be much interested by Jim's explanations, and eyed the young man closely whenever he had an opportunity.

'And I hope trade is prosperous with you this year,' said the Baron.

'Very, my noble lord,' replied Jim, who, in his uncertainty on the proper method of address, wisely concluded that it was better to err by giving too much honour than by giving too little. 'In short, trade is looking so well that I've become a partner in the firm.'

'Indeed; I am glad to hear it. So now you are settled in life.'

'Well, my lord; I am hardly settled, even now. For I've got to finish it – I mean, to get married.'

'That's an easy matter, compared with the partnership.'

'Now a man might think so, my baron,' said Jim, getting more confidential. 'But the real truth is, 'tis the hardest part of all for me.'

'Your suit prospers, I hope?'

'It don't,' said Jim. 'It don't at all just at present. In short, I can't for the life o' me think what's come over the young woman lately.' And he fell into deep reflection.

Though Jim did not observe it, the Baron's brow became shadowed with self-reproach as he heard those simple words, and his eyes had a look of pity. 'Indeed – since when?' he asked.

'Since yesterday, my noble lord.' Jim spoke meditatively. He was resolving upon a bold stroke. Why not make a confidant of this kind gentleman, instead of the parson, as he had intended? The thought was no sooner conceived than acted on. 'My lord,' he resumed, 'I have heard that you are a nobleman of great scope and talent, who has seen more strange countries and characters than I have ever heard of, and know the insides of men well. Therefore I would fain put a question to your noble lordship, if I may so trouble you, and having nobody else in the world who could inform me so trewly.'

'Any advice I can give is at your service, Hayward. What do you wish to know?'

'It is this, my baron. What can I do to bring down a young woman's ambition that's got to such a towering height there's no reaching it or compassing it: how get her to be pleased with me and my station as she used to be when I first knew her?'

'Truly, that's a hard question, my man. What does she aspire to?'

'She's got a craze for fine furniture.'

'How long has she had it?'

'Only just now.'

Tha Baron seemed still more to experience regret. 'What furniture does she specially covet?' he asked.

'Silver candlesticks, work-tables, looking-glasses, gold tea-things, silver tea-pots, gold clocks, curtains, pictures, and I don't know what all – things I shall never get if I live to be a hundred – not so much that I couldn't raise the money to buy 'em, as that I ought to put it to other uses, or save it for a rainy day.'

'You think the possession of those articles would make her happy?'

'I really think they might, my lord.'

'Good. Open your pocket-book and write as I tell you.'

Jim in some astonishment did as commanded, and elevating his pocket-book against the garden-wall, thoroughly mois-tened his pencil, and wrote at the Baron's dictation:

'Pair of silver candlesticks: inlaid work-table and work-box: one large mirror: two small ditto: one gilt china tea and coffee service: one silver tea-pot, coffee-pot, sugar-basin, jug, and dozen spoons: French clock: pair of curtains: six large pic-tures.'

'Now,' said the Baron, 'tear out that leaf and give it to me. Keep a close tongue about this; go home, and don't be surprised at anything that may come to your door.'

'But, my noble lord, you don't mean that your lordship is going to give –'

'Never mind what I am going to do. Only keep your own counsel. I perceive that, though a plain countryman, you are by no means deficient in tact and understanding. If sending these things to you gives me pleasure, why should you object? The fact is, Hayward, I occasionally take an interest in people, and like to do a little for them. I take an interest in you. Now go home, and a week hence invite Marg – the young woman and her father, to tea with you. The rest is in your own hands.'

A question often put to Jim in after times was why it had not occurred to him at once that the Baron's liberal conduct must have been dictated by something more personal than sudden spontaneous generosity to him, a stranger. To which Jim always answered that, admitting the existence of such

generosity, there had appeared nothing remarkable in the
Baron selecting himself as its object. The Baron had told him
that he took an interest in him; and self-esteem, even with the
most modest, is usually sufficient to over-ride any little
difficulty that might occur to an outsider in accounting for a
preference. He moreover considered that foreign noblemen,
rich and eccentric, might have habits of acting which were
quite at variance with those of their English compeers.

So he drove off homeward with a lighter heart than he had
known for several days. To have a foreign gentleman take a
fancy to him – what a triumph to a plain sort of fellow, who
had scarcely expected the Baron to look in his face. It would
be a fine story to tell Margery when the Baron gave him
liberty to speak out.

Jim lodged at the house of his cousin and partner, Richard
Vine, a widower of fifty odd years. Having failed in the
development of a household of direct descendants this tradesman had been glad to let his chambers to his much younger
relative, when the latter entered on the business of lime
manufacture; and their intimacy had led to a partnership. Jim
lived upstairs; his partner lived down, and the furniture of all
the rooms was so plain and old fashioned as to excite the
special dislike of Miss Margery Tucker, and even to prejudice
her against Jim for tolerating it. Not only were the chairs and
tables queer, but, with due regard to the principle that a man's
surroundings should bear the impress of that man's life and
occupation, the chief ornaments of the dwelling were a
curious collection of calcinations, that had been discovered
from time to time in the lime-kiln – misshapen ingots of
strange substance, some of them like Pompeian remains.

The head of the firm was a quiet-living, narrow-minded,
though friendly, man of fifty; and he took a serious interest in
Jim's love-suit, frequently inquiring how it progressed, and
assuring Jim that if he chose to marry he might have all the
upper floor at a low rent, he, Mr. Vine, contenting himself
entirely with the ground level. It had been so convenient for
discussing business matters to have Jim in the same house, that
he did not wish any change to be made in consequence of a
change in Jim's domestic estate. Margery knew of this wish,
and of Jim's concurrent feeling; and did not like the idea at all.

About four days after the young man's interview with the Baron, there drew up in front of Jim's house at noon a waggon laden with cases and packages, large and small. They were all addressed to 'Mr. Hayward,' and they had come from the largest furnishing warehouses in that part of England.

Three-quarters of an hour were occupied in getting the cases to Jim's rooms. The wary Jim did not show the amazement he felt at his patron's munificence; and presently the senior partner came into the passage, and wondered what was lumbering upstairs.

'Oh – it's only some things of mine,' said Jim coolly.

'Bearing upon the coming event – eh?' said his partner.

'Exactly,' replied Jim.

Mr. Vine, with some astonishment at the number of cases, shortly after went away to the kiln; whereupon Jim shut himself into his rooms, and there he might have been heard ripping up and opening boxes with a cautious hand, afterwards appearing outside the door with them empty, and carrying them off to the outhouse.

A triumphant look lit up his face when, a little later in the afternoon, he sent into the vale to the dairy, and invited Margery and her father to his house to supper.

She was not unsociable that day, and, her father expressing a hard and fast acceptance of the invitation, she perforce agreed to go with him. Meanwhile at home, Jim made himself as mysteriously busy as before in those rooms of his, and when his partner returned he too was asked to join in the supper.

At dusk Hayward went to the door, where he stood till he heard the voices of his guests from the direction of the low grounds, now covered with their frequent fleece of fog. The voices grew more distinct, and then on the white surface of the fog there appeared two trunkless heads, from which bodies and a horse and cart gradually extended as the approaching pair rose towards the house.

When they had entered Jim pressed Margery's hand and conducted her up to his rooms, her father waiting below to say a few words to the senior lime-burner.

'Bless me,' said Jim to her, on entering the sitting-room; 'I quite forgot to get a light beforehand; but I'll have one in a jiffy.'

Margery stood in the middle of the dark room, while Jim struck a match; and then the young girl's eyes were conscious of a burst of light, and the rise into being of a pair of handsome silver candlesticks containing two candles that Jim was in the act of lighting.

'Why – where – you have candlesticks like that?' said Margery. Her eyes flew round the room as the growing candle-flames showed other articles. 'Pictures too – and lovely china – why I knew nothing of this, I declare.'

'Yes – a few things that came to me by accident,' said Jim in quiet tones.

'And a great gold clock under a glass, and a cupid swinging for a pendulum; and O what a lovely work-table – woods of every colour – and a work-box to match. May I look inside that work-box, Jim? – whose is it?'

'Oh yes; look at it, of course. It is a poor enough thing, but 'tis mine; and it will belong to the woman I marry, whoever she may be, as well as all the other things here.'

'And the curtains and the looking-glasses: why I declare I can see myself in a hundred places.'

'That tea-set,' said Jim, placidly pointing to a gorgeous china service and a large silver tea-pot on the side table, 'I don't use at present, being a bachelor-man; but, says I to myself, "whoever I marry will want some such things for giving her parties; or I can sell em" – but I haven't took steps for't yet –'

'Sell 'em – no, I should think not,' said Margery with earnest reproach. 'Why, I hope you wouldn't be so foolish! Why, this is exactly the kind of thing I was thinking of when I told you of the things women could want – of course not meaning myself particularly. I had no idea that you had such valuable –' Margery was unable to speak coherently, so much was she amazed at the wealth of Jim's possessions.

At this moment her father and the lime-burner came upstairs; and to appear womanly and proper to Mr. Vine, Margery repressed the remainder of her surprise. As for the two elderly worthies, it was not till they entered the room and sat down that their slower eyes discerned anything brilliant in the appointments. Then one of them stole a glance at some article, and the other at another; but each being unwilling to express his wonder in the presence of his neighbours, they received the objects before them with quite an accustomed air; the lime-burner inwardly trying to conjecture what all this meant, and the dairyman musing that if Jim's business allowed him to accumulate at this rate, the sooner Margery became his wife the better. Margery retreated to the work-table, work-box, and tea-service, which she examined with hushed exclamations.

An entertainment thus surprisingly begun could not fail to progress well. Whenever Margery's crusty old father felt the need of a civil sentence, the flash of Jim's fancy articles inspired him to one; while the lime-burner, having reasoned away his first ominous thought that all this had come out of the firm, also felt proud and blithe.

Jim accompanied his dairy friends part of the way home before they mounted. Her father, finding that Jim wanted to speak to her privately, and that she exhibited some elusiveness, turned to Margery and said, 'Come, come, my lady; no more of this nonsense. You just step behind with that young man, and I and the cart will wait for you.'

Margery, a little scared at her father's peremptoriness, obeyed. It was plain that Jim had won the old man by that night's stroke, if he had not won her.

'I know what you are going to say, Jim,' she began, less ardently now, for she was no longer under the novel influence of the shining silver and glass. 'Well, as you desire it, and as my father desires it, and as I suppose it will be the best course for me, I will fix the day – not this evening, but as soon as I can think it over.'

VIII

Notwithstanding a press of business, Jim went and did his duty in thanking the Baron. The latter saw him in his fishing-tackle room, an apartment littered with every appliance that a votary of the rod could require.

'And when is the wedding-day to be, Hayward?' the Baron asked, after Jim had told him that matters were settled.

'It is not quite certain yet, my noble lord,' said Jim cheerfully. 'But I hope 'twill not be long after the time when God A'mighty christens the little apples.'

'And when is that?'

'St. Swithin's – the middle of July. 'Tis to be some time in that month, she tells me.'

When Jim was gone the Baron seemed meditative. He went out, ascended the mount, and entered the weather-screen, where he looked at the seats, as though re-enacting in his fancy the scene of that memorable morning of fog. He turned his eyes to the angle of the shelter, round which Margery had suddenly appeared like a vision, and it was plain that he would not have minded her appearing there then. The juncture had indeed been such an impressive and critical one that she must have seemed rather a heavenly messenger than a passing milkmaid, more especially to a man like the Baron, who, despite the mystery of his origin and life, revealed himself to be a melancholy, emotional character – the Jacques of this forest and stream.

Behind the mount the ground rose yet higher, ascending to a plantation which sheltered the house. The Baron strolled up here, and bent his gaze over the distance. The valley of the Exe lay before him, with its shining river, the brooks that fed it, and the trickling springs that fed the brooks. The situation of Margery's house was visible, though not the house itself; and the Baron gazed that way for an infinitely long time, till, remembering himself, he moved on.

Instead of returning to the house he went along the ridge till he arrived at the verge of Chillington Wood, and in the same desultory manner roamed under the trees, not pausing till he had come to Three-Walks-End, and the hollow elm hard by. He peeped in at the rift. In the soft dry layer of touch-wood that floored the hollow Margery's tracks were still visible, as she had made them there when dressing for the ball.

'Little Margery!' murmured the Baron.

In a moment he thought better of this mood, and turned to go home. But behold, a form stood behind him – that of the girl whose name had been on his lips.

She was in utter confusion. 'I – I – did not know you were here, sir!' she began. 'I was out for a little walk.' She could get no further; her eyes filled with tears. That spice of wilfulness, even hardness, which characterized her in Jim's company, magically disappeared in the presence of the Baron.

'Never mind, never mind,' said he, masking under a severe manner whatever he felt. 'The meeting is awkward, and ought not to have occurred, especially if, as I suppose, you are shortly to be married to James Hayward. But it cannot be helped now. You had no idea I was here, of course. Neither had I of seeing you. Remember you cannot be too careful,' continued the Baron in the same grave tone; 'and I strongly request you as a friend to do your utmost to avoid meetings like this. When you saw me before I turned, why did you not go away?'

'I did not see you, sir. I did not think of seeing you. I was walking this way, and I only looked in to see the tree.'

'That shows you have been thinking of things you should not think of,' returned the Baron. 'Good morning.'

Margery could answer nothing. A browbeaten glance, almost of misery, was all she gave him. He took a slow step away from her; then turned suddenly back and, stooping, impulsively kissed her cheek, taking her as much by surprise as ever a woman was taken in her life.

Immediately after he went off with a flushed face and rapid strides, which he did not check till he was within his own boundaries.

The haymaking season now set in vigorously, and the weir-hatches were all drawn in the meads to drain off the water. The streams ran themselves dry, and there was no longer any difficulty in walking about among them. The Baron could very well witness from the elevations about his house the activity which followed these preliminaries. The white shirt-sleeves of the mowers glistened in the sun, the scythes flashed, voices echoed, snatches of song floated about, and there were glimpses of red waggon-wheels, purple gowns, and many-coloured handkerchiefs.

The Baron had been told that the haymaking was to be followed by the wedding, and had he gone down the vale to the dairy he would have had evidence to that effect. Dairyman Tucker's house was in a whirlpool of bustle, and among other difficulties was that of turning the cheese-room into a genteel apartment for the time being, and hiding the awkwardness of having to pass through the milk-house to get to the parlour door. These household contrivances appeared to interest Margery much more than the great question of dressing for the ceremony and the ceremony itself. In all relating to that she showed an indescribable backwardness, which later on was well remembered.

'If it were only somebody else, and I was one of the bridesmaids, I really think I should like it better!' she murmured one afternoon.

'Away with thee – that's only your shyness!' said one of the milkmaids.

It is said that about this time the Baron seemed to feel the effects of solitude strongly. Solitude revives the simple instincts of primitive man, and lonely country nooks afford rich soil for wayward emotions. Moreover, idleness waters those unconsidered impulses which a short season of turmoil would stamp out. It is difficult to speak with any exactness of the bearing of such conditions on the mind of the Baron – a man of whom so little was ever truly known – but there is no doubt that his mind ran much on Margery as an individual, without reference to her rank or quality, or to the question whether she would marry Jim Hayward that summer. She was the single lovely human thing within his present horizon, for he lived in absolute seclusion; and her image unduly affected him.

But, leaving conjecture, let me state what happened. One Saturday evening, two or three weeks after his accidental meeting with her in the wood, he wrote the note following:–

Dear Margery,

You must not suppose that, because I spoke somewhat severely to you at our chance encounter by the hollow tree, I have any feeling against you. Far from it. Now, as ever, I have the most grateful sense of your considerate kindness to me on a momentous occasion which shall be nameless.

You solemnly promised to come and see me whenever I should send for you. Can you call for five minutes as soon as possible and disperse those plaguy glooms from which I am so unfortunate as to suffer? If you refuse I will not answer for the consequences. I shall be in the summer shelter of the mount tomorrow morning at half-past ten. If you come I shall be grateful. I have also something for you.

Yours,

X.

In keeping with the tenor of this epistle the desponding, self-oppressed Baron ascended the mount on Sunday morning and sat down. There was nothing here to signify exactly the hour, but before the church bells had begun he heard somebody approaching at the back. The light footstep moved timidly, first to one recess, and then to another; then to the third, where he sat in the shade. Poor Margery stood before him.

She looked worn and weary, and her little shoes and the skirts of her dress were covered with dust. The weather was sultry, the sun being already high and powerful, and rain had not fallen for weeks. The Baron, who walked little, had thought nothing of the effects of this heat and drought in inducing fatigue. A distance which had been but a reasonable excercise on a foggy morning was a drag for Margery now. She was out of breath; and anxiety, even unhappiness was written on her everywhere.

He rose to his feet, and took her hand. He was vexed with himself at sight of her. 'My dear little girl!' he said. 'You are tired – you should not have come.'

'You sent for me, sir; and I was afraid you were ill; and my promise to you was sacred.'

He bent over her, looking upon her downcast face, and still holding her hand; then he dropped it, and took a pace or two backwards.

'It was a whim, nothing more,' he said, sadly. 'I wanted to see my little friend, to express good wishes – and to present her with this.' He held forward a small morocco case, and showed her how to open it, disclosing a pretty locket, set with pearls. 'It is intended as a wedding present,' he continued. 'To be returned to me again if you do not marry Jim this summer – it is to be this summer, I think?'

'It was, sir,' she said with agitation. 'But it is so no longer.' And, therefore, I cannot take this.'

'What do you say?'

'It was to have been today; but now it cannot be.'

'The wedding today – Sunday?' he cried.

'We fixed Sunday not to hinder much time at this busy season of the year,' replied she.

'And have you, then, put it off – surely not?'

'You sent for me, and I have come,' she answered humbly, like an obedient familiar in the employ of some great enchanter. Indeed, the Baron's power over this innocent girl was curiously like enchantment, or mesmeric influence. It was so masterful that the sexual element was almost eliminated. It was that of Prospero over the gentle Ariel. And yet it was probably only that of the cosmopolite over the recluse, of the experienced man over the simple maid.

'You have come – on your wedding-day! – O Margery, this is a mistake. Of course, you should not have obeyed me, since, though I thought your wedding would be soon, I did not know it was today.'

'I promised you, sir; and I would rather keep my promise to you than be married to Jim.'

'That must not be – the feeling is wrong!' he murmured, looking at the distant hills. 'There seems to be a fate in all this; I get out of the frying-pan into the fire. What a recompense to you for your goodness! The fact is, I was out of health and out of spirits, so I – but no more of that. Now instantly to repair this tremendous blunder that we have made – that's the question.'

After a pause, he went on hurriedly, 'Walk down the hill; get into the road. By that time I shall be there with a phaeton. We may get back in time. What time is it now? If not, no doubt the wedding can be tomorrow; so all will come right again. Don't cry, my dear girl. Keep the locket, of course – you'll marry Jim.'

IX

He hastened down towards the stables, and she went on as directed. It seemed as if he must have put in the horse himself, so quickly did he reappear with the phaeton on the open road.

Margery silently took her seat, and the Baron seemed cut to the quick with self-reproach as he noticed the listless indifference with which she acted. There was no doubt that in her heart she had preferred obeying the apparently important mandate that morning to becoming Jim's wife; but there was no less doubt that had the Baron left her alone she would quietly have gone to the altar.

He drove along furiously, in a cloud of dust. There was much to contemplate in that peaceful Sunday morning – the windless trees and fields, the shaking sunlight, the pause in human stir. Yet neither of them heeded, and thus they drew near to the dairy. His first expressed intention had been to go indoors with her, but this he abandoned as impolitic in the highest degree.

'You may be soon enough,' he said, springing down, and helping her to follow. 'Tell the truth: say you were sent for to receive a wedding present – that it was a mistake on my part – a mistake on yours; and I think they'll forgive. . . . And, Margery, my last request to you is this: that if I send for you again, you do not come. Promise solemnly, my dear girl, that any such request shall be unheeded.'

Her lips moved, but the promise was not articulated. 'O, sir, I cannot promise it!' she said at last.

'But you must; your salvation may depend on it!' he insisted almost sternly. 'You don't know what I am.'

'Then, sir, I promise,' she replied. 'Now leave me to myself, please, and I'll go indoors and manage matters.'

He turned the horse and drove away, but only for a little distance. Out of sight he pulled rein suddenly. 'Only to go back and propose it to her, and she'd come!' he murmured.

He stood up in the phaeton, and by this means he could see over the hedge. Margery still sat listlessly in the same place; there was not a lovelier flower in the field. 'No,' he said; 'no, no – never!' He reseated himself, and the wheels sped lightly back over the soft dust to Mount Lodge.

Meanwhile Margery had not moved. If the Baron could dissimulate on the side of severity she could dissimulate on the side of calm. He did not know what had been veiled by the quiet promise to manage matters indoors. Rising at length she first turned away from the house; and, by-and-by, having apparently forgotten till then that she carried it in her hand, she opened the case, and looked at the locket. This seemed to give her courage. She turned, set her face towards the dairy in good earnest, and though her heart faltered when the gates came in sight, she kept on and drew near the door.

On the threshold she stood listening. The house was silent. Decorations were visible in the passage, and also the carefully swept and sanded path to the gate, which she was to have trodden as a bride; but the sparrows hopped over it as if it were abandoned; and all appeared to have been checked at its climacteric, like a clock stopped on the strike. Till this moment of confronting the suspended animation of the scene she had not realized the full shock of the convulsion which her disappearance must have caused. It is quite certain – apart from her own repeated assurances to that effect in later years – that in hastening off that morning to her sudden engagement, Margery had not counted the cost of such an enterprise; while a dim notion that she might get back again in time for the ceremony, if the message meant nothing serious, should also be mentioned in her favour. But, upon the whole, she had obeyed the call with an unreasoning obedience worthy of a disciple in primitive times. A conviction that the Baron's life might depend upon her presence – for she had by this time divined the tragical event she had interrupted on the foggy morning – took from her all will to judge and consider calmly. The simple affairs of her and hers seemed nothing beside the possibility of harm to him.

A well-known step moved on the sanded floor within, and she went forward. That she saw her father's face before, just within the door, can hardly be said: it was rather Reproach and Rage in a human mask.

'What! ye have dared to come back alive, hussy, to look upon the dupery you have practised on honest people! You've mortified us all; I don't want to see 'ee; I don't want to hear 'ee; I don't want to know anything!' He walked up and down the room, unable to command himself. 'Nothing but being dead could have excused 'ee for not meeting and marrying that man this morning; and yet you have the brazen impudence to stand there as well as ever! What be you here for?'

'I've come back to marry Jim, if he wants me to,' she said faintly. 'And if not – perhaps so much the better. I was sent for this morning early. I thought –' She halted. To say that she had thought a man's death might happen by his own hand if she did not go to him would never do. 'I was obliged to go,' she said. 'I had given my word.'

'Why didn't you tell us then, so that the wedding could be put off, without making fools o' us?'

'Because I was afraid you wouldn't let me go, and I had made up my mind to go.'

'To go where?'

She was silent; till she said, 'I will tell Jim all, and why it was; and if he's any friend of mine he'll excuse me.'

'Not Jim – he's no such fool. Jim had put all ready for you, Jim had called at your house, a-dressed up in his new wedding clothes, and a-smiling like the sun; Jim had told the parson, had got the ringers in tow, and the clerk awaiting; and then – you was *gone*! Then Jim turned as pale as rendlewood, and busted out, "If she don't marry me today," 'a said, "she don't marry me at all! No; let her look elsewhere for a husband. For tew years I've put up with her haughty tricks and her takings," 'a said, " I've droudged and I've traipsed, I've bought and I've sold, all wi' an eye to her; I've suffered horseflesh," he says – yes, them was his noble words – "but I'll suffer it no longer. She shall go!" "Jim," says I, "you be a man. If she's alive, I commend 'ee; if she's dead, pity my old age." "She isn't dead," says he "for I've just heard she was seen walking off across the fields this morning, looking all of a scornful triumph." He turned round and went, and the rest o' the neighbours went; and here be I left to the reproach o't.'

'He was too hasty,' murmured Margery. 'For now he's said this I can't marry him tomorrow, as I might ha' done; and perhaps so much the better.'

'You can be so calm about it, can ye? Be my arrangements nothing, then, that you should break 'em up, and say off hand what wasn't done today might ha' been done tomorrow, and such flick-flack? Out o' my sight! I won't hear any more. I won't speak to 'ee any more.'

'I'll go away, and then you'll be sorry!'

'Very well, go. Sorry – not I.'

He turned and stamped his way into the cheese-room. Margery went upstairs. She too was excited now, and instead of fortifying herself in her bedroom till her father's rage had blown over, as she had often done on lesser occasions, she packed up a bundle of articles, crept down again, and went out of the house. She had a place of refuge in these cases of necessity, and her father knew it, and was less alarmed at seeing her depart than he might otherwise have been. This place was Rook's Gate, the house of her grandmother, who always took Margery's part when that young woman was particularly in the wrong.

The devious way she pursued, to avoid the vicinity of Mount Lodge, was tedious, and she was already weary. But the cottage was a restful place to arrive at, for she was her own mistress there – her grandmother never coming down stairs – and Edy, the woman who lived with and attended her, being a cipher except in muscle and voice. The approach was by a straight open road, bordered by thin lank trees, all sloping away from the south-west wind-quarter, and the scene bore a strange resemblance to certain bits of Dutch landscape which have been imprinted on the world's eye by Hobbema and his school.

Having explained to her granny that the wedding was put off, and that she had come to stay, one of Margery's first acts was carefully to pack up the locket and case, her wedding present from the Baron. The conditions of the gift were unfulfilled, and she wished it to go back instantly. Perhaps, in the intricacies of her bosom, there lurked a greater satisfaction with the reason for returning the present than she would have felt just then with a reason for keeping it.

To send the article was difficult. In the evening she wrapped herself up, searched and found a gauze veil that had been used by her grandmother in past years for hiving swarms of bees, buried her face in it, and sallied forth with a palpitating heart till she drew near the tabernacle of her demi-god the Baron. She ventured only to the back-door where she handed in the parcel addressed to him, and quickly came away.

Now it seems that during the day the Baron had been unable to learn the result of his attempt to return Margery in time for the event he had interrupted. Wishing, for obvious reasons, to avoid direct inquiry by messenger, and being too unwell to go far himself, he could learn no particulars. He was sitting in thought after a lonely dinner when the parcel intimating failure was brought in. The footman, whose curiosity had been excited by the mode of its arrival, peeped through the keyhole after closing the door, to learn what the packet meant. Directly the Baron had opened it he thrust out his feet vehemently from his chair, and began cursing his ruinous conduct in bringing about such a disaster, for the return of the locket denoted not only no wedding that day, but none tomorrow, or at any time.

'I have done that innocent woman a great wrong!' he murmured. 'Deprived her of, perhaps, her only opportunity of becoming mistress of a happy home!'

X

A considerable period of inaction followed among all concerned.

Nothing tended to dissipate the obscurity which veiled the life of the Baron. The position he occupied in the minds of the country folk around was one which combined the mysteriousness of a legendary character with the unobtrusive deeds of a modern gentleman. To this day whoever takes the trouble to go down to Silverthorn in Lower Wessex and make inquiries will find existing there almost a superstitious feeling for the moody melancholy stranger who resided in the Lodge some forty years ago.

Whence he came, whither he was going, were alike unknown. It was said that his mother had been an English lady of noble family who had married a foreigner not unheard of in circles where men pile up 'the cankered heaps of strange-achieved gold' – that he had been born and educated in England, taken abroad, and so on. But the facts of a life in such cases are of little account beside the aspect of a life; and hence though doubtless the years of his existence contained their share of trite and homely circumstance, the curtain which masked all this was never lifted to gratify such a theatre of spectators as those of Silverthorn. Therein lay his charm.

His life was a vignette, of which the central strokes only were drawn with any distinctness, the environment shading away to a blank.

He might have been said to resemble that solitary bird the heron. The still, lonely stream was his frequent haunt: on its banks he would stand for hours with his rod, looking into the water, beholding the tawny inhabitants with the eye of a philosopher, and seeming to say, 'Bite or don't bite it's all the same to me.' He was often mistaken for a ghost by children; and for a pollard willow by men, when, on their way home in the dusk, they saw him motionless by some rushy bank, unobservant of the decline of the day.

Why did he come to fish near Silverthorn? That was never explained. As far as was known he had no relatives near; the fishing there was not exceptionally good; the society thereabout was decidedly meagre. That he had committed some folly or hasty act, that he had been wrongfully accused of some crime, thus rendering his seclusion from the world desirable for a while, squared very well with his frequent melancholy. But such as he was there he lived, well supplied with fishing-tackle, and tenant of a furnished house, just suited to the requirements of such an eccentric being as he.

Margery's father, having privately ascertained that she was living with her grandmother, and getting into no harm, refrained from communicating with her, in the hope of seeing her contrite at his door. It had, of course, become known about Silverthorn that at the last moment Margery refused to wed Hayward, by absenting herself from the house. Jim was pitied, yet not pitied much, for it was said that he ought not to have been so eager for a woman who had shown no anxiety for him.

And where was Jim himself? It must not be supposed that that tactician had all this while withdrawn from mortal eye to tear his hair in silent indignation and despair. He had, in truth, merely retired up the lonesome defile between the downs to his smouldering kiln, and the ancient ramparts above it; and there, after his first hours of natural discomposure, he quietly waited for overtures from the possibly repentant Margery. But no overtures arrived, and then he meditated anew on the absorbing problem of her skittishness, and how to set about another campaign for her conquest, notwithstanding his late disastrous failure. Why had he failed? To what was her strange conduct owing? That was the thing which puzzled him.

He had made no advance in solving the riddle when, one morning, a stranger appeared on the down above him, looking as if he had lost his way. The man had a good deal of black hair below his felt hat, and carried under his arm a case containing a musical instrument. Descending to where Jim stood, he asked if there were not a short cut across that way to Tivworthy, where a fête was to be held.

'Well, yes, there is,' said Jim. 'But 'tis an enormous distance for 'ee.'

'Oh, yes,' replied the musician. 'I wish to intercept the carrier on the highway.'

The nearest way was precisely in the direction of Rook's Gate where Margery, as Jim knew, was staying. Having some time to spare, Jim was strongly impelled to make a kind act to the lost musician a pretext for taking observations in that neighbourhood, and telling his acquaintance that he was going the same way, he started without further ado.

They skirted the long length of meads, and in due time arrived at the back of Rook's Gate, where the path joined the high road. A hedge divided the public way from the cottage garden. Jim drew up at this point and said, 'Your road is straight on: I turn back here.'

But the musician was standing fixed, as if in great perplexity. Thrusting his hand into his forest of black hair, he murmured, 'Surely it is the same – surely!'

Jim, following the direction of his neighbour's eyes, found them to be fixed on a figure till that moment hidden from himself – Margery Tucker – who was crossing the garden to an opposite gate with a little cheese in her arms, her head thrown back, and her face quite exposed.

'What of her?' said Jim.

'Two months ago I formed one of the band at the Yeomanry Ball given by Lord Toneborough in the next county. I saw that young lady dancing the polka there in robes of gauze and lace. Now I see her carry a cheese!'

'Never!' said Jim incredulously.

'But I do not mistake. I say it is so!'

Jim ridiculed the idea; the bandsman protested, and was about to lose his temper, when Jim gave in with the good-nature of a person who can afford to despise opinions; and the musician went his way.

As he dwindled out of sight Jim began to think more carefully over what he had said. The young man's thoughts grew quite to an excitement, for there came into his mind the Baron's extraordinary kindness in regard to furniture, hitherto accounted for by the assumption that the nobleman had taken a fancy to him. Could it be, among all the amazing things of life, that the Baron was at the bottom of this mischief, and that he had amused himself by taking Margery to a ball?

Doubts and suspicions which distract some lovers to imbecility only served to bring out Jim's great qualities. Where he trusted he was the most trusting fellow in the world; where he doubted he could be guilty of the slyest strategy. Once suspicious, he became one of those subtle, watchful characters who, without integrity, make good thieves; with a little, good jobbers; with a little more, good diplomatists. Jim was honest, and he considered what to do.

Retracing his steps, he peeped again. She had gone in; but she would soon reappear, for it could be seen that she was carrying little new cheeses one by one to a spring-cart and horse tethered outside the gate – her grandmother, though not a regular dairywoman, still managing a few cows by means of a man and maid. With the lightness of a cat Jim crept round to the gate, took a piece of chalk from his pocket, and wrote upon the boarding 'The Baron.' Then he retreated to the other side of the garden where he had just watched Margery.

In due time she emerged with another little cheese, came on to the garden-door, and glanced upon the chalked words which confronted her. She started; the cheese rolled from her arms to the ground, and broke into pieces like a pudding.

She looked fearfully round, her face burning like sunset, and, seeing nobody, stooped to pick up the flaccid lumps. Jim, with a pale face, departed as invisibly as he had come. He had proved the bandsman's tale to be true. On his way back he formed a resolution. It was to beard the lion in his den – to call on the Baron.

Meanwhile Margery had recovered her equanimity, and gathered up the broken cheese. But she could by no means account for the handwriting. Jim was just the sort of fellow to play her such a trick at ordinary times, but she imagined him to be far too incensed against her to do it now; and she suddenly wondered if it were any sort of signal from the Baron himself.

Of him she had lately heard nothing. If ever monotony pervaded a life it pervaded hers at Rook's Gate; and she had begun to despair of any happy change. But it is precisely when the social atmosphere seems stagnant that great events are brewing. Margery's quiet was broken first, as we have seen, by a slight start, only sufficient to make her drop a cheese; and then by a more serious matter.

She was inside the same garden one day when she heard two watermen talking without. The conversation was to the effect that the strange gentleman who had taken Mount Lodge for the season was seriously ill.

'How ill?' cried Margery through the hedge, which screened her from recognition.

'Bad abed,' said one of the watermen.

'Inflammation of the lungs,' said the other.

'Got wet, fishing,' the first chimed in.

Margery could gather no more. An ideal admiration rather than any positive passion existed in her breast for the Baron: she had of late seen too little of him to allow any incipient views of him as a lover to grow to formidable dimensions. It was an extremely romantic feeling, delicate as an aroma, capable of quickening to an active principle, or dying to 'a painless sympathy,' as the case might be.

This news of his illness, coupled with the mysterious chalking on the gate, troubled her, and revived his image much. She took to walking up and down the garden-paths, looking into the hearts of flowers, and not thinking what they were. His last request had been that she was not to go to him if he should send for her; and now she asked herself, was the name on the gate a hint to enable her to go without infringing the letter of her promise? Thus unexpectedly had Jim's manœuvre operated.

Ten days passed. All she could hear of the Baron were the

same words, 'Bad abed,' till one afternoon, after a gallop of the physician to the Lodge, the tidings spread like lightning that the Baron was dying.

Margery distressed herself with the question whether she might be permitted to visit him and say her prayers at his bedside; but she feared to venture; and thus eight-and-forty hours slipped away, and the Baron still lived. Despite her shyness and awe of him she had almost made up her mind to call when, just at dusk on that October evening, somebody came to the door and asked for her.

She could see the messenger's head against the low new moon. He was a man-servant. He said he had been all the way to her father's, and had been sent thence to her here. He simply brought a note, and, delivering it into her hands, went away.

DEAR MARGERY TUCKER (ran the note) – They say I am not likely to live, so I want to see you. Be here at eight o'clock this evening. Come quite alone to the side-door, and tap four times softly. My trusty man will admit you. The occasion is an important one. Prepare yourself for a solemn ceremony, which I wish to have performed while it lies in my power.

VON XANTEN.

XI

Margery's face flushed up, and her neck and arms glowed in sympathy. The quickness of youthful imagination, and the assumptiveness of woman's reason sent her straight as an arrow this thought: 'He wants to marry me!'

She had heard of similar strange proceedings, in which the orange-flower and the sad cypress were intertwined. People sometimes wished on their death-beds from motives of esteem, to form a legal tie which they had not cared to establish as a domestic one during their active life.

For a few minutes Margery could hardly be called excited; she was excitement itself. Between surprise and modesty she blushed and trembled by turns. She became grave, sat down in the solitary room, and looked into the fire. At seven o'clock she rose resolved, and went quite tranquilly upstairs, where she speedily began to dress.

In making this hasty toilet nine-tenths of her care were given to her hands. The summer had left them slightly brown, and she held them up and looked at them with some misgiving, the fourth finger of her left hand more especially. Hot washings and cold washings, certain products from bee and flower known only to country girls, everything she could think of, were used upon those little sunburnt hands, till she persuaded herself that they were really as white as could be wished by a husband with a hundred titles. Her dressing completed, she left word with Edy that she was going for a long walk, and set out in the direction of Mount Lodge.

She no longer tripped like a girl, but walked like a woman. While crossing the park she murmured 'Baroness von Xanten' in a pronunciation of her own. The sound of that title caused her such agitation that she was obliged to pause, with her hand upon her heart.

The house was so closely neighboured by shrubberies on three of its sides that it was not till she had gone nearly round it that she found the little door. The resolution she had been an hour in forming failed her when she stood at the portal. While pausing for courage to tap, a carriage drove up to the front entrance a little way off, and peeping round the corner she saw alight a clergyman, and a gentleman in whom Margery fancied that she recognized a well-known solicitor from the neighbouring town. She had no longer any doubt of the nature of the ceremony proposed. 'It is sudden – but I must obey him!' she murmured: and tapped four times.

The door was opened so quickly that the servant must have been standing immediately inside. She thought him the man who had driven them to the ball – the silent man who could be trusted. Without a word he conducted her up the back staircase, and through a door at the top, into a wide corridor. She was asked to wait in a little dressing-room, where there was a fire and an old metal-framed looking-glass over the mantel-piece, in which she caught sight of herself. A red spot burnt in each of her cheeks; the rest of her face was pale; and her eyes were like diamonds of the first water.

Before she had been seated many minutes the man came back noiselessly, and she followed him to a door covered by a red and black curtain, which he lifted, and ushered her into a large chamber. A screened light stood on a table before her, and on her left the hangings of a tall dark four-post bedstead obstructed her view of the centre of the room. Everything here seemed of such a magnificent type to her eyes that she felt confused, diminished to half her height, half her strength, half her prettiness. The man who had conducted her retired at once, and some one came softly round the angle of the bed-curtains. He held out his hand kindly – rather patronisingly: it was the solicitor whom she knew by sight. The gentleman led her forward, as if she had been a lamb rather than a woman, till the occupant of the bed was revealed.

The Baron's eyes were closed, and her entry had been so noiseless that he did not open them. The pallor of his face nearly matched the white bed-linen and his dark hair and heavy black moustache were like dashes of ink on a clean page. Near him sat the parson and another gentleman, whom she afterwards learnt to be a London physician; and on the parson whispering a few words the Baron opened his eyes. As soon as he saw her he smiled faintly, and held out his hand.

Margery would have wept for him, if she had not been too overawed and palpitating to do anything. She quite forgot what she had come for, shook hands with him mechanically, and could hardly return an answer to his weak 'Dear Margery, you see how I am – how are you?'

In preparing for marriage she had not calculated on such a scene as this. Her affection for the Baron had too much of the vague in it to afford her trustfulness now. She wished she had not come. On a sign from the Baron the lawyer brought her a chair, and the oppressive silence was broken by the Baron's words.

'I am pulled down to death's door, Margery,' he said; 'and I suppose I soon shall pass through. . . . My peace has been much disturbed in this illness, for just before it attacked me I received – that present you returned, from which, and in other ways, I learnt that you had lost your chance of marriage. . . . Now it was I who did the harm, and you can imagine how the news has affected me. It has worried me all the illness through, and I cannot dismiss my error from my mind. . . . I want to right the wrong I have done you before I die. Margery, you have always obeyed me, and, strange as the request may be, will you obey me now?'

She whispered 'Yes.'

'Well, then,' said the Baron, 'these three gentleman are here for a special purpose: one helps the body – he's called a physician; another helps the soul – he's a parson; the other helps the understanding – he's a lawyer. They are here partly on my account, and partly on yours.'

The speaker then made a sign to the lawyer, who went out of the door. He came back almost instantly, but not alone. Behind him, dressed up in his best clothes, with a flower in his buttonhole and a bridegroom's air, walked – Jim.

XII

Margery could hardly repress a scream. As for flushing and blushing, she had turned hot and turned pale so many times already during the evening, that there was really now nothing of that sort left for her to do; and she remained in complexion much as before. O, the mockery of it! That secret dream – that sweet word 'Baroness!' – which had sustained her all the way along. Instead of a Baron there stood Jim, white waistcoated, demure, every hair in place, and, if she mistook not, even a deedy spark in his eye.

Jim's surprising presence on the scene may be briefly accounted for. His resolve to seek an explanation with the Baron at all risks had proved unexpectedly easy: the interview had at once been granted, and then, seeing the crisis at which matters stood, the Baron had generously revealed to Jim the whole of his indebtedness to and knowledge of Margery. The truth of the Baron's statement, the innocent nature as yet of the acquaintanceship, his sorrow for the rupture he had produced, was so evident that, far from having any further doubts of his patron, Jim frankly asked his advice on the next step to be pursued. At this stage the Baron fell ill, and, desiring much to see the two young people united before his death, he had sent anew to Hayward, and proposed the plan which they were now about to attempt – a marriage at the bedside of the sick man by special licence. The influence at Lambeth of some friends of the Baron's, and the charitable bequests of his late mother to several deserving Church funds, were generally supposed to be among the reasons why the application for the licence was not refused.

This, however, is of small consequence. The Baron probably knew, in proposing this method of celebrating the marriage, that his enormous power over her would outweigh any sentimental obstacles which she might set up – inward objections that, without his presence and firmness, might prove too much for her acquiescence. Doubtless he foresaw, too, the advantage of getting her into the house before making the individuality of her husband clear to her mind.

Now, the Baron's conjectures were right as to the event, but wrong as to the motives. Margery was a perfect little dissembler on some occasions, and one of them was when she wished to hide any sudden mortification that might bring her into ridicule. She had no sooner recovered from her first fit of discomfiture than pride bade her suffer anything rather than reveal her absurd disappointment. Hence the scene progressed as follows:

'Come here, Hayward,' said the invalid. Hayward came near. The Baron, holding her hand in one of his own, and her lover's in the other, continued, 'Will you, in spite of your recent vexation with her, marry her now if she does not refuse?'

'I will, sir,' said Jim promptly.

'And Margery, what do you say? It is merely a setting of things right. You have already promised this young man to be his wife, and should, of course, perform your promise. You don't dislike Jim?'

'O, no sir,' she said, in a low, dry voice.

'I like him better than I can tell you,' said the Baron. 'He is an honourable man, and will make you a good husband. You must remember that marriage is a life contract, in which general compatability of temper and wordly position is of more importance than fleeting passion, which never long survives. Now, will you, at my earnest request, and before I go to the South of Europe to die, agree to make this good man happy? I have expressed your views on the subject, haven't I, Hayward?'

'To a T, sir,' said Jim emphatically; with a motion of raising his hat to his influential ally, till he remembered he had no hat on. 'And, though I could hardly expect Margery to gie in for my asking, I feels she ought to gie in for yours.'

'And you accept him, my little friend?'

'Yes, sir,' she murmured, 'if he'll agree to a thing or two.'

'Doubtless he will – what are they?'

'That I shall not be made to live with him till I am in the mind for it; and that my having him shall be kept unknown for the present.'

'Well, what do you think of it, Hayward?'

'Anything that you or she may wish I'll do my noble lord,' said Jim.

'Well, her request is not unreasonable, seeing that the proceedings are, on my account, a little hurried. So we'll proceed. You rather expected this, from my allusion to a ceremony in my note, did you not, Margery?'

'Yes, sir,' said she, with an effort.

'Good; I thought so; you looked so little surprised.'

We now leave the scene in the bedroom for a spot not many yards off.

When the carriage seen by Margery at the door was driving up to Mount Lodge it arrested the attention not only of the young girl, but of a man who had for some time been moving slowly about the opposite lawn, engaged in some operation while he smoked a short pipe. A short observation of his doings would have shown that he was sheltering some delicate plants from an expected frost, and that he was the gardener. When the light at the door fell upon the entering forms of parson and lawyer – the former a stranger, the latter known to him – the gardener walked thoughtfully round the house. Reaching the small side-entrance he was further surprised to see it noiselessly open to a young woman, in whose momentarily illuminated features he discerned those of Margery Tucker.

Altogether there was something curious in this. The man returned to the lawn front, and perfunctorily went on putting shelters over certain plants, though his thoughts were plainly otherwise engaged. On the grass his footsteps were noiseless, and the night moreover being still, he could presently hear a murmuring from the bedroom window over his head.

The gardener took from a tree a ladder that he had used in nailing that day, set it under the window, and ascended half-way hoodwinking his conscience by seizing a nail or two with his hand and testing their twig-supporting powers. He soon heard enough to satisfy him. The words of a church-service in the strange parson's voice were audible in snatches through the blind: they were words he knew to be part of the solemnization of matrimony, such as 'wedded wife,' 'richer for poorer,' and so on; the less familiar parts being a more or less confused sound.

Satisfied that a wedding was in progress there, the gardener did not for a moment dream that one of the contracting parties could be other than the sick Baron. He descended the ladder and again walked round the house, waiting only till he saw Margery emerge from the same little door; when fearing that he might be discovered, he withdrew in the direction of his own cottage.

This building stood at the lower corner of the garden, and as soon as the gardener entered he was accosted by a hand-some woman in a widow's cap, who called him father, and said that supper had been ready for a long time. They sat down, but during the meal the gardener was so abstracted and silent that his daughter put her head winningly to one side and said, 'What is it, father dear?'

'Ah – what is it!' cried the gardener. 'Something that makes very little difference to me, but may be of great account to you, if you play your cards well. *There's been a wedding at the Lodge tonight!*' He related to her, with a caution to secrecy, all that he had heard and seen.

'We are folk that have got to get their living,' he said, 'and such ones mustn't tell tales about their betters, – Lord forgive the mockery of the word! – but there's something to be made of it. She's a nice maid; so, Harriet, do you take the first chance you get for honouring her, before others know what has happened. Since this is done so privately it will be kept private for some time – till after his death, no question; when I expect she'll take this house for herself, and blaze out as a widow-lady ten thousand pound strong. You being a widow, she may make you her company-keeper; and so you'll have a home by a little contriving.'

While this conversation progressed at the gardener's Margery was on her way out of the Baron's house. She was, indeed, married. But, as we know, she was not married to the Baron. The ceremony over she seemed but little discomposed, and expressed a wish to return alone as she had come. To this, of course, no objection could be offered under the terms of the agreement, and wishing Jim a frigid good-bye, and the Baron a very quiet farewell, she went out by the door which had admitted her. Once safe and alone in the darkness of the park she burst into tears, which dropped upon the grass as she passed along. In the Baron's room she had seemed scared and helpless; now her reason and emotions returned. The further she got away from the glamour of that room, and the influence of its occupant, the more she became of the opinion that she had acted foolishly. She had disobediently left her father's house, to obey him here. She had pleased everybody but herself.

However, thinking was now too late. How she got into her grandmother's house she hardly knew; but without a supper, and without confronting either her relative or Edy, she went to bed.

XIII

On going out into the garden next morning, with a strange sense of being another person than herself, she beheld Jim leaning mutely over the gate.

He nodded. 'Good morning, Margery,' he said civilly.

'Good morning,' said Margery in the same tone.

'I beg your pardon,' he continued. 'But which way was you going this morning?'

'I am not going anywhere just now, thank you. But I shall go to my father's by-and-by with Edy.' She went on with a sigh, 'I have done what he has all along wished, that is, married you; and there's no longer reason for enmity atween him and me.'

'Trew – trew. Well, as I am going the same way, I can give you a lift in the trap, for the distance is long.'

'No thank you – I am used to walking,' she said.

They remained in silence, the gate between them, till Jim's convictions would apparently allow him to hold his peace no longer. 'This is a bad job!' he murmured.

'It is,' she said, as one whose thoughts have only too readily been identified. 'How I came to agree to it is more than I can tell!' And tears began rolling down her cheeks.

'The blame is more mine than yours, I suppose,' he returned. 'I ought to have said No, and not backed up the gentleman in carrying out this scheme. 'Twas his own notion entirely, as perhaps you know. I should never have thought of such a plan; but he said you'd be willing, and that it would be all right; and I was too ready to believe him.'

'The thing is, how to remedy it,' said she bitterly. 'I believe, of course, in your promise to keep this private, and not to trouble me by calling.'

'Certainly,' said Jim. 'I don't want to trouble you. As for that, why, my dear Mrs. Hayward –'

'Don't Mrs. Hayward me!' said Margery sharply. 'I won't be Mrs. Hayward!'

Jim paused. 'Well, you are she by law, and that was all I meant,' he said mildly.

'I said I would acknowledge no such thing, and I won't. A thing can't be legal when it's against the wishes of the persons the laws are made to protect. So I beg you not to call me that any more.'

'Very well, Miss Tucker,' said Jim deferentially. 'We can live on exactly as before. We can't marry anybody else, that's true; but beyond that there's no difference, and no harm done. Your father ought to be told, I suppose, even if nobody else is? It will partly reconcile him to you and make your life smoother.'

Instead of directly replying, Margery exclaimed in a low voice:

'O, it is a mistake – I didn't see it all, owing to not having time to reflect! I agreed, thinking that at least I should get reconciled to father by the step. But perhaps he would as soon have me not married at all as married and parted. I must ha'' been enchanted – bewitched – when I gave my consent to this! I only did it to please that dear good dying nobleman – though why he should have wished it so much I can't tell!'

'Nor I neither,' said Jim. 'Yes, we've been fooled into it, Margery,' he said, with extraordinary gravity. 'He's had his way wi' us, and now we've got to suffer for it. Being a gentleman of patronage and having bought several loads of lime o' me, and having given me all that splendid furniture, I could hardly refuse –'

'What, did he give you that?'

'Ay sure – to help me win ye.'

Margery covered her face with her hands; whereupon Jim stood up from the gate and looked critically at her. ''Tis a footy plot between you two men to – snare me!' she exclaimed. 'Why should you have done it – why should he have done it – when I've not deserved to be treated so. He bought the furniture – did he! O, I've been taken in – I've been wronged!' The grief and vexation of finding that long ago, when fondly believing the Baron to have lover-like feelings himself for her, he was still conspiring to favour Jim's suit, was more than she could endure.

Jim with distant courtesy waited, nibbling a straw, till her paroxysm was over. 'One word, Miss Tuck – Mrs. – Margery,' he then recommenced gravely. 'You'll find me man enough to respect your wish, and to leave you to yourself – for ever and ever, if that's all. But I've just one word of advice to render 'ee. That is, that before you go to Silverthorn Dairy yourself you let me drive ahead and call on your father. He's friends with me, and he's not friends with you. I can break the news, a little at a time, and I think I can gain his good will for you now, even though the wedding be no natural wedding at all. At any count, I can hear what he's got to say about 'ee, and come back here and tell 'ee.'

She nodded a cool assent to this, and he left her strolling about the garden in the sunlight while he went on to reconnoitre as agreed. It must not be supposed that Jim's dutiful echoes of Margery's regret at her precipitate marriage were all gospel; and there is no doubt that his private intention, after telling the dairy-farmer what had happened, was to ask his temporary assent to her caprice, till, in the course of time, she should be reasoned out of her whims and induced to settle down with Jim in a natural manner. He had, it is true, been somewhat nettled by her firm objection to him, and her keen sorrow for what she had done to please another; but he hoped for the best.

But, alas for the astute Jim's calculations! He drove on to the dairy, whose white walls now gleamed in the morning sun; made fast the horse to a ring in the wall, and entered the barton. Before knocking, he perceived the dairyman walking across from a gate in the other direction, as if he had just come in. Jim went over to him. Since the unfortunate incident on the morning of the intended wedding they had merely been on nodding terms, from a sense of awkwardness in their relations.

'What – is that thee?' said Dairyman Tucker, in a voice which unmistakably startled Jim by its abrupt fierceness. 'A pretty fellow thou be'st!'

It was a bad beginning for the young man's life as a son-in-law, and augured ill for the delicate consultation he desired.

'What's the matter?' said Jim.

'Matter! I wish some folks would burn their lime without burning other folks' property along wi' it. You ought to be ashamed of yourself. You call yourself a man, Jim Hayward, and an honest lime-burner, and a respectable, market-keeping Christen, and yet at six o'clock this morning, instead o' being where you ought to ha' been – at your work, there was neither vell or mark o' thee to be seen!'

'Faith, I don't know what you are raving at,' said Jim.

'Why – the sparks from thy couch-heap blew over upon my hay-rick, and the rick's burnt to ashes; and all to come out o' my well-squeezed pocket. I'll tell thee what it is, young man. There's no business in thee. I've known Silverthorn folk, quick and dead, for the last couple-o'-score year, and I've never knew one so three-cunning for harm as thee, my gentleman lime-burner; and I reckon it one o' the luckiest days o' my life when I 'scaped having thee in my family. That maid of mine was right; I was wrong. She seed thee to be a drawlacheting rogue, and 'twas her wisdom to go off that morning and get rid o' thee. I commend her for't, and I'm going to fetch her home tomorrow.'

'You needn't take the trouble. She's coming home-along tonight of her own accord. I have seen her this morning, and she told me so.'

'So much the better. I'll welcome her warm. Nation! I'd sooner see her married to the parish fool than thee. Not you – you don't care for my hay. Tarrying about where you shouldn't be, in bed, no doubt; that's what you was a-doing. Now, don't you darken my doors again, and the sooner you be off my bit o' ground the better I shall be pleased.'

Jim looked as he felt, stultified. If the rick had been really destroyed, a little blame certainly attached to him, but he could not understand how it had happened. However, blame or none, it was clear he could not, with any self-respect, declare himself to be this peppery old gaffer's son-in-law in the face of such an attack as this.

For months – almost years – the one transaction that had seemed necessary to compose these two families satisfactorily was Jim's union with Margery. No sooner had it been completed than it appeared on all sides as the gravest mishap for both. Stating coldly that he would discover how much of the accident was to be attributed to his negligence and pay the damage, he went out of the barton, and returned the way he had come.

Margery had been keeping a look-out for him, particularly wishing him not to enter the house, lest others should see the seriousness of their interview; and as soon as she heard wheels she went to the gate, which was out of view.

'Surely father has been speaking roughly to you!' she said, on seeing his face.

'Not the least doubt that he have,' said Jim.

'But is he still angry with me?'

'Not in the least. He's waiting to welcome 'ee.'

'Ah! because I've married you.'

'Because he thinks you have *not* married me! He's jawed me up hill and down. He hates me; and for your sake I have not explained a word.'

Margery looked towards home with a sad, severe gaze. 'Mr. Hayward,' she said, 'we have made a great mistake, and we are in a strange position.'

'True, but I'll tell you what, mistress – I won't stand –' He stopped suddenly. 'Well, well; I've promised!' he quietly added.

'We must suffer for our mistake,' she went on. 'The way to suffer least is to keep our own counsel on what happened last evening, and not to meet. I must now return to my father.

He inclined his head in indifferent assent, and she went indoors, leaving him there.

XIV

Margery returned home, as she had decided, and resumed her old life at Silverthorn. And seeing her father's animosity towards Jim, she told him not a word of the marriage.

Her inner life, however, was not what it once had been. She had suffered a mental and emotional displacement – a shock, which had set a shade of astonishment on her face as a permanent thing.

Her indignation with the Baron for collusion with Jim, at first bitter, lessened with the lapse of a few weeks, and at length vanished in the interest of some tidings she received one day.

The Baron was not dead, but he was no longer at the Lodge. To the surprise of the physicians, a sufficient improvement had taken place in his condition to permit his removal before the cold weather came. His desire for removal had been such, indeed, that it was advisable to carry it out at almost any risk. The plan adopted had been to have him borne on men's shoulders in a sort of palanquin to the shore near Idmouth, a distance of several miles, where a yacht lay awaiting him. By this means the noise and jolting of a carriage, along irregular bye-roads, were avoided. The singular procession over the fields took place at night, and was witnessed by but few people, one being a labouring man, who described the scene to Margery. When the seaside was reached a long, narrow gangway was laid from the deck of the yacht to the shore, which was so steep as to allow the yacht to lie quite near. The men, with their burden, ascended by the light of lanterns, the sick man was laid in the cabin, and, as soon as his bearers had returned to the shore, the gangway was removed, a rope was heard skirring over wood in the darkness, the yacht quivered, spread her woven wings to the air, and moved away. Soon she was but a small, shapeless phantom upon the wide breast of the sea.

It was said that the yacht was bound for Algiers.

When the inimical autumn and winter weather came on, Margery wondered if he were still alive. The house being shut up, and the servants gone, she had no means of knowing, till, on a particular Saturday, her father drove her to Exonbury market. Here, in attending to his business, he left her to herself for awhile. Walking in a quiet street in the professional quarter of the town, she saw coming towards her the solicitor who had been present at the wedding and who had acted for the Baron in various small local matters during his brief residence at the Lodge.

She reddened to peony hues, averted her eyes, and would have passed him. But he crossed over and barred the pavement, and when she met his glance he was looking with friendly severity at her. The street was quiet, and he said in a low voice, 'How's the husband?'

'I don't know, sir,' said she.

'What – are your stipulations about secrecy and separate living still in force?'

'They will always be,' she replied decisively. 'Mr. Hayward and I agreed on the point, and we have not the slightest wish to change the arrangement.'

'H'm. Then 'tis Miss Tucker to the world; Mrs. Hayward to me and one or two others only?'

Margery nodded. Then she nerved herself by an effort, and, though blushing painfully, asked, 'May I put one question, sir? Is the Baron dead?'

'He is dead to you and to all of us. Why should you ask?'

'Because, if he's alive, I am sorry I married James Hayward. If he is dead I do not much mind my marriage.'

'I repeat, he is dead to you,' said the lawyer emphatically. 'I'll tell you all I know. My professional services for him ended with his departure from this country; but I think I should have heard from him if he had been alive still. I have not heard at all: and this, taken in connection with the nature of his illness, leaves no doubt in my mind that he is dead.'

Margery sighed, and thanking the lawyer she left him with a tear for the Baron in her eye. After this incident she became more restful; and the time drew on for her periodical visit to her grandmother.

A few days subsequent to her arrival her aged relative asked her to go with a message to the gardener at Mount Lodge (who still lived on there, keeping the grounds in order for the landlord). Margery hated that direction now, but she went. The Lodge, which she saw over the trees, was to her like a skull from which the warm and living flesh had vanished. It was twilight by the time she reached the cottage at the bottom of the Lodge garden, and, the room being illuminated within, she saw through the window a woman she had never seen before. She was dark, and rather handsome and when Margery knocked she opened the door. It was the gardener's widowed daughter, who had been advised to make friends with Margery.

She now found her opportunity. Margery's errand was soon completed, the young widow, to her surprise treating her with preternatural respect, and afterwards offering to accompany her home. Margery was not sorry to have a companion in the gloom, and they walked on together. The widow, Mrs. Peach, was demonstrative and confidential; and told Margery all about herself. She had come quite recently to live with her father – during the Baron's illness, in fact – and her husband had been captain of a ketch.

'I saw you one morning, ma'am,' she said. 'But you didn't see me. It was when you were crossing the hill in sight of the Lodge. You looked at it, and sighed. 'Tis the lot of widows to sigh, ma'am, is it not?'

'Widows – yes, I suppose; but what do you mean?'

Mrs. Peace lowered her voice. 'I can't say more, ma'am, with proper respect. But there seems to be no question of the poor Baron's death; and though these foreign princes can take (as my poor husband used to tell me) what they call left-handed wives, and leave them behind when they go abroad, widowhood is widowhood, left-handed or right. And really, to be the left-handed wife of a foreign baron is nobler than to be married all round to a common man. You'll excuse my freedom, ma'am; but being a widow myself, I have pitied you from my heart; so young as you are, and having to keep it a secret and (excusing

me) having no money out of his vast riches because 'tis
swallowed up by Baroness Number One.'

Margery did not understand a word more of this than the
bare fact that Mrs. Peach suspected her to be the Baron's
undowered widow, and such was the milkmaid's nature that
she did not deny the widow's impeachment. The latter continued –

'But ah, ma'am, all your troubles are straight backward in
your memory – while I have troubles before as well as grief
behind.'

'What may they be, Mrs. Peach?' inquired Margery, with an
air of the Baroness.

The other dropped her voice to revelation tones: 'I have been
forgetful enough of my first man to lose my heart to a second!'

'You shouldn't do that – it is wrong. You should control
your feelings.'

'But how am I to control my feelings?'

'By going to your dead husband's grave, and things of that
sort.'

'Do you go to your dead husband's grave?'

'How can I go to Algiers?'

'Ah – too true! Well, I've tried everything to cure myself –
read the words against it, gone to the Table the first Sunday of
every month, and all sorts. But, avast, my shipmate! – as my
poor man used to say – there 'tis just the same. In short, I've
made up my mind to encourage the new one. 'Tis flattering that
I, a new-comer, should have been found out by a young man so
soon.'

'Who is he?' said Margery listlessly.

'A master lime-burner.'

'A master lime-burner?'

'That's his profession. He's a partner-in-co., doing very well
indeed.'

'But what's his name?'

'I don't like to tell you his name, for, though 'tis night, that
covers all shame-facedness, my face is as hot as a 'Talian iron, I
declare! Do you just feel it.'

Margery put her hand on Mrs. Peach's face, and, sure
enough, hot it was. 'Does he come courting?' she asked
quickly.

'Well – only in the way of business. He never comes unless lime is wanted in the neighbourhood. He's in the Yeomanry, too, and will look very fine when he comes out in regimentals for drill in May.'

'Oh – in the Yeomanry,' Margery said, with a slight relief. 'Then it can't – is he a young man?'

'Yes, junior partner-in-co.'

The description had an odd resemblance to Jim, of whom Margery had not heard a word for months. He had promised silence and absence, and had fulfilled his promise literally, with a gratuitous addition that was rather amazing, if indeed it were Jim whom the widow loved. One point in the description puzzled Margery: Jim was not in the Yeomanry, unless, by a surprising development of enterprise, he had entered it recently.

At parting Margery said, with an interest quite tender, 'I should like to see you again, Mrs. Peach, and hear of your attachment. When can you call?'

'Oh – any time, dear Baroness, I'm sure – if you think I am good enough.'

'Indeed, I do, Mrs. Peach. Come as soon as you've seen the lime-burner again.'

XV

Seeing that Jim lived several miles from the widow, Margery was rather surprised, and even felt a slight sinking of the heart, when her new acquaintance appeared at her door so soon as the evening of the following Monday. She asked Margery to walk out with her, which the young woman readily did.

'I am come at once,' said the widow breathlessly, as soon as they were in the lane, 'for it is so exciting that I can't keep it. I must tell it to somebody, if only a bird, or a cat, or a garden snail.'

'What is it?' asked her companion.

'I've pulled grass from my husband's grave to cure it – wove the blades into true lover's knots; took off my shoes upon the sod; but avast, my shipmate, –'

'Upon the sod – why?'

'To feel the damp earth he's in, and make the sense of it

enter my soul. But no. It has swelled to a head; he is going to meet me at the Yeomanry Review.'

'The master lime-burner?'

The widow nodded.

'When is it to be?'

'Tomorrow. He looks so lovely in his accoutrements! He's such a splendid soldier; that was the last straw that kindled my soul to say yes. He's home from Exonbury for a night between the drills,' continued Mrs. Peach. 'He goes back tomorrow morning for the Review, and when it's over he's going to meet me. . . . But, guide my heart, there he is!'

Her exclamation had rise in the sudden appearance of a brilliant red uniform through the trees, and the tramp of a horse carrying the wearer thereof. In another half-minute the military gentleman would have turned the corner, and faced them.

'He'd better not see me; he'll think I know too much,' said Margery precipitately. 'I'll go up here.'

The widow, whose thoughts had been of the same cast, seemed much relieved to see Margery disappear in the plantation, in the midst of a spring chorus of birds. Once among the trees, Margery turned her head, and, before she could see the rider's person she recognised the horse as Tony, the lightest of three that Jim and his partner owned, for the purpose of carting out lime to their customers.

Jim, then, had joined the Yeomanry since his estrangement from Margery. A man who had worn the young Queen Victoria's uniform for seven days only could not be expected to look as if it were part of his person, in the manner of long-trained soldiers; but he was a well-formed young fellow, and of an age when few positions came amiss to one who has the capacity to adapt himself to circumstances.

Meeting the blushing Mrs. Peach (to whom Margery in her mind sternly denied the right to blush at all), Jim alighted and moved on with her, probably at Mrs. Peach's own suggestion; so that what they said, how long they remained together, and how they parted, Margery knew not. She might have known some of these things by waiting; but the presence of Jim had bred in her heart a sudden disgust for the widow, and a general sense of discomfiture. She went away in an opposite direction, turning her head and saying to the unconscious Jim, 'There's a fine rod in pickle for you, my gentleman, if you carry out that pretty scheme!'

Jim's military *coup* had decidedly astonished her. What he might do next she could not conjecture. The idea of his doing anything sufficiently brilliant to arrest her attention would have seemed ludicrous, had not Jim by entering the Yeomanry, revealed a capacity for dazzling exploits which made it unsafe to predict any limitation to his powers.

Margery was now excited. The daring of the wretched Jim in bursting into scarlet amazed her as much as his doubtful acquaintanceship with the demonstrative Mrs. Peach. To go to that Review, to watch the pair, to eclipse Mrs. Peach in brilliancy, to meet and pass them in withering contempt – if she only could do it! But, alas! she was a forsaken woman. 'If the Baron were alive, or in England,' she said to herself (for sometimes she thought he might possibly be alive), 'and he were to take me to this Review, wouldn't I show that forward Mrs. Peach what a lady is like, and keep among the select company, and not mix with the common people at all.'

It might at first sight be thought that the best course for Margery at this juncture would have been to go to Jim, and nip the intrigue in the bud without further scruple. But her own declaration in after days was that whoever could say that was far from realizing her situation. It was hard to break such ice as divided their two lives now, and to attempt it at that moment was a too humiliating proclamation of defeat. The only plan she could think of – perhaps not a wise one in the circumstances – was to go to the Review herself, and be the gayest there.

A method of doing this with some propriety soon occurred to her. She dared not ask her father, who scorned to waste time in sight-seeing, and whose animosity towards Jim knew no abatement; but she might call on her old acquaintance, Mr. Vine, Jim's partner, who would probably be going with the rest of the holiday folk, and ask if she might accompany him in his spring-trap. She had no sooner perceived the feasibility of this, through her being at her grandmother's, than she decided to meet with the old man early the next morning.

In the meantime Jim and Mrs. Peach had walked slowly along the road together, Jim leading the horse, and Mrs.

Peach informing him that her father, the gardener, was at
Jim's village further on, and that she had come to meet him.
Jim, for reasons of his own, was going to sleep at his partner's
that night, and thus their route was the same. The shades of eve
closed in upon them as they walked, and by the time they
reached the lime-kiln, which it was necessary to pass to get to
the village, it was quite dark. Jim stopped at the kiln, to see if
matters had progressed rightly in his seven days' absence, and
Mrs. Peach, who stuck to him like a teazle, stopped also, saying
she would wait for her father there.

She held the horse while he ascended to the top of the kiln.
Then rejoining her, and not quite knowing what to do, he
stood beside her looking at the flames, which tonight burnt up
brightly, shining a long way into the dark air, even up to the
ramparts of the earthwork above them, and overhead into the
bosoms of the clouds.

It was during this proceeding that a carriage, drawn by a pair
of dark horses, came along the turnpike road. The light of the
kiln caused the horses to swerve a little, and the occupant of the
carriage looked out. He saw the bluish, lightning-like flames
from the limestone, rising from the top of the furnace, and hard
by the figures of Jim Hayward, the widow, and the horse
standing out with spectral distinctness against the mass of night
behind. The scene wore the aspect of some unholy assignation
in Pandaemonium, and it was all the more impressive from the
fact that both Jim and the woman were quite unconscious of the
striking spectacle they presented. The gentleman in the carriage
watched them till he was borne out of sight.

Having seen to the kiln, Jim and the widow walked on again,
and soon Mrs. Peach's father met them, and relieved Jim of the
lady. When they had parted, Jim, with an expiration not unlike
a breath of relief, went on to Mr. Vine's, and, having put the
horse into the stable entered the house. His partner was seated
at the table, solacing himself after the labours of the day by
luxurious alternations between a long clay pipe and a mug of
perry.

'Well,' said Jim eagerly, 'what's the news – how do she take
it?'

'Sit down – sit down,' said Vine. ''Tis working well; not but
that I deserve something o' thee for the trouble I've had in

watching her. The soldiering was a fine move; but the
woman is a better! – who invented it?'

'I myself,' said Jim modestly.

'Well; jealousy is making her rise like a thunderstorm, and
in a day or two you'll have her for the asking, my sonny.
What's the next step?'

'The widow is getting rather a weight upon a feller, worse
luck,' said Jim. 'But I must keep it up until tomorrow, at any
rate. I have promised to see her at the Review, and now the
great thing is that Margery should see we a-smiling together
– I in my full-dress uniform and clinking arms o' war. 'Twill
be a good strong sting, and will end the business, I hope.
Couldn't you manage to put the hoss in and drive her there?
She'd go if you were to ask her.'

'With all my heart,' said Mr. Vine, moistening the end of a
new pipe in his perry. 'I can call at her grammer's for her –
'twill be all in my way.'

XVI

Margery duly followed up her intention by arraying herself
the next morning in her loveliest guise, and keeping watch
for Mr. Vine's appearance upon the high road, feeling certain
that his would form one in the procession of carts and
carriages which set in towards Exonbury that day. Jim had
gone by at a very early hour, and she did not see him pass.
Her anticipation was verified by the advent of Mr. Vine
about eleven o'clock, dressed to his highest effort; but
Margery was surprised to find that, instead of her having to
stop him, he pulled in towards the gate of his own accord.
The invitation planned between Jim and the old man on the
previous night was now promptly given, and, as may be
supposed, as promptly accepted. Such a strange coincidence,
she had never before known. She was quite ready, and they
drove onward at once.

The Review was held on some high ground a little way
out of the city, and her conductor suggested that they should
put up the horse at the inn, and walk to the field – a plan
which pleased her well, for it was more easy to take preli-

minary observations on foot without being seen herself than
when sitting elevated in a vehicle.

They were just in time to secure a good place near the front,
and in a few minutes after their arrival the reviewing officer
came on the ground. Margery's eye had rapidly run over the
troop in which Jim was enrolled, and she discerned him in one
of the ranks, looking remarkably new and bright, both as to
uniform and countenance. Indeed, if she had not worked
herself into such a desperate state of mind she would have felt
proud of him then and there. His shapely upright figure was
quite noteworthy in the row of rotund yeomen on his right
and left; while his charger Tony expressed by his bearing,
even more than Jim, that he knew nothing about lime-carts
whatever, and everything about trumpets and glory. How Jim
could have scrubbed Tony to such shining blackness she could
not tell, for the horse in his natural state was ingrained with
lime-dust, that burnt the colour out of his coat as it did out of
Jim's hair. Now he pranced martially, and was a war-horse
every inch of him.

Having discovered Jim her next search was for Mrs. Peach,
and, by dint of some oblique glancing Margery indignantly
discovered the widow in the most forward place of all, her
head and bright face conspicuously advanced; and, what was
more shocking, she had abandoned her mourning for a violet
drawn-bonnet and a gay spencer, together with a parasol
luxuriously fringed in a way Margery had never before seen.
'Where did she get the money?' said Margery, under her
breath. 'And to forget that poor sailor so soon!'

These general reflections were precipitately postponed by
her discovering that Jim and the widow were perfectly alive to
each other's whereabouts, and in the interchange of telegraphic
signs of affection, which on the latter's part took the form of a
playful fluttering of her handkerchief or waving of her parasol.
Richard Vine had placed Margery in front of him, to protect
her from the crowd, as he said, he himself surveying the scene
over her bonnet. Margery would have been even more surprised than she was if she had known that Jim was not only
aware of Mrs. Peach's presence, but also of her own, the
treacherous Mr. Vine having drawn out his flame-coloured
handkerchief and waved it to Jim over the young woman's

head as soon as they had taken up their position.

'My partner makes a tidy soldier, eh – Miss Tucker?' said the senior lime-burner. 'It is my belief as a Christian that he's got a party here that he's making signs to – that handsome figure o' fun straight over-right him.'

'Perhaps so,' she said.

'And it's growing warm between 'em if I don't mistake,' continued the merciless Vine.

Margery was silent, biting her lip; and the troops being now set in motion, all signalling ceased for the present between soldier Hayward and his pretended sweetheart.

'Have you a piece of paper that I could make a memorandum on, Mr. Vine?' said Margery.

Vine took out his pocket-book and tore a leaf from it, which he handed her with a pencil.

'Don't move from here – I'll return in a minute,' she continued, with the innocence of a woman who means mischief. And, withdrawing herself to the back, where the grass was clear, she pencilled the words

'JIM'S MARRIED.'

Armed with this document she crept into the throng behind the unsuspecting Mrs. Peach, slipped the paper into her pocket on the top of her handkerchief, and withdrew unobserved, rejoining Mr. Vine with a bearing of *nonchalance*.

By-and-by the troops were in different order, Jim taking a left-hand position almost close to Mrs. Peach. He bent down and said a few words to her. From her manner of nodding assent it was surely some arrangement about a meeting by-and-by when Jim's drill was over, and Margery was more certain of the fact when, the Review having ended, and the people having strolled off to another part of the field where sports were to take place, Mrs. Peach tripped away in the direction of the city.

'I'll just say a word to my partner afore he goes off the ground, if you'll spare me a minute,' said the old lime-burner. 'Please stay here till I'm back again.' He edged along the front till he reached Jim.

'How is she?' said the latter.

'In a trimming sweat,' said Mr. Vine. 'And my counsel to

'ee is to carry this larry no further. 'Twill do no good. She's as ready to make friends with 'ee as any wife can be; and more showing off can only do harm.'

'But I must finish off with a spurt,' said Jim. 'And this is how I am going to do it. I have arranged with Mrs. Peach that, as soon as we soldiers have entered the town and been dismissed, I'll meet her there. It is really to say good-bye, but she don't know that; and I wanted it to look like a lopement to Margery's eyes. When I'm clear of Mrs. Peach I'll come back here and make it up with Margery on the spot. But don't say I'm coming, or she may be inclined to throw off again. Just hint to her that I may be meaning to be off to London with the widow.'

The old man still insisted that this was going too far.

'No, no, it isn't,' said Jim. 'I know how to manage her. 'Twill just mellow her heart nicely by the time I come back. I must bring her down real tender, or 'twill all fail.'

His senior reluctantly gave in and returned to Margery. A short time afterwards the Yeomanry band struck up, and Jim with the regiment followed towards Exonbury.

'Yes, yes; they are going to meet,' said Margery to herself, perceiving that Mrs. Peach had so timed her departure as to be in the town at Jim's dismounting.

'Now we will go and see the games,' said Mr. Vine; 'they are really worth seeing. There's greasy poles, and jumping in sacks and other trials of the intellect, that nobody ought to miss who wants to be abreast of his generation.'

Margery felt so indignant at the apparent assignation, which seemed about to take place despite her anonymous writing, that she helplessly assented to go anywhere, dropping behind Vine, that he might not see her mood.

Jim followed out his programme with literal exactness. No sooner was the troop dismissed in the city than he sent Tony to stable and joined Mrs. Peach, who stood on the edge of the pavement expecting him. But this acquaintance was to end: he meant to part from her for ever and in the quickest time, though civilly; for it was important to be with Margery as soon as possible. He had nearly completed the manœuvre to his satisfaction when, in drawing her handkerchief from her pocket to wipe the tears from her eyes, Mrs. Peach's hand grasped the paper, which she read at once.

'What! is that true?' she said, holding it out to Jim.

Jim started and admitted that it was, beginning an elaborate explanation and apologies. But Mrs. Peach was thoroughly roused, and then overcome. 'He's married, he's married!' she said, and swooned, or feigned to swoon, so that Jim was obliged to support her.

'He's married, he's married!' said a boy hard by who had watched the scene with interest.

'He's married, he's married!' said a hilarious group of other boys near, with smiles several inches broad, and shining teeth; and so the exclamation echoed down the street.

Jim cursed his ill-luck; the loss of time that this dilemma entailed grew serious; for Mrs. Peach was now in such a hysterical state that he could not leave her with any good grace or feeling. It was necessary to take her to a refreshment room, lavish restoratives upon her, and altogether to waste nearly half an hour. When she had kept him as long as she chose, she forgave him; and thus at last he got away, his heart swelling with tenderness towards Margery. He at once hurried up the street to effect the reconciliation with her.

'How shall I do it?' he said to himself. 'Why, I'll step round to her side, fish for her hand, draw it through my arm as if I wasn't aware of it. Then she'll look in my face, I shall look in hers, and we shall march off the field triumphant, and the thing will be done without takings or tears.'

He entered the field and went straight as an arrow to the place appointed for the meeting. It was at the back of a refreshment tent outside the mass of spectators, and divided from their view by the tent itself. He turned the corner of the canvas, and there beheld Vine at the indicated spot. But Margery was not with him.

Vine's hat was thrust back into his poll. His face was pale, and his manner bewildered. 'Hullo? what's the matter?' said Jim. 'Where's my Margery?'

'You've carried this footy game too far, my man!' exclaimed Vine, with the air of a friend who has 'always told you so.' 'You ought to have dropped it several days ago, when she would have come to 'ee like a cooing dove. Now this is the end o't!'

'Hey! what, my Margery? Has anything happened, for God's sake?'

'She's gone.'

'Where to?'

'That's more than earthly man can tell! I never see such a thing! 'Twas a stroke o' the black art – as if she were sperrited away. When we got to the games I said – mind, you told me to! – I said, "Jim Hayward thinks o' going off to London with that widow woman" – mind you told me to! She showed no wonderment though a' seemed very low. Then she said to me, "I don't like standing here in this slummocky crowd. I shall feel more at home among the gentlepeople." And then she went to where the carriages were drawn up, and near here there was a grand coach, a-blazing with lions and unicorns, and hauled by two coal-black horses. I hardly thought much of it then, and by degrees lost sight of her behind it. Presently the other carriages moved off, and I thought still to see her standing there. But no, she had vanished; and then I saw the grand coach rolling away, and glimpsed Margery in it, beside a fine dark gentleman with black mustachios, and a very pale prince-like face. As soon as the horses got into the hard road they rattled on like hell-and-skimmer and went out of sight in the dust, and – that's all. If you'd come back a little sooner you'd ha' caught her.'

Jim had turned whiter than his pipeclay 'O, this is too bad – too bad!' he cried in anguish, striking his brow. 'That paper and that fainting woman kept me so long. Who could have done it? But 'tis my fault. I've stung her too much. I shouldn't have carried it so far.'

'You shouldn't – just what I said,' replied his senior.

'She thinks I've gone off with that cust widow; and to spite me she's gone off with the man. Do you know who that stranger wi' the lions and unicorns is? Why, 'tis that foreigner who calls himself a Baron, and took Mount Lodge for six months last year to make mischief – a villain! O, my Margery – that it should come to this! She's lost, she's ruined! – Which way did they go?'

Jim turned to follow in the direction indicated, when, behold, there stood at his back her father, Dairyman Tucker.

'Now look here, young man,' said Dairyman Tucker. 'I've just heard all that wailing – and straightway will ask 'ee to stop it sharp. 'Tis like your brazen impudence to teave and wail

when you be another woman's husband; yes, faith, I see'd her
a-fainting in yer arms when you wanted to get away from her,
and honest folk a-standing round who knew you'd married
her, and said so. I heard it, though you didn't see me. "He's
married!" they say. Some sly register-office business, no
doubt; but sly doings will out. As for Margery – who's to be
called higher titles in these parts hencefor'ard – I'm her father,
and I say it's all right what she's done. Don't I know private
news, hey? Haven't I just learnt that secret weddings of high
people can happen at expected deathbeds by special licence, as
well as low people at registrars' offices? And can't husbands
come back and claim their own when they choose? Begone,
young man, and leave noblemen's wives alone; and I thank
God I shall be rid of a numskull!'

Swift words of explanation rose to Jim's lips, but they
paused there and died. At that last moment he could not, as
Margery's husband, announce Margery's shame and his own,
and transform her father's triumph to wretchedness at a blow.

'I – I – must leave here,' he stammered. Going from the
place in an opposite course to that of the fugitives, he doubled
when out of sight, and in an incredibly short space had entered
the town. Here he made inquiries for the emblazoned carriage,
and gained from one or two persons a general idea of its route.
They thought it had taken the highway to London. Saddling
poor Tony before he had half eaten his corn, Jim galloped
along the same road.

XVII

Now Jim was quite mistaken in supposing that by leaving the
field in a roundabout manner he had deceived Dairyman
Tucker as to his object. That astute old man immediately
divined that Jim was meaning to track the fugitives, in
ignorance (as the dairyman supposed) of their lawful relation.
He was soon assured of the fact, for, creeping to a remote
angle of the field, he saw Jim hastening into the town.
Vowing vengeance on the young lime-burner for his mischievous interference between a nobleman and his secretly-
wedded wife, the dairy-farmer determined to balk him.

Tucker had ridden on to the Review ground, so that there was no necessity for him, as there had been for poor Jim, to re-enter the town before starting. The dairyman hastily untied his mare from the row of other horses, mounted, and descended to a bridle-path which would take him obliquely into the London road a mile or so ahead. The old man's route being along one side of an equilateral triangle, while Jim's was along two sides of the same, the former was at the point of intersection long before Hayward.

Arrived here, the dairyman pulled up and looked around. It was a spot at which the highway forked; the left arm, the more important, led on through Sherton Abbas and Melchester to London; the right to Idmouth and the coast. Nothing was visible on the white track to London; but on the other there appeared the back of a carriage, which rapidly ascended a distant hill and vanished under the trees. It was the Baron's who, according to the sworn information of the gardener at Mount Lodge, had made Margery his wife.

The carriage having vanished, the dairyman gazed in the opposite direction, towards Exonbury. Here he beheld Jim in his regimentals, laboriously approaching on Tony's back.

Soon he reached the forking roads, and saw the dairyman by the wayside. But Jim did not halt. Then the dairyman practised the greatest duplicity of his life.

'Right along the London road, if you want to catch 'em!' he said.

'Thank 'ee, dairyman, thank 'ee!' cried Jim, his pale face lighting up with gratitude, for he believed that Tucker had learnt his mistake from Vine, and had come to his assistance. Without drawing rein he diminished along the road not taken by the flying pair. The dairyman rubbed his hands with delight, and returned to the city as the cathedral clock struck five.

Jim pursued his way through the dust, up hill and down hill; but never saw ahead of him the vehicle of his search. That vehicle was passing along a diverging way at a distance of many miles from where he rode. Still he sped onwards, till Tony showed signs of breaking down; and then Jim gathered from inquiries he made that he had come the wrong way. It burst upon his mind that the dairyman, still ignorant of the truth, had misinformed him. Heavier in his heart than words can describe he turned Tony's drooping head, and resolved to drag his way home.

But the horse was now so jaded that it was impossible to proceed far. Having gone about half a mile back he came again to a small roadside hamlet and inn, where he put up Tony for a rest and feed. As for himself, there was no quiet in him. He tried to sit and eat in the inn kitchen; but he could not stay there. He went out, and paced up and down the road.

Standing in sight of the white way by which he had come he beheld advancing towards him the horses and carriage he sought, now black and daemonic against the slanting fires of the western sun.

The why and wherefore of this sudden appearance he did not pause to consider. His resolve to intercept the carriage was instantaneous. He ran forward, and doggedly waiting barred the way to the advancing equipage.

The Baron's coachman shouted, but Jim stood firm as a rock, and on the former attempting to push past him Jim drew his sword, resolving to cut the horses down rather than be displaced. The animals were nearly thrown back upon their haunches, and at this juncture a gentleman looked out of the window. It was the Baron himself.

'Who's there?' he inquired.

'James Hayward!' replied the young man fiercely, 'and he demands his wife.'

The Baron leapt out, and told the coachman to drive back out of sight and wait for him.

'I was hastening to find you,' he said to Jim. 'Your wife is where she ought to be, and where you ought to be also – by your own fireside. Where's the other woman?'

Jim, without replying, looked incredulously into the carriage as it turned. Margery was certainly not there. 'The other woman is nothing to me,' he said bitterly. 'I used her to warm up Margery; I have now done with her. The question I ask, my lord, is, what business had you with Margery today?'

'My business was to help her regain the husband she had seemingly lost. I saw her; she told me you had eloped by the London road with another. I, who have – mostly – had her happiness at heart, told her I would help her to follow you if she wished. She gladly agreed; we drove after, but could hear no tidings of you in front of us. Then I took her – to your house – and there she awaits you. I promised to send you to her if human effort could do it, and was tracking you for that purpose.'

'Then you've been a-pursuing after me?'

'You and the widow.'

'And I've been pursuing after you and Margery! . . . My noble lord, your actions seem to show that I ought to believe you in this; and when you say you've her happiness at heart, I don't forget that you've formerly proved it to be so. Well, Heaven forbid that I should think wrongfully of you if you don't deserve it! A mystery to me you have always been, my noble lord, and in this business more than in any.'

'I am glad to hear you say no worse. In one hour you'll have proof of my conduct – good or bad. Can I do anything more? Say the word, and I'll try.'

Jim reflected. 'Baron,' he said, 'I am a plain man, and wish only to lead a quiet life with my wife, as a man should. You have great power over her – power to any extent, for good or otherwise. If you command her anything on earth, righteous or questionable, that she'll do. So that, since you ask me if you can do more for me, I'll answer this, you can promise never to see her again. I mean no harm, my lord; but your presence can do no good; you will trouble us. If I return to her, will you for ever stay away?'

'Hayward,' said the Baron, 'I swear to you that I will disturb you and your wife by my presence no more.' And he took Jim's hand, and pressed it within his own upon the hilt of Jim's sword.

In relating this incident to the present narrator Jim used to declare that, to his fancy, the ruddy light of the setting sun burned with more than earthly fire on the Baron's face as the words were spoken; and that the ruby flash of his eye in the same light was what he never witnessed before nor since in the eye of mortal man. After this there was nothing more to do or say in that place. Jim accompanied his never-to-be-forgotten acquaintance to the carriage, closed the door after him, waved his hat to him, and from that hour he and the Baron met not again on earth.

A few words will suffice to explain the fortunes of Margery while the foregoing events were in action elsewhere. On leaving her companion Vine she had gone distractedly among the carriages, the rather to escape his observation than of any set purpose. Standing here she thought she heard her name pronounced, and turning, saw her foreign friend, whom she had supposed to be, if not dead, a thousand miles off. He beckoned, and she went close. 'You are ill – you are wretched,' he said, looking keenly in her face. 'Where's your husband?'

She told him her sad suspicion that Jim had run away from her. The Baron reflected, and inquired a few other particulars of her late life. Then he said: 'You and I must find him. Come with me.' At this word of command from the Baron she had entered the carriage as docilely as a child, and there she sat beside him till he chose to speak, which was not till they were some way out of the town, at the forking ways, and the Baron had discovered that Jim was certainly not, as they had supposed, making off from Margery along that particular branch of the fork that led to London.

'To pursue him in this way is useless, I perceive,' he said. 'And the proper course now is that I should take you to his house. That done I will return and bring him to you if mortal persuasion can do it.'

'I didn't want to go to his house without him, sir,' said she, tremblingly.

'Didn't want to!' he answered. 'Let me remind you, Margery Hayward, that your place is in your husband's house. Till you are there you have no right to criticize his conduct, however wild it may be. Why have you not been there before?'

'I don't know, sir,' she murmured, her tears falling silently upon her hand.

'Don't you think you ought to be there?'

She did not answer.

'Of course you ought.'

Still she did not speak.

The Baron sank into silence, and allowed his eye to rest on her. What thoughts were all at once engaging his mind after those moments of reproof? Margery had given herself into his hands without a remonstrance. Her husband had apparently deserted her. She was absolutely in his power, and they were on the high road.

That his first impulse in inviting her to accompany him had been the legitimate one denoted by his words cannot reasonably be doubted. That his second was otherwise soon became revealed, though not at first to her, for she was too bewildered to notice where they were going. Instead of turning and taking the road to Jim's, the Baron, as if influenced suddenly by her reluctance to return thither if Jim was playing truant, signalled to the coachman to take the branch road to the right, as her father had discerned.

They soon approached the coast near Idmouth. The carriage stopped. Margery awoke from her reverie.

'Where are we?' she said, looking out of the window, with a start. Before her was an inlet of the sea, and in the middle of the inlet rode a yacht, its masts repeating as if from memory the rocking they had practised in their native forest.

'At a little sea-side nook, where my yacht lies at anchor,' he said tentatively. 'Now Margery, in five minutes we can be aboard, and in half an hour we can be sailing away all the world over. Will you come?'

'I cannot decide,' she said in low tones.

'Why not?'

'Because –'

Then on a sudden, Margery seemed to see all contingencies: she became white as a fleece, and a bewildered look came into her eyes. With clasped hands she leant on the Baron.

Baron von Xanten observed her distracted look, averted his face, and coming to a decision opened the carriage door, quickly mounted outside, and in a second or two the carriage left the shore behind, and ascended the road by which it had come.

In about an hour they reached Jim Hayward's home. The Baron alighted, and spoke to her through the window. 'Margery, can you forgive a lover's bad impulse, which I swear was unpremeditated?' he asked. 'If you can, shake my hand.'

She did not do it, but eventually allowed him to help her out of the carriage. He seemed to feel the awkwardness keenly; and seeing it, she said, 'Of course I forgive you, sir, for I felt for a moment as you did. Will you send my husband to me?'

'I will, if any man can,' said he. 'Such penance is milder than I deserve! God bless you and give you happiness! I shall never see you again!' He turned, entered the carriage, and was gone; and having found out Jim's course, came up with him upon the road as described.

In due time the latter reached his lodging at his partner's. The woman who took care of the house in Vine's absence at once told Jim that a lady who had come in a carriage was waiting for him in his sitting-room. Jim proceeded thither with agitation, and beheld, shrinkingly ensconced in the large slippery chair, and surrounded by the brilliant articles that had so long awaited her, his long-estranged wife.

Margery's eyes were round and fear-stricken. She essayed to speak, but Jim, strangely enough, found the readier tongue then. 'Why did I do it, you would ask,' he said. 'I cannot tell. Do you forgive my deception? O Margery – you are my Margery still! But how could you trust yourself in the Baron's hands this afternoon, without knowing him better?'

'He said I was to come, and I went,' she said, as well as she could for tearfulness.

'You obeyed him blindly.'

'I did. But perhaps I was not justified in doing it.'

'I don't know,' said Jim musingly. 'I think he's a good man.' Margery did not explain. And then a sunnier mood succeeded her tremblings and tears, till old Mr. Vine came into the house below, and Jim went down to declare that all was well, and sent off his partner to break the news to Margery's father, who as yet remained unenlightened.

The dairyman bore the intelligence of his daughter's untitled state as best he could, and punished her by not coming near her for several weeks, though at last he grumbled his forgiveness, and made up matters with Jim. The handsome Mrs. Peach vanished to Plymouth, and found another sailor, not without a reasonable complaint against Jim and Margery both that she had been unfairly used.

As for the mysterious gentleman who had exercised such an influence over their lives, he kept his word, and was a stranger to Lower Wessex thenceforward. Baron or no Baron, Englishman or foreigner, he had shown a genuine interest in Jim, and real sorrow for a certain reckless phase of his acquaintance with Margery. That he had a more tender feeling toward the young girl than he wished her or any one else to perceive there could be no doubt. That he was strongly tempted at times to adopt other than conventional courses with regard to her is also clear, particularly at that critical hour when she rolled along the high road with him in the carriage, after turning from the fancied pursuit of Jim. But at other times he schooled impassioned sentiments into fair conduct, which even erred on the side of harshness. In after years there was a report that another attempt on his life with a pistol, during one of those fits of moodiness to which he seemed constitutionally liable, had been effectual; but nobody in Silverthorn was in a position to ascertain the truth.

There he is still regarded as one who had something about him magical and unearthly. In his mystery let him remain; for a man, no less than a landscape, who awakens an interest under uncertain lights and touches of unfathomable shade, may cut but a poor figure in a garish noontide shine.

When she heard of his mournful death Margery sat in her nursing-chair, gravely thinking for nearly ten minutes, to the total neglect of her infant in the cradle. Jim, from the other side of the fireplace, said: 'You are sorry enough for him, Margery. I am sure of that.'

'Yes, yes,' she murmured, 'I am sorry.' After a moment she added: 'Now that he's dead I'll make a confession, Jim, that I have never made to a soul. If he had pressed me – which he did not – to go with him when I was in the carriage that night beside his yacht, I would have gone. And I was disappointed that he did not press me.'

'Suppose he were to suddenly appear now, and say in a voice of command, "Margery, come with me!"'

'I believe I should have no power to disobey,' she returned, with a mischievous look. 'He was like a magician to me. I think he was one. He could move me as a loadstone moves a speck of steel. . . . Yet no,' she added, hearing the infant cry, 'he would not move me now. It would be so unfair to baby.'

'Well,' said Jim, with no great concern (for '*la jalousie rétrospective*,' as George Sand calls it, had nearly died out of him), 'however he might move 'ee, my love, he'll never come. He swore it to me: and he was a man of his word.'

Midsummer, 1883

THOMAS HARDY

A GROUP OF NOBLE DAMES

The ten stories contained in *A Group of Noble Dames* ranged around a '. . . store of ladies, whose bright eyes rain influence'.

Hardy plumbs the hidden depths of county families to reveal what went on behind the scenes, transforming half-remembered incidents into palpitating drama. Barbara of the House of Grebe, Lady Mottisfont, Anna, Lady Baxly, The Lady Penelope and The Honourable Laura, together with the other Noble Dames, will live long in the mind of the reader.

THOMAS HARDY

LIFE'S LITTLE IRONIES

Hardy considered 'The Son's Veto' to be his best short story, whilst 'On The Western Circuit' was Florence Hardy's favourite. It is difficult to argue with either judgement, but each of the tales in *Life's Little Ironies* will be championed by different readers. Suffice it to say that they show Hardy at his characteristic best in the Wessex countryside he made his own.

As a pendant to the tales, Hardy added a series of stories linked under the heading 'A Few Crusted Characters', harking back to an earlier age. The characters are here in good measure – Tony Kytes, Andrey Satchel and the rest – their stories told to a returning native by Burthen, the Longpuddle Carrier, during a golden afternoon in autumn.

CHARLES DICKENS
THE MUDFOG PAPERS

Mudfog is a pleasant town situated in a charming hollow by the side of a river from which it derives an agreeable scent of pitch, tar, coals, and rope-yarn, a roving population in oilskin hats, a steady influx of drunken bargemen, and a great many other maritime advantages.

The public buildings too are very imposing and the town hall is one of the finest examples of shed architecture extant: it is a combination of the pig-sty and tea-garden-box orders. The idea of placing a large window on one side of the door, and a small one on the other, is particularly happy. In this room do the corporation, headed by that well-known coal-dealer, Nicholas Tulrumble, assemble together in solemn council for the public good.

ANTHONY TROLLOPE

THE SPOTTED DOG & OTHER STORIES

Here is a fine assortment, as good as anything that came from Trollope's pen. These stories are presented as if collected by London magazine editors, gleaned over the years in their search for new material for their readers; tales of sorrow and mirth, suffering and delight.

The title story takes the reader into the dark world of Victorian London, with its squalid back streets surrounding The Spotted Dog public house. In the five remaining tales, a stream of characters is given life by the author, each with a story to tell as fascinating and diverse as anything likely to pass through an editor's hands; little fair-haired Mary Gresley, Mr Michael Molloy, Josephine de Montmorenci and her sister-in-law Mrs Puffle, Lieutenant and Mrs Brumby and a host of others. All are guaranteed to delight the reader.

MARIA EDGEWORTH

ORMOND

It is a sharp knock at the window which alerts Lady O'Shane to the pale, bloodstained figure of Harry Ormond standing outside. During a drunken brawl he has shot his provoker, Moriarty Carroll. Though Carroll survives, this is not enough to prevent Ormond's scheming guardian, Sir Ulick O'Shane, from banishing his ward from Castle Hermitage.

Thus Ormond starts out on his adventures, travelling to the isolated Black Islands, home of the benevolent King Corny, back to Castle Hermitage and the passionately anti-Papist Mrs McCrule, then on to Paris, with its vibrant literary scene, and the regal splendours of the Court of Versailles.

Penetrating characterization, a lively plot and vivid description combine in this exciting story of underhand dealings and the search for love in eighteenth-century Ireland.

ARNOLD BENNETT

TALES OF THE FIVE TOWNS

After a drink with Mr Gordon, 'a municipal mediocrity', Mr Curtenty, the Deputy-Mayor, makes the decision to purchase a flock of geese and drive them back to his residence. The problems he encounters soon become common knowledge and when the *Signal* reveals that the Mayor has resigned, it appears that 'His Worship the Goosedriver' will become a laughing-stock.

In 'The Hungarian Rhapsody' Edward Norris, under the impression that he is about to die, reveals to his wife that he has not been honest in a deal with her deceased father. Although she forgives him, the atmosphere remains tense, until May Norris says that she has something to tell her husband . . .

'His Worship the Goosedriver' and 'The Hungarian Rhapsody' are two of the stories in *Tales of the Five Towns*, in which Bennett tells of life in the Potteries and its citizens' adventures in London.

WILKIE COLLINS

THE BITER BIT
& OTHER STORIES

Here are tales of detection, mystery and suspense, from the author of *The Moonstone* and *The Woman in White*.

The title story is an investigation into an unusual robbery, revealing Wilkie Collins' little known comic talents. Others selected for inclusion are *Mad Monckton*, a fine thriller; *Gabriel's Marriage*, set at the time of the French Revolution and an intriguing mystery, *The Lady of Glenwith Grange*.